H

in Ontario

Trace

3rd Edi

Author: Tracey Arial
Editor: Pierre Ledoux
Copy Editors: Pierre Daveluy, Matthew McLauchlin
Computer Graphics: Pascal Biet, Marie-France Denis, Philippe Thomas
Editing Assistance: Annie Gilbert
Front cover photo: Front cover, George Lake, Killarney Provincial Park: © HP Canada / Alamy

This work was produced under the direction of Olivier Gougeon.

Acknowledgements:

Author: Thanks so much for all of the outdoors enthusiasts who've shared Ontario's natural wonders with me over the last several years. In particular, I'd like to thank the people who answer the phone and greet visitors at parks and conservation areas. These unsung heroes share their passion for a place with everyone who visits and many of them helped me discover highlights I might have overlooked. Thanks also to the staff at great local bookstores, who really care about their customers, including Terry Needham from Novack's and Nancy Frater at Booklore. Thanks also to three exceptional high school teachers: John Nephew for introducing me to glaciers, Hal Babcock for helping me appreciate history and the late Ina Healey, for inspiring my love of words. Thanks also to mom, dad, Lorrey, Kimm, Keelan, Chloe, Manny, Pedro, Paul and Arial for exploring the trails with me.
Publisher: Thank you to Lori Waldbrook of Ontario Parks, Jeff Truscott and Guy Thériault of Parks Canada and Suzanne McFarlane of the Morris Island Conservation Area for their help in updating this guide's maps. We acknowledge the financial support of the Government of Canada through the Book Publishing Industry Development Program (BPIDP) for ur publishing activities. We would also like to thank the Government of Québec – Tax credit for book publishing – Administered by SODEC.

Note to Readers

The information contained in this guide was correct at press time. However, mistakes may slip by, omissions are always possible, establishments may move, etc. The authors and publisher hereby disclaim any liability for loss or damage resulting from omissions or errors.

Write to Us

We value your comments, corrections and suggestions, as they allow us to keep each guide up to date. You can send your comments to us in writing at the following address; the best contributions will be rewarded with a free book from Ulysses Travel Guides (please indicate which title you would like to receive).

Ulysses Travel Guides
4176 St. Denis Street, Montréal, Québec, Canada H2W 2M5, www.ulyssesguides.com
text@ulysses.ca

Bibliothèque et Archives nationales du Québec and Library and Archives Canada cataloguing in publication
Arial, Tracey, 1963-
Hiking in Ontario
3rd ed.
(Ulysses green escapes)
Includes index.
ISBN 978-2-89464-827-8 (print version)
1. Hiking - Ontario - Guidebooks. 2. Trails - Ontario - Guidebooks. I. Title. II. Series: Ulysses green escapes.
GV199.44.C220582 2010 796.5109713 C2009-941717-0

Printed in Canada
ISBN 978-2-89464-827-8 (print version)
ISBN 978-2-89665-007-1 (digital version)

100%

This book was printed on 100% post-consumer EcoLogo certified paper, processed chlorine free and made with biogas energy.

Table of Contents

List of Maps

Map Symbols

	Hiking trail		Trans Canada Highway
	Road		Highway

	Beach		Park
	Bridge		Parking lot
	Campsite		Picnic area
	Car ferry		Provincial or regional border
	Cemetery		Provincial or state capital
	Forest or park		Regional airport
	Golf course		Sea, lake, river
	International airport		Tourist information
	International border		Trail location
	Landmark		Train track
	Lookout		Washroom
	Medical clinic		Wildlife reserve
	National capital		

Other Symbols Used in This Guide

Telephone number

Easy trail

Moderate trail

Difficult trail

Trail identified as a favourite location

Favourite Trails and Custom Hikes

Our Favourite Hiking Trails

Multi-Regional Trails

- Bruce Trail, p. 57
- Oak Ridges Trail, p. 66
- Trans Canada Trail (particularly the Orange Corners Trestle and Midland), p. 55

Southern Ontario

- Bruce Peninsula National Park, p. 86
- Point Pelee National Park, p. 106

Greater Toronto and the Niagara Peninsula

- Dundas Valley and Tiffany Fall Conservation Areas, p. 129
- Niagara Glen, p. 141

Central Ontario

- Algonquin Provincial Park, p. 152
- Old Nipissing Colonization Road, p. 172
- Mono Cliffs Provincial Park, p. 169

Eastern Ontario

- Bon Echo Provincial Park, p. 185
- Murphys Point Provincial Park, p. 203
- Silent Lake Provincial Park, p. 214

Northeastern Ontario

- Killarney Provincial Park, p. 228
- Lake Superior Provincial Park, p. 231

Northwestern Ontario

- Pukaskwa National Park, p. 253
- Sleeping Giant Provincial Park, p. 259

Animal Lover Walks

- Algonquin Provincial Park (moose and wolf howls from any of the trails along Frank McDougall Parkway, see p. 152)
- Darlington Provincial Park (butterfly migration in September, see p. 125)
- Frontenac Provincial Park (Doe Lake Trail, see p. 193)
- Glen Haffy Conservation Area (Falconry Centre, see p. 136)
- Haliburton Forest (Wolf Centre, see p. 168)
- Hawk's Ridge, Craig's Bluff and Craig's Pit (soaring hawks, see p. 248)
- Mountsberg Conservation Area (Raptor Centre, elk, bison, see p. 139)
- Perth Wildlife Reserve (geese and duck migration, see p. 210)
- Point Pelee National Park (spring bird migration, see p. 106)
- Springwater Provincial Park (wounded animal shelter, see p. 177)
- Wye Marsh Wildlife Centre (trumpeter swan sanctuary, see p. 179)

Bog and Marsh Hikes

- Algonquin Provincial Park (Bat Lake Trail, see p. 157; Spruce Bog Trail, see p. 155; Track and Tower, see p. 159)
- Backus Heritage Conservation Area (Wetlands Trail, see p. 84)
- Bruce Peninsula National Park (Horse Lake Trail, see p. 89)
- Charleston Lake Provincial Park (Quiddity Trail, see p. 188)
- Cootes Paradise, Royal Botanical Gardens (Captain Cootes, Marshwalk, Macdonell and Pinetum trails, North Shore, see p. 122; Hopkins Trail, see p. 122; Calebs Walk, see p. 123)
- Darlington Provincial Park, see p. 125
- Foley Mountain Conservation Area (Beaver Trail, see p. 189)
- Frontenac Provincial Park (Arab Lake Gorge, see p. 192; Arkon Lake Loop, see p. 193
- Killarney Provincial Park (Cranberry Bog Trail, see p. 229)
- Lake Superior Provincial Park (Trapper's Trail, see p. 232)
- Luther Marsh Wildlife Management Area, see p. 97
- Mac Johnson Wildlife Area, see p. 199
- McLaughlin Bay Wildlife Reserve and Second Marsh Wildlife Area, see p. 138
- Mountsberg Conservation Area, see p. 139
- Ottawa Greenbelt Trails (Mer Bleue Trail and Trails 50-53, Mer Bleue Bog, see p. 206; Beaver and Chipmunk Trail, Old Quarry Trail, Jack Pine Trail and Trails 20-29, Stony Swamp, see p. 207)

- Ouimet Canyon Provincial Nature Reserve (Marsh Trail, see p. 252)
- Point Pelee National Park, see p. 106
- Quetico Provincial Park (Beaver Meadows and Pond Trails, see p. 256; Pickerel River and Point Trails, see p. 256; Whiskey Jack Trail, see p. 257)
- Rondeau Provincial Park (Marsh Trail, see p. 111)
- St. Catharines Trail System (Green Ribbon Trail, see p. 147)
- Seguin Trail, see p. 176
- Wye Marsh, see p. 179

Forest Adventures

- Algonquin Provincial Park (Bat Lake Trail, see p. 157; Eastern Pines Backpacking Trail, see p. 158; Hardwood Lookout Trail, see p. 155; Hemlock Bluff, see p. 158)
- Awenda Provincial Park (Brûlé Trail, see p. 162; Nipissing Trail, see p. 162)
- Backus Heritage Conservation Area (Flood Plain Trail, see p. 85; Sassafras Trail, see p. 86; Sugar Bush Trail, see p. 85;)
- Ball's Falls Conservation Area (Twenty Mile Creek Valley Trail, see p. 120)
- Bon Echo Provincial Park (High Pines Trail, see p. 186)
- Charleston Lake Provincial Park (Hemlock Ridge Trail, see p. 188; Beech Woods Trail, see p. 188)
- Cootes Paradise, Royal Botanical Gardens (Arnotts Walk and Chegwin Trails, see p. 122)
- Durham Regional Forest, see p. 134
- Fanshawe Conservation Area (Blue Trail, see p. 93; Green Trail, see p. 92)
- Frontenac Provincial Park (Arab Lake Gorge, see p. 192)
- Ganaraska Forest, see p. 135
- Glen Haffy Conservation Area, see p. 136
- Greenwood Lake Conservation Reserve, see p. 246
- Haliburton Forest (Canopy Trail, see p. 168)
- Kap-Kig-Iwan Provincial Park, see p. 228
- Kawartha Highlands, see p. 151
- Lake Superior Provincial Park (Crescent Lake Trail, see p. 232)
- Old Nipissing Colonization Road (through the French/Severn Forest, see p. 172)
- Ottawa Greenbelt Trails (NCC Trail 30 and 31, Pinhey Forest, see p. 206; Trails 44 to 46, MNR Logging Forest, see p. 209)

- Rondeau Provincial Park, see p. 109
- Shabomeka Legpower Pathfinders, see p. 215

Glacial Feature Hikes

- Albion Hills Conservation Area, see p. 118
- Algonquin Provincial Park (Barron Canyon, see p. 156; Brent Crater, see p. 156; Eastern Pines Backpacking Trail, see p. 158)
- Arrowhead Provincial Park (Beaver Meadow Trail, see p. 161)
- Awenda Provincial Park (Wendat Trail, see p. 163)
- Bruce Trail, see p. 57
- Charleston Lake Provincial Park (Tallow Rock Bay, see p. 188)
- Cootes Paradise, Royal Botanical Gardens (Ginger Valley Trail, see p. 123)
- Crawford Lake Conservation Area and Iroquoian Village, see p. 123
- Cup and Saucer Trail, see p. 222
- Dundas Valley and Tiffany Falls conservation areas, see p. 129
- Elliot Lake Hiking Trails, see p. 223
- Ferris Provincial Park (Drumlin Trail, see p. 164)
- Glen Haffy Conservation Area, see p. 136
- Humber Valley Trail, see p. 137
- Lake Superior Provincial Park (South Old Woman River Trail, see p. 234)
- Mono Cliffs Provincial Park, see p. 169
- Niagara Glen, see p. 141
- Oak Ridges Trail, see p. 66
- Petroglyphs Provincial Park, see p. 173
- Samuel de Champlain Provincial Park, see p. 238
- Warsaw Caves Conservation Area, see p. 178

Historical Journeys

- Lake Superior Provincial Park (Agawa Rock Pictographs Trail, see p. 232; Nokomis Trail, see p. 234)
- Algonquin Provincial Park (Booth's Rock Trail, see p. 157; Track and Tower, see p. 159)
- Arrowhead Provincial Park (Beaver Meadow Trail, see p. 161; Homesteader and Mayflower Lake Trails, see p. 161)

- Awenda Provincial Park (Beaver Pond Trail, see p. 162; Dunes Trail, see p. 162; Wendat Trail, see p. 163)
- Backus Heritage Conservation Area (Heritage Village Tour, see p. 85)
- Ball's Falls Conservation Area (Cataract Trail, see p. 120; Twenty Mile Creek Valley Trail, see p. 120)
- Bon Echo Provincial Park (Cliff Top Trail, see p. 186; Shield Trail, see p. 187)
- Charleston Lake Provincial Park (Sandstone Island Trail, see p. 188)
- Cootes Paradise, Royal Botanical Gardens (Captain Cootes, Marshwalk, Macdonell and Pinetum trails, North Shore, see p. 122)
- Crawford Lake Conservation Area and Iroquoian Village, see p. 123
- Darlington Provincial Park, see p. 125
- Dufferin Islands, Niagara Falls, see p. 128
- Dundas Valley and Tiffany Falls conservation areas (G. Donald Side Trail, see p. 133, Heritage Trail, see p. 132, Orchard Side Trail, see p. 131; Sulphur Creek Side Trail, see p. 131)
- Fanshawe Conservation Area (Fanshawe Lake Trail, see p. 92)
- Frontenac Provincial Park (Arab Lake Gorge, see p. 192; Doe Lake Trail, see p. 193; Big Salmon Lake Loop, see p. 194; Hemlock Lake Loop, see p. 195; Little Clear Lake Loop, see p. 194)
- Georgian Bay Islands National Park (Brebeuf Lighthouse Trail, see p. 165; Southern Loop, see p. 166)
- Gould Lake Conservation Area (Mica Loop, see p. 197; Mine Loop, see p. 197)
- Hell Holes Nature Trails, Caves & Ravines, see p. 198
- Humber Valley Trail, see p. 137
- Kakabeka Falls Provincial Park (Mountain Portage Trail, see p. 249)
- Killarney Provincial Park (Chikanishing Trail, see p. 229)
- Magpie Falls and Fort Friendship, see p. 235
- McKeough Conservation Area and Floodway, see p. 101
- Mississagi Provincial Park (Cobre Lake Trail, see p. 237; Flack Lake Nature Trail, see p. 237; MacKenzie Trail, see p. 238)
- Murphys Point Provincial Park (McParlan House Trail and Loon Lake Loop, see p. 204)
- Niagara River Recreation Trail, see p. 143
- Old Nipissing Colonization Road, see p. 172
- Ottawa Greenbelt Trails (Trail 26, Stony Swamp, see p. 209)

- Petroglyphs Provincial Park, see p. 173
- Rideau Trail, see p. 211
- Samuel de Champlain Provincial Park, see p. 238
- Sandbanks Provincial Park, see p. 212
- Seguin Trail, see p. 176
- St. Catharines Trail System (Merritt Trail, see p. 146; Welland Canals Parkway Trail, see p. 147)

Multi-Day Hikes

- Algonquin Provincial Park (Bruton Farm Trail, see p. 159; Eastern Pines Backpacking Trail, see p. 158; Highland Backpacking Trail, see p. 159; Scorch Lake Lookout Trail, see p. 159; Western Uplands Backpacking Trail, see p. 160)
- Avon Trail, see p. 82
- Bon Echo Provincial Park (Abes and Essens Trail, see p. 186)
- Bruce Trail, see p. 57
- Casque-Isles Hiking Trail, see p.244
- Elgin Trail, see p. 89
- Frontenac Provincial Park (Arkon Lake Loop, see p. 193; Cedar Lake Trail, see p. 195; Little Salmon Lake Loop, see p. 194; Big Salmon Lake Loop, see p. 194; Gibson Lake Loop, see p. 195; Little Clear Lake Loop, see p. 194; Slide Lake Loop, see p. 196; Tetsmine Lake Trail, see p. 195)
- Ganaraska Trail, see p. 61
- Grand Valley Trail, see p. 64
- Killarney Provincial Park (La Cloche Silhouette Trail, see p. 230)
- Lake Superior Provincial Park (Coastal Hiking Trail, see p. 235; Towab Trail, see p. 235)
- Lynn Valley Trail, see p. 99
- Maitland Trail, see p. 100
- Mississagi Provincial Park (MacKenzie Trail, see p. 238)
- National Trail, see p. 55
- Oak Ridges Trail, see p. 66
- Pukaskwa National Park (Coastal Hiking Trail, see p. 254)
- Rideau Trail, see p. 211
- Thames Valley Trail, see p. 112
- Trans Canada Trail, see p. 55
- Quetico Provincial Park (Pines Trail, see p. 257)

- Voyageur Trail, see p. 70
- Waterfront Trail, see p. 71

Scenic Views from Above

- Algonquin Provincial Park (Barron Canyon, see p. 156; Centennial Ridges, see p. 158; Eastern Pines Backpacking Trail, see p. 158; Hardwood Lookout, see p. 155; Hemlock Bluff, see p. 158; Lookout Trail, see p. 156; Two Rivers Trail, see p. 157)
- Awenda Provincial Park (Bluff Trail, see p. 162; Dunes Trail, see p. 162; Nipissing Trail, see p. 162)
- Bon Echo Provincial Park (Cliff Top Trail, see p. 186; High Pines Trail, see p. 186)
- Charleston Lake Provincial Park (Blue Mountain Trail, see p. 188; Sandstone Island Trail, see p. 188; Tallow Rock Bay, see p. 188)
- Dundas Valley and Tiffany Falls conservation areas (Hilltop Side Trail, see p. 133; Lookout Side Trail, see p. 133, Spring Creek Trail, see p. 134)
- Foley Mountain Conservation Area (Blue Circle Trail, see p. 189; Red Oak Trail, see p. 191; White Pine Trail, see p. 191)
- Gould Lake Conservation Area (Point Spur, see p. 196)
- Hawk's Ridge, Craig's Bluff and Craig's Pit, see p. 248
- Hiawatha Highlands Conservation Area (Lookout Trail , see p. 226)
- Kakabeka Falls Provincial Park (Beaver Meadows Trail, see p. 250; River Terrace Loop, see p. 250)
- Killarney Provincial Park (Granite Ridge Trail, see p. 229)
- Lake Superior Provincial Park (Awausee Trail, see p. 234; Orphan Lake Trail, see p. 234; Peat Mountain Trail, see p. 234)
- Mississagi Provincial Park (Helenbar Lookout Trail, see p. 237)
- Murphys Point Provincial Park (Sylvan Trail, see p. 204)
- Ouimet Canyon Provincial Nature Reserve, see p. 251
- Pukaskwa National Park (Southern Headland Trail, see p. 254)
- Rainbow Falls Provincial Park (Back 40 Trail, see p. 259)

Trails over Sand Dunes

- Bruce Peninsula National Park (Singing Sands Trail, see p. 88)
- Long Point World Biosphere Reserve, see p. 95
- Pinery Provincial Park, see p. 101
- Sandbanks Provincial Park, see p. 212

Waterfall Trails

- Algonquin Provincial Park (Brent Crater, see p. 156; Eastern Pines Backpacking Trail, see p. 158)
- Arrowhead Provincial Park (Stubbs Falls Trail, see p. 160)
- Ball's Falls Conservation Area (Cataract Trail, see p. 120)
- Chutes Provincial Park, see p.222
- Ferris Provincial Park (Gorge Trail, see p. 163; Ranney Falls Trail, see p. 164)
- Hiawatha Highlands Conservation Area (Crystal Creek Trail, see p. 226)
- Kap-Kig-Iwan Provincial Park, see p. 228
- Kakabeka Falls Provincial Park (Boardwalk, see p. 249; Contact Trail, see p. 249; Little Falls Trail, see p. 250)
- Lake Superior Provincial Park (Orphan Lake Trail, see p. 234; Pinguisibi Trail, see p. 232)
- Magpie Falls and Fort Friendship, see p. 235
- Niagara River Recreation Trail, see p. 143
- Quetico Provincial Park (French Falls Trail, see p. 256)
- Rainbow Falls Provincial Park (Falls Boardwalk, see p. 258)

Wheelchair Accessible Trails

- Charleston Lake Provincial Park (Tallow Rock Bay, see p. 188)
- Foley Mountain Conservation Area (Mobility Trail, see p. 191)
- Hiawatha Highlands Conservation Area (Kinsmen Lit, see p. 226)
- Kakabeka Falls Provincial Park (Boardwalk, see p. 249; Little Falls Trail, see p. 250; Mountain Portage Trail, see p. 249)
- Morris Island Conservation Area (Accessible Track, see p. 200; Old CN Causeway, see p. 202)
- Niagara River Recreation Trail, see p. 143
- Ouimet Canyon Provincial Nature Reserve (Ouimet Canyon Lookout, see p. 251)
- Ottawa Greenbelt Trails (Greenbelt Pathway, see p. 210; Sarsaparilla Trail, Stony Swamp, see p. 205; Watts Creek Pathway, Shirley's Bay, see p. 206)
- Quetico Provincial Park (Pickerel River Trail, see p. 256)

Introduction

As late I rambled in the happy fields—
What time the skylark shakes the tremulous dew
From his lush clover covert, when anew
Adventurous knights take up their dinted shields—
I saw the sweetest flower wild nature yields,
A fresh-blown musk-rose; 'twas the first that threw
Its sweets upon the summer: graceful it grew
As is the wand that Queen Titania wields.
And, as I feasted on its fragrancy,
I thought the garden-rose it far excelled:
But when, O Wells! thy roses came to me
My sense with their deliciousness was spelled:
Soft voices had they, that with tender plea
Whispered of peace, and truth, and friendliness unquelled.

John Keats wrote this in 1816 to express the extraordinary experience of walking on a trail when the first fragrant flowers bud, a feeling that can only be exceeded by the kind action of a friend. It's now 200 years later, but the same joyful experience in the outdoors can still be had on any trail in Ontario, with a little guidance from us. In this, the third edition of our hiking guide, we've carefully outlined 98 of the province's most interesting hiking locations in detail. All of them are worth driving a day or more to get to, either because of an unusual geological feature or because there are many, many diverse walking experiences nearby. Plan on spending at least one full day in each of these major locations. Some are conservation areas, others are provincial parks or nature reserves, and others are longer trails through several towns. Each section describes all the recommended hiking trails in the location..

Locations are listed within regional sections to make it easier to select the length of hike you wish to do, whether that means doing two or three sections of a long trail or a couple of trails in one region. An additional chapter lists the eight long trails in Ontario that go through two or more regions. These trails will take you to some of Ontario's most impressive land formations, such as the Niagara Escarpment, the Oak Ridges Moraine, Elora Gorge, Ouimet Canyon, the Sleeping Giant, the La Cloche Mountains and Bon Echo rock. They'll enable you to view important heritage landmarks and monuments, like the Backhouse Mill, the Hermitage or the gravestone of Canada's first prime minister. You'll explore the most beautiful areas near Niagara Falls, along Long Point and on the Bruce Peninsula. The best places to view bird and butterfly migrations are here, as are the most likely locations for seeing nesting species. The trails around Ontario's most important wetlands are included, as are those that border the famous Great Lakes. If an unusual plant species can be seen in Ontario, you'll find a trail that leads to it in this guide. Naturalists will particularly appreciate the bird and plant species mentioned within each listing, while budding geologists will want to hike the trails that lead past potholes, kettle lakes and drumlins. You'll also find several wheelchair-accessible trails listed so that people who are less mobile can also explore Ontario's best natural features.

We've created a number of lists to help guide you through the province (see p. 7). The most important of these are our 17 favourite locations, which are specially marked throughout this guide with the Ulysses Label: . Although it was extremely difficult to limit our selection, these trails are the ones with the most awe-inspiring locations, either because of the type of landscape, the importance of a cultural site, the plants or animals that live within the location or simply for the unique experience they provide. If your time is limited, you may want to begin with these.

Our other lists were created with specific hikers in mind. **Wheelchair Accessible Trails** are important ways for people with limited mobility to explore the outdoors. Lists of **Scenic Views from Above** and **Waterfall Trails** feature these popular outdoor attractions. **Animal Lover Walks** will attract those who want to see other species along the way. **Bog and Marsh Hikes** will attract bird watchers, frog lovers, plant enthusiasts and those who appreciate calm, diverse scenery. **Forest Adventures** are for those wishing to wander among trees growing in their natural habitats. **Historical Journeys** retrace the steps of our ancestors. **Multi-Day Hikes** will appeal to those looking to retreat into the wild. **Trails over Sand Dunes** offer ways for hikers to explore these unusual features. And last but not least, although most trails in Ontario feature at least one or two **Glacial Features**, we've listed places where such landmarks are numerous or spectacular.

Chapter Overview

The **Practical Information** chapter helps you get ready for a typical day hike, and includes a checklist of the most important items you'll need.

To help you identify hikes that match your own passions, the **Ontario Overview** chapter provides a big-picture look at Ontario. Along with size and climate, it mentions major physical landforms, unusual flora and fauna and unique historical landmarks throughout the province.

The **Multi-Regional Trails** chapter provides basic information about any trail that crosses through two or more regions.

The rest of the book is divided into six major regions, which are roughly based on telephone area codes. They include Southern Ontario (519 area code), Greater Toronto and the Niagara Peninsula (416 and 905 area codes), Central Ontario (705 area code), Eastern Ontario (613 area code), Northeastern Ontario (705 area code north of Lake Huron) and Northwestern Ontario (807 area code). A short list of other hiking trails in the region is also listed at the back of each chapter so you can choose your own path, no matter which part of Ontario you decide to visit.

Southern Ontario lies between Lake Erie and Lake Huron. Major towns in the area include Goderich, Guelph, Kitchener, Leamington, London, Orangeville, Sarnia, Stratford, Tobermory, Wasaga Beach, Windsor and Woodstock. This relatively flat region is known for Carolinian forests, oak savanna, vast farms, sandy beaches, and flowing rivers.

The **Greater Toronto and the Niagara Peninsula** chapter includes Aurora, Bolton, Bradford, Brampton, Brantford, Burlington, Cambridge, Hamilton, Oshawa, Port Hope, Pickering, Markham, Milton, Mississauga, Newmarket, Niagara Falls, St. Catharines and Toronto. The area is known for the Niagara Escarpment, the Oak Ridges Moraine, the Welland Canal, Carolinian forests and an incredible variety of bird species.

Central Ontario includes the Kawartha Lakes region, Algonquin Park and the northern coast of Georgian Bay. Major towns include Barrie, Bracebridge, Collingwood, Gravenhurst, Haliburton, Huntsville, Lindsay, Midland, Orillia, Peterborough, and the Town of the Blue Mountains. This region, pitted with caves and lakes, has great Aboriginal significance and is the best place for viewing drumlins, potholes and moraines.

Eastern Ontario is the area just north of Lake Ontario and along the St. Lawrence River next to the Québec border. Major towns include Belleville, Brockville, Cornwall, Gananoque, Kanata, Kingston, Nepean, Ottawa, and Trenton. This ancient marine bed is known for pink granite, rock paintings, abandoned mines, farming estates, vast marshes and the Rideau Canal.

Northeastern Ontario includes the northern coast of Georgian Bay and Lake Huron north to James Bay. Major towns include North Bay, Sault Ste. Marie, Sudbury and Timmins. This region, which also includes Manitoulin Island, has become known for its landscape of rock ridges, wild water, and stunted trees that was made famous by the Group of Seven.

Northwestern Ontario is the area north of Lake Superior through to Lake of the Woods and the Manitoba border. Major towns include Atikokan, Dryden, Fort Frances, Kenora, Marathon, Nipigon and Thunder Bay. Only a few trails have pierced this vast mysterious region of impenetrable rock, huge canyons and waterfalls, making it a prime hiking location for daring adventurers.

How to Use This Guide

Within each chapter, hiking locations are placed in alphabetical order. In each location, trails appear in recommended order. The only exception to this is for trails that begin in the middle or at the end of another trail. In those cases, the trails are listed in the order they are encountered.

The description of each trail includes everything needed to plan a trip, including **interesting features**, **trailheads**, **services and facilities** in the area and **contact information** for the organization or club in charge of trail maintenance. When **dogs** are permitted on a trail, this is mentioned. Most parks allow dogs on trails as long as they are kept on a short leash.

The length of the trail, in kilometres and miles, is followed by either the word **linear** or **loop** to indicate how a hiker will travel.

The **estimated time** for completion is extremely **generous** and often includes time for lunch and sightseeing. It is often followed by **return** to indicate that the hiker is completing a loop and expected to return to the trailhead in the time specified, or **each way** when a hiker will likely double back along the same trail, or begin another trail rather than returning to the trailhead.

We hope that, with this guidebook, you'll have a meaningful personal journey hiking through the natural splendour of Ontario.

Happy trails!

Trail Rating Information

Easy trails can be completed by just about anybody, including a four-year-old child or a parent wearing a child carrier.

Moderate trails have uneven, rocky or root-covered pathways or include sections that might be difficult for children, backpackers or someone with a mild knee injury, for example.

Difficult trails attract experienced hikers, who don't mind rocky climbs and uneven or wet paths. They often include dangerous sections.

Practical Information

This chapter covers what you need to do to prepare for a hike, including what to wear, day-trip and backpacking necessities, potential problems you might encounter on a trail, and trail ethics.

Equipment

What to Wear

Dressing for a hike depends in part on the weather, but you'll want to include a number of layers to stay comfortable should the weather change, as it invariably does.

A **light**, **loose-fitting long-sleeved shirt** and **comfortable pants** are best, in case insects become numerous.

Wear **socks** to protect your feet from blistering and your ankles from ticks, fleas, mosquitoes and other insects. Good **running shoes** or **foot-bearing sandals** are fine for many hikes, although **hiking boots** are better on difficult trails. Wear a **hat** with a good brim to keep the sun off your face.

Day Trip Necessities

- Antiseptic towelettes, hand sanitizer or baby wipes
- Baby carrier (if needed), with diaper bag
- Backpack or daypack
- Extra clothes for children (if needed)
- Extra socks
- Facial tissue or toilet paper
- First-aid kit (acetaminophen, adhesive bandages, alcohol, antiseptic towelettes, candle, first-aid cream, gauze, sting relief, matches, scissors, tensor bandage)
- Flashlight
- Fleece jacket
- Garbage bags
- Gloves
- High-energy snacks (dried fruit, nuts, cookies, chocolate, soda crackers, sports drink)
- Insect repellent
- Rain gear
- Sun screen
- Water: at least one litre (three in the summer) per person

Other Handy Items

- Binoculars
- Cash
- Camera
- Compass
- Field guides (plants, birds, butterflies, spiders, reptiles, amphibians)
- Hiking boots
- Hunter orange vest (for spring and fall hiking)
- Lip balm
- Maps
- Noise-maker for pack (bell, pots, wind chimes)

- Notebook and pencil
- Sun screen
- Pocket knife
- Toilet paper
- Whistle
- Walking stick

Overnight Necessities

All items previously listed, plus:

- Camp stove, with appropriate fuel
- Candles (to replace the intimacy of a campfire)
- Clothing
- Cooking pot and bowl
- Food and drink (no cans or bottles)
- Insulating mattress
- Muscle cream
- Sleeping bag
- Sleepwear
- Soap
- Utensils
- Tent
- Toothbrush and toothpaste
- Towel

Potential Health Risks on the Trail

Heat Exhaustion and Stroke

A lack of water and salt can cause heat exhaustion, which can turn into heat stroke. Early signs include red cheeks, muscle weakness, mild confusion, headache and nausea. Children feel dizzy and faint. Vomiting is common. Drinking enough water throughout the hike should prevent heat exhaustion from occurring, but if you begin to feel dizzy or light headed, stop hiking. Get out of the sun. If possible, lie flat and raise your feet. Sprinkle yourself with cool water. Drink a high energy drink or as much water as possible. Eat something salty. Stop hiking until you feel better, and even then, hike only as long as necessary to get off the trail and back home.

Hypothermia

Any prolonged exposure to cold air or water can cause your body temperature to drop below a normal level, a condition known as hypothermia. Tired, hungry children easily suffer this condition, even in the summer. Symptoms include a persistent chill, uncontrollable shivering, skin numbness and a change in muscle coordination. Confusion, lethargy and frequent falls follow the initial symptoms. Treatment includes changing into warm clothes, drinking warm beverages and applying an external source of heat.

Poison Ivy

Poison ivy—a plant with a volatile oil that causes severe skin reactions—can grow as ground cover, plant, bush or vine, depending on the location in Ontario. It has three leaflets that can be either glossy or dull; small white flower clusters appear from May until

July and small white berries from August until November. It turns a brilliant red in the fall, but the only way to distinguish it from other three-leaved plants during the rest of the year is an extended stem on the centre leaf.

If you suspect that you've touched poison ivy, wash your skin immediately with soap or rub it with alcohol. After ten minutes, the resin can't be washed off. It can take anywhere from three hours to three days after contact for the itching and inflammation to begin.

Poison Oak

Touching poison oak also results in an itchy rash, although the plant is much less common than poison ivy. It grows as a shrub and resembles poison ivy, except that the three leaflets are lobed like oak leaves.

Poison Sumac

Poison sumac grows in swampy, partially wooded areas and is even less common than poison ivy and poison oak. It grows as a shrub or small tree. Leaves consist of seven to 13 smooth pointed leaflets.

Lyme Disease

A bacteria spread by deer ticks can cause nausea, headaches, vomiting and fever anywhere from three days or three weeks after the initial bite. Use tweezers to remove the tiny dots from exposed skin within 24 hours of contact. Pull slowly and steadily so you don't squeeze or twist the tick. If you notice a bull's-eye rash around the bite, consult a doctor immediately.

Bee, Wasp and Hornet Stings

Remove the stinger of a bee, wasp or hornet by scraping it gently away from the skin. Do not pull.

Snake Bites

The only venomous snake in Ontario is the massasauga rattlesnake in the Georgian Bay area. If you are bitten, stop hiking immediately and lie down to keep the bitten limb at the same level as the heart. Wash the bite with soap and water. Place a flat tight bandage between the bite mark and the heart, but do not stop blood circulation. Call or send for medical help. All the hospitals in the Georgian Bay area carry anti-venom vaccine.

Rabies

Bats, coyotes, foxes, skunks and raccoons are all potential rabies carriers. Hikers should avoid any animal that easily approaches them, especially if they seem to be moving erratically or salivating. If a hiker—or a hiker's dog—is bitten, clean the wound with antiseptic and get to a hospital immediately.

Black Bear Attack

Hikers in black bear country should consider wearing noisemakers on their packs. Also, be careful around berry patches, beech trees and dead animals. If you approach a bear that hasn't run away, back away slowly and take a different route.

West Nile Virus

Birds with West Nile Virus (WNV) are now prevalent in Ontario. The disease spreads to humans through mosquitoes that bite after having bitten infected birds. Infections cause no symptoms in 80% of those bitten, but others suffer from aches, fever or encephalitis between 3 and 15 days after contact. Mosquito netting offers some protection, as does repellent lotion.

Trail Ethics

Avoid Wildlife

Scaring a bird away from a nest is a death sentence for its young.

Touching insects and amphibians can kill or hurt them, especially if you have insect repellent or other chemicals on your hands. Moving rocks or logs to see them can destroy their homes.

Don't feed wildlife. Canada geese no longer migrate south for the winter because they've been fed over the years. Chipmunks, raccoons, pigeons and squirrels become very aggressive when campers feed them.

Don't Touch Plants

Many of the conservation areas don't publicize the rare plants, flowers, sedges and bushes in their parks to avoid visitors stealing plant and grass specimens for gardens, picking flowers for decoration, cutting branches for floral displays, or picking edible plants and berries. Consider growing your own specimens from seed or looking in potential construction sites for this purpose.

Follow Trail Markers

Provincial parks, conservation areas and trail associations frequently improve, change and temporarily close trails for habitat improvement, species protection or other reasons.

Take Out What You Bring In

Many locations, including Algonquin Park, ban bottles and cans from their interior sites. Take along a garbage bag for your refuse and carry it home for disposal.

Hunting Seasons

Hunting is very popular in Ontario, especially in the spring and autumn. Moose and turkey seasons occur in the spring, while bear and waterfowl seasons are in the late summer and fall. Some provincial parks and most conservation areas allow hunting within their territories, so be sure to check in with authorities prior to hiking. When in doubt, wear a hunter orange vest to be certain that you will be visible to hunting parties.

ONTARIO
Hudson Bay
James Bay
Akimiski Island
LABRADOR (NEWFOUNDLAND)
MANITOBA
ONTARIO
QUÉBEC
CANADA
N.B.
MAINE
NEW HAMPSHIRE
VERMONT
MASS.
NEW YORK
NORTH DAKOTA
MINNESOTA
WISCONSIN
MICHIGAN
UNITED STATES
ATLANTIC OCEAN
Lake Winnipeg
Lake Superior
Lake Michigan
Lake Huron
Lake Ontario
Lake Erie
St. Lawrence River
Fort Seven
Winisk
Lake River
Big Trout Lake
Attawapiskat
Fort Albany
Moosonee
Kuujjuarapik
Chisasibi
Waskaganish
Chibougamau
Saguenay
Tadoussac
Rivière-du-Loup
Havre-Saint-Pierre
Sept-Îles
Port-Cartier
Baie-Comeau
Matane
Gaspé
Percé
Fredericton
Saint John
Québec City
Trois-Rivières
Montréal
Gatineau
Ottawa
Kingston
Peterborough
Toronto
Niagara Falls
London
Windsor
Detroit
Owen Sound
Sudbury
North Bay
Sault Ste. Marie
Agawa Bay
Wawa
Marathon
Gogama
Kirkland Lake
Timmins
Geraldton
Armstrong
Thunder Bay
English River
Hudson
Kenora
Fort Frances
Winnipeg
Grand Forks
Fargo
Duluth
Minneapolis
Sioux Falls
Green Bay
Waterville
Boston
Albany
New York
1
17
71
11
53
66
2
69
7
401
75
94
35
21
40
20
15
95
87
89
138
132
0
150
300km
©ULYSSES

Ontario Overview

A hike is the best way to begin appreciating the subtle beauty of Ontario's landscape. With careful observation you can detect evidence of the last glacier retreat. This incredible event took place over an 8,000-year-long period that began 18,000 years ago and remains a modern-day mystery.

By using modern landforms as clues, you can guess how this land became what it is today. The biggest clues include the Great Lakes and the Niagara Escarpment, but you'll identify some smaller ones too, including hills that are actually drumlins, ridges called moraines and mounds known as eskers. You'll see deep, perfectly round holes with smooth walls called potholes, cobble beaches, kettle lakes, boulder fields and a multitude of other treasures.

Most major hiking trails in Ontario include glacial landforms as some of their most interesting features, but glaciers aren't the only important natural forces that have left their mark. Ontario is a very large province with a diverse geology, multiple climates and an abundance of fresh water which make it home to a variety of types of flora and fauna. These natural forces combine with human intervention to provide Ontario hikers with a great variety of experiences.

That's the big picture you'll discover in this chapter.

Geography

Size

Ontario covers 1,068,580km² (412,579 sq mi), 10.7% of Canada's total landmass. Land makes up 83% of the province's total area, while water makes up the remaining 17%. This extensive territory encompasses cities and countryside, 807,000km² (31,158 sq mi) of vast forests and 17,610km² (6,799 sq mi) of rocky tundra beyond the tree line.

The province borders on five U.S. states (Minnesota, Michigan, Ohio, Pennsylvania and New York), two Canadian provinces (Manitoba and Québec), four of the five Great Lakes (Superior, Huron, Erie, and Ontario), and two vast bays (Hudson Bay and James Bay).

Climatic Zones

Because of its large size, the number of climatic zones in Ontario ranges from a minimum of three to at least 17, depending on which variables are considered. Wladimir Köppen's system, for instance, divides Ontario into three distinct regions based on a comparison with worldwide precipitation, temperature and vegetation. The zones include: warm summer (the very southern tip of the province), cool summer (the north shore of Lake Huron and areas to the south) and subarctic (north of Lake Superior).

When the U.S. Department of Agriculture published a map of climatic zones for North America, however, they were most concerned with plant hardiness and chose to consider only one variable: minimum winter temperature. That map divides Ontario into five zones.

When Agriculture Canada performed the same exercise in the 1960s, the department compared low winter temperatures, frost-free period length, summer and winter precipitation, summer high temperatures, snow depth, wind speed and the hardiness of 174 shrubs at 108 stations throughout Canada. Its map divides Ontario into 14 zones. Natural Resources Canada recently updated this map and added elevation as a new variable. The new version includes 17 subzones.

All this is to say that the more you know about Ontario, the more local variations in climate you find. Because of the effects of latitude, summers are generally hot in the south, and cooler towards the north. Average summer temperatures range from 16.8°C (62.2°F) in the northeast region (Kapuskasing) to 20.6°C (69°F) in the central (Toronto) and eastern (Ottawa) regions. Thunder Bay, in the northwest, has the greatest amount of sunshine per year, with an average annual total of 2,203hrs.

Winter temperatures vary to an even greater degree. While winter is cold across the province, it is absolutely frigid in the north. Average winter temperatures vary from -18.5°C (-1.3°F) in Kapuskasing to 6.7°C (44.1°F) in Toronto. Local wind speeds exacerbate the effects.

Humidity exacerbates the effect of cold and hot temperatures on hikers. The level of humidity in a region depends on its proximity to large bodies of water and the prevailing winds. The latter are a significant factor because they carry moisture as they move from west to east. Perhaps not surprisingly, humidity is very high in the south and on coastal areas and lower in the northwest.

Southern and coastal areas also receive an increased level of annual rain and snowfall, although there is also a snowbelt arc that stretches east from Georgian Bay. Annual precipitation is highest in southwestern Ontario (London), with 909.4mm (36in), and lowest in the northwest (Thunder Bay). Average annual snowfall ranges from a low of 131.2cm (51in) in Toronto to 319.9cm (125in) in Kapuskasing. Most places average about 200cm (78in) a year.

Despite all these variations, Ontario's weather is generally quite predictable, although frequently changing. When preparing for your hike, call ahead to the region you want to visit and ask locals what the weather is like.

Topography

Ontario includes four major topographic regions: the Canadian Shield (also known as the Precambrian Shield), the Hudson

Bay Lowland, the Great Lakes Lowland and the St. Lawrence Lowland.

The largest of these regions is the Canadian Shield, which covers about two-thirds of the province in an arc around Hudson Bay. The ancient plateau once held towering mountains of hardened volcanic magma and tough bedrock hardened by heat or a combination of heat, water and pressure. Known as the La Cloche range, these mountains were thrust up by volcanoes 3.8 million years ago. Since then, the tops of the mountains have disappeared, as a result of erosion by four glaciers, wind and water. The result is a layer of rock that lies very close to the surface and slopes gently toward the north. A southeast extension of the Canadian Shield, known as the Frontenac Axis or Arch, separates the St. Lawrence and Great Lakes lowlands. The Frontenac Axis forms the Thousand Islands in the St. Lawrence River and ends as the Adirondack Mountains of New York. Hikers in the southern portion of the Canadian Shield and along the Frontenac Arch can see jagged outcrops of some of the oldest rock on the planet.

The Hudson Bay Lowland is a subarctic area of flat bogs and small trees that circles Hudson Bay. There are no roads through the region and much of it is inaccessible to hikers, except by canoe or train.

The St. Lawrence Lowland is a flat—less than 91m-high (300ft)—plain of sand and clay that extends along the St. Lawrence River into Québec. The sand and clay deposits that don't come from the St. Lawrence River itself were left behind after the melting of the Champlain Sea, a vast, cold body of water that once covered much of the area.

The Great Lakes Lowland region is that portion of Ontario that lies south of the Niagara Escarpment. A deep layer of fertile soil and a moderate climate make the area one of the three most fertile regions in all of Canada. Hikers in this region will be able to stock up on fresh peaches, cherries and grapes.

Major Glacial Landforms

Ontario has several major landforms left behind by glaciers. Some of the most significant for hikers include the Niagara Escarpment, the Oak Ridges Moraine and the Sleeping Giant.

The Niagara Escarpment

Glaciers left a 736km-long (442mi) horseshoe-shaped ridge between Queenston and Tobermory that is now called the Niagara Escarpment. The northern portion of the escarpment, some 80km (50mi) in length, juts out into Lake Huron and forms the Bruce Peninsula. This area is known for the wide variety of ferns and 43 species of wild orchids that grow here. The United Nations proclaimed the Niagara Escarpment a UNESCO World Biosphere Reserve in 1990. Ontario's longest trail, the **Bruce Trail** (see p. 57), follows the entire escarpment.

The Oak Ridges Moraine

Another ridge, the Oak Ridges Moraine, runs for about 200km (124mi) from the Niagara Escarpment in the west to the Trent River in the east. Volunteers are currently working on completing a trail (see p. 67) along the top of the moraine.

The Sleeping Giant

Glaciers and erosion have helped create a giant rock formation that looks exactly like Gulliver in the land of the Lilliputians. The formation is now protected within **Sleeping Giant Provincial Park** (see p. 259). Trails lead up to the giant's knees and chest for a panoramic view of Lake Superior.

Other Major Landforms

Glaciers aren't the only mysteries hidden within Ontario's geography for hikers to consider. Earthquakes, volcanoes and perhaps even meteorites have also created some interesting landforms, including the Sudbury Basin, Ouimet Canyon and Agawa Canyon.

The Sudbury Basin

No one is quite sure about the origin of the Sudbury basin, a crater 56km (35mi) long and 27km (17mi) wide. Hypotheses include that it was caused by the impact of a giant meteorite, or that an ancient volcano subsequently got buried, leaving only the depression from which it spewed.

Ouimet Canyon

Subarctic plants grow in Ontario in the shade of **Ouimet Canyon** (see p. 251), a 3.2km (2mi) gorge that is 107m (351ft) deep and 132m (440ft) wide. The canyon is located near the town of Nipigon.

Agawa Canyon

Earthquakes wrenched apart the tough bedrock of the Canadian Shield to form Agawa Canyon, Agawa Rock and Old Woman Bay. All three of these land formations are part of **Lake Superior Provincial Park** (see p. 231), south of Wawa, near Sault St. Marie. The area falls into a transitional zone between mixed and boreal forest ranges, which attracts an abundance of wildlife, including moose, timber wolves, Canada lynx and bears.

Lakes

Freshwater covers 17% of Ontario, although some residents also have access to saltwater along the 1,094km (680mi) shoreline of James and Hudson bays.

Much of that area consists of Lake of the Woods and four of the five Great Lakes, which are jointly controlled by Canada and the United States. Together, the five Great Lakes make up the world's biggest continuous body of fresh water. A boardwalk and trails run along Lake Ontario as part of the Lake Ontario **Waterfront Trail** (see p. 71).

The province also includes some 250,000 other lakes, many of them in the western part. Among the largest are Lake Nipigon, Lac Seul, Lake Abitibi (shared with Québec), Lake Nipissing, Lake Simcoe, Rainy Lake, and Big Trout Lake.

Rivers

Rivers in southern Ontario, including the Niagara, Ottawa, French, Grand, and Thames rivers, flow into the Atlantic Ocean by way of the Great Lakes and the St. Lawrence River system. Most northern Ontario rivers, including the Severn, Winisk, Attawapiskat, Albany, and Abitibi, empty into James Bay and Hudson Bay. A few of the rivers in northwestern Ontario flow westward into Manitoba.

Heritage Rivers

Of the 39 Heritage Rivers in Canada, 11 are in Ontario:

The **Bloodvein River** links Woodland Caribou Provincial Park near Thunder Bay to Atikaki Provincial Park in Manitoba. Since the region through which the Bloodvein passes has no roads, the river runs for 300km (186mi) through unspoiled plant and animal communities that have remained virtually intact since the glacier age.

The "**Boundary Waters**" are all the lakes, rivers and portages used by the Voyageurs to get from Lake Superior to Lac La Croix. Most of the 250km (155mi) corridor is protected both in Minnesota and by Ontario's Quetico, La Verendrye and Middle Falls provincial parks, designated in 1996.

The **Detroit River**'s important role as transportation and food for settlers began in 400 A.D. It has also served as a strategic location during battles and escapes, particularly for loyalists during the American Revolution, slaves during the Underground Railway era and draft dodgers and deserters during many different wars. Ecologically, it is important in Canada as the only river that lies totally within the Carolinian zone. It was designated as an American Heritage River in 1998 and a Canadian Heritage River in 2001.

The **French River** became a Canadian Heritage River in 1986, in part because it was one of the country's best examples of a glaciated Canadian Shield river environment. Located 60km (37mi) south of Sudbury, the river flows through a landscape that remains largely unchanged from when the first Europeans explored it more than 300 years ago. French River Provincial Park covers 51,000ha (125,970 acres) and includes the French River's 110km (68mi) corridor plus an additional 200km (124mi) of navigable water courses and channels which vary from narrow, enclosed steep-walled gorges, falls and rapids, to broad expanses of open water.

At 7,000km² (2,600 sq mi), the **Grand River** watershed represents southern Ontario's largest and most important inland water resource. The river, whose watershed covers an area equal in size to Prince Edward Island, was designated a Canadian Heritage River under a joint federal, provincial and territorial program in

1993. The Grand River Trail will eventually enable hikers to walk the entire length of the river.

The 100km (62mi) long **Humber River** begins at the junction of the Niagara Escarpment and the Oak Ridges Moraine and runs through the city of Toronto's Hyde Park to the Humber Marshes at the edge of Lake Ontario. It became a designated Heritage River in 1999. The entire 908km² watershed has been known as one of the most populated areas in Canada as far back as with the Paleo-Indians in 10,000 BC.

Like the French River, the **Mattawa River** provides a link to the voyageurs of the 17th century. Designated in 1988, the Mattawa River runs through a 600-million-year-old fissure in the earth's crust and through Samuel de Champlain Provincial Park. Forests of red and white pine or secluded groves of hemlock and yellow birch border the river. This pristine ecosystem grows a unique hybrid of wild rye bottlebrush grass, fragrant smooth roses, and cardinal flowers. Moose, wolves, and bears live in Samuel de Champlain Park all year, while white-tailed deer feed there in winter.

The **Missinaibi River**, which was designated as a Heritage River in 2004, has a distinguished history as the main transportation route for fur traders moving between Lake Superior and James Bay. Signs of this significant past include former trading posts and pictograph sites which can be found all along the river. The river also houses important ecological sites such as the Thunderhouse and Split Rock waterfalls and the Peterbell bog and marsh.

The **Rideau Waterway** encompasses all the rivers, lakes and canals for 202km (125mi) between Canada's capital city, Ottawa, and the former capital city of Kingston. Built as a freight canal between 1826 and 1832, the waterway includes 24 still-operating lock stations. A particularly scenic section cuts through the Precambrian rock that makes up the Frontenac Axis. It was designated a Canadian Heritage River in 2000, and a UNESCO World Heritage Site in 2007.

St. Mary's River, which was designated in 2000, links lakes Superior, Michigan and Huron. It begins at Gros Cap, continues through Sault Ste. Marie and divides into two at St. Joseph Island. The area along the river is known to have been settled as far back as 2500 BC. A prime hiking trail, the **Voyageur Trail** (see p. 70), runs along the shores of much of the river.

The **Thames River** was designated in 2000 to commemorate human settlement going back to 90 BC. The 273km (169mi) river runs from Mitchell, Hickson and Tavistock through the cities of London and Chatham and four First Nations Reserves (Chippewa, Moravian, Munsee Delaware and Oneida) until it ends at Lake St. Clair. Heritage sites marking the war of 1812, agricultural clearings of the 1850s and Underground Railway can be found along its shores.

Waterfalls

The Niagara River flows between Lake Erie and Lake Ontario, creating the legendary Niagara Falls along the way. Other towns also have waterfalls to be proud of. **Kakabeka Falls** (see p. 248) near Thunder Bay are the northern version of Niagara. Owen Sound is home to three scenic waterfalls—Inglis Falls, Jones Falls and Indian Falls—while Healey Falls is located in Campbellford.

Sixteen Mile Creek tumbles over the escarpment to form Hilton Falls, in a conservation area of the same name near Milton.

There's also Recollet Falls on the French River, **Ball's Falls** (see p. 119) on the Niagara Peninsula and plenty of others.

Wetlands

Ontario is home to several important wetland areas that protect bog plants and sustain insects and birds. These include the Beverly Swamp, Lee Brown Waterfowl Management Area and **Luther Marsh** (see p. 97).

Presqu'ile Provincial Park (see p. 72) contains several coastal wet meadows called "pannes." These internationally significant areas support several endemic species of plants and insects.

A bog in **Sleeping Giant Provincial Park** (see p. 259) supports two unusual orchids, the adder's mouth and the striped round-leafed orchid.

Wet meadows in **Pinery Provincial Park** (see p. 101) provide the only ecosystem in Canada where the blue heart (*Buchnera americana*) can grow.

Extensive wetlands at the mouth of the French River on Georgian Bay provide a habitat for the most abundant population of Virginia chain fern in Canada.

Canals

Each of Ontario's four canals—the Welland Canal, the Rideau Canal, the Sault Ste. Marie Canal and the Trent-Severn Waterway—offer hiking routes along their banks.

Originally built to serve as a protected supply route after the War of 1812, the **Rideau Canal** connects Ottawa and Kingston. The **Rideau Trail** (see p. 211) follows part of the 202km (126mi) route of 47 locks and 24 dams that allows ships to traverse this part of the Canadian Shield.

The **Sault Ste. Marie Canal** through the St. Mary's Rapids was considered the world's most advanced when it opened as the Canadian Sault Ship Canal in 1895. Unique features included on-site electricity generation and an Emergency Swing Bridge Dam.

The **Trent-Severn Waterway** runs for 386km (240mi) from Trenton to Port Severn. A system of 44 locks connects Lakes Rice, Lovesick, Buckhorn, Pigeon, Sturgeon, Stony, Balsam, Simcoe and Couchiching.

The **Welland Canal** bypasses Niagara Falls to link Lake Erie with Lake Ontario. As a result of the Niagara Escarpment, Lake

Erie is 99.5m (326.5ft) higher that Lake Ontario. The modern-day canal runs 42km (26mi) from Lock 1 in St. Catharines to Lock 8 at Port Colborne, but three older locks still exist.

Flora

Bioregions

Ontario's five bioregions are determined by the type or absence of trees on the land. Three quarters of Ontario, 807,000km² (311,583 sq mi), is forested with boreal forest or deciduous trees, with the vast mixed forests in the middle part of the province containing both types. Permafrost in the north creates a fourth bioregion called tundra. A large marsh just south of the tundra area stunts the conifers into a barren boreal forest.

The **tundra** area of Ontario is a very narrow band of permanently frozen subarctic land next to Hudson Bay.

The area of Ontario to the north of the tree line is known as the **boreal barrens**. It stretches in a band from the Québec border to the Manitoba border, and from Pickle Lake north to James Bay and Hudson Bay.

The largest forest type in Ontario is the **boreal forest** region, which stretches from the north shore of Lake Superior to the tree-line. In this region, you'll mainly find black and white spruce, jack pine, aspen and white birch trees.

The second-largest forest type is the mixed forest of the **Great Lakes-St. Lawrence mixed forest** region. This region covers central Ontario from Ottawa to Sault Ste. Marie and includes a small band near the Rainy River along the Minnesota border in the northwest. These forests contain vast quantities of sugar maple, beech, yellow birch, red oak, and red and white pine. In fact, white pine is so prevalent, it's been chosen as Ontario's official tree. The tallest white pine in Ontario—in Gillies Grove, near Arnprior—stands at 50m (163.5ft) high. Red pine also grows very tall. Caliper Lake, near Nestor Falls in Northern Ontario, features an impressive stand of 12- to 18m-high (40 to 60ft) red pine. The mixed forest also contains black and white spruce, aspen, ash, hemlock, red maple and white cedar. The mixed forest is also where you'll find numerous beautiful drifts of trillium. Although there are red and drooping trilliums, the white version is more numerous and claims status as Ontario's official flower. The three-petalled beauty blooms for about four weeks in May.

The **deciduous forest** includes pure maple and birch forests, beech forests and oak forests. There are only rare stands of this forest in the very southern portion of Ontario.

While the small stands of deciduous forest dotted throughout the extreme southwest region of the province don't cover a large area, they do have a special status. Known as **Carolinian Canada**, the areas contain a wide variety of interesting flora that do not grow naturally anywhere else in Canada. Sample specimens include: American crab apple (*Pyrus coronaria*), black walnut (*Juglans nigra*), chestnut (*Castanea dentata*), flowering dogwood (*Cornus florida*), pawpaw (*Asimina triloba*), sassafras (*Sassafras variifolium*), sour gum (*Nyssa sylvatica*), sycamore (*Platanus occidentalis*), and tulip tree (*Liriodendron tulipifera*). Carolinian Canada also contains six species of hickories and 10 species of oak. Many of the trees that grow in this area are at risk of extinction. (See rare trees below.)

Southern Ontario also contains one of the largest remaining examples of **oak savanna**, an ecosystem that has become even more rare than rain forests. Located in **Pinery Provincial Park** (see p. 101) on the southern shores of Lake Huron and on the **Oak Ridges Moraine** (see p. 31) south of Rice Lake, the savanna contains massive oak trees, prairie grasses, wildflowers and shrubs in broad meadows. These are the last remnants of an ecosystem that used to cover huge tracts of land along the border of the grasslands of the Great American Plains.

Killbear Provincial Park, on the shore of Georgian Bay north of Perry Sound, protects a **sedge meadow**, a **black spruce bog**, a **floating sphagnum bog** and **sand dunes**. Hikers can wander along kilometres of sandy beach or along three different trails.

Long Point Provincial Park (see p. 95), south of Brantford, protects a sandy spit that juts out for 40km (25mi) into Lake Erie. Southwesterly winds and shore currents have been depositing sediment along the spit for the last 4,000 years. The area is so unique that the United Nations has recognized it as a biosphere reserve. Many native plant species live in the marshes and wet meadows, including grass-of-Parnassus, fringed and bottle gentians, lady's-tresses orchids and sneezeweed.

Rare Trees

The blue ash (*Fraxinus quadrangulata*) is a Carolinian tree that is named for the colour of dye that Aboriginals produced by mashing its inner tree bark. Southwestern Ontario is the northern limit of its range and it is considered vulnerable in the province.

The cucumber tree (*Magnolia acuminata*), Canada's only native magnolia, is on both the provincial and national endangered species list. Only nine stands of this tree remain in southwestern Ontario and only three of those are of significant size.

Fewer than 200 mature **Kentucky coffee trees** (*Gymnocladus dioica*) remain in Ontario. The tree was so named by early North American settlers who used the poisonous seeds as a coffee substitute. This tree is easy to recognize in woodlands and at the edge of marshes, because it spends nine months of the year without leaves and has the largest leaves of any tree in Canada.

The **Shumard oak** (*Quercus shumardii*) grows in the swampy areas along the shores of Lake Erie, primarily in conservation areas. Some specimens are 12m (40ft) tall.

Thanks to hybridization with Asia's white mulberry (*Morus alba*), Ontario's **red mulberry** (*Morus rubra*) population has just about been eliminated. Red mulberries can grow up to 9m (30ft) tall and have blackberry-like fruit.

The sun-loving **dwarf hackberry** (*Celtis tenuifolia*) dies when shaded. In Ontario, this elm can be found on Pelee Island, at Point Pelee and on the shores of Lake Huron. Birds love its orange-coloured fruit.

In Ontario, the **hoptree** (*Ptelea trifoliata*) can only be found on sandy beaches along the shore of Lake Erie, particularly on the west shore of Point Pelee in **Point Pelee National Park** (see p. 106). Beer brewers used its fruit as a hop substitute in the 1800s. It's an important food for giant swallowtail butterfly caterpillars.

A fungus called chestnut blight destroyed most of the **American chestnut** (*Castanea dentata*) stands in North America in the early 20th century. Although the tree once grew throughout Carolinian Canada, fewer than 200 specimens remain, most on private land.

Rare Plants

Canada's last remaining stands of **Pitcher's thistle** (*Cirsium pitcheri*) grow along Lake Huron south of the Bruce Peninsula, on Manitoulin Island, and at one location on Lake Superior.

Only two stands of the white or maroon **drooping trillium** (*Trillium flexipes*) grow in Ontario, and the species is endangered throughout North America.

Golden seal (*Hydrastis canadensis*) is also known as yellow paint, yellow puccoon and turmeric root because of its bright yellow rootstalk. Feathery white flowers bloom in spring, followed by an inedible fruit that resembles raspberries. Avid collectors seeking to make a medicinal tea from the roots have over-collected this plant to the point where it now can only be found on private land.

The triangular fronds of the **broad beech fern** (*Phegopteris hexagonoptera*) can grow as long as 40cm (16in). Although the fern is vulnerable, it can still be found in southern Muskoka, along the shores of Lake Erie, and in the St. Lawrence lowland. It is not a protected species.

Each flower on an **eastern prairie white-fringed orchid** (*Platanthera leucophaea*) lasts for about 10 days. If a stalk on a plant has several flowers, the display can last for up to three weeks. Although this species can grow throughout southern Ontario, the scarcity of brush fires, which stimulate flowering, has led to its decline.

Although the blue and yellow **wild hyacinth** (*Camassia scilloides*) does not grow on mainland Ontario, it can be found on several islands in Lake Erie, including Pelee Island. Aboriginals used to depend on wild hyacinth bulbs as an important food source, but today, collectors tend to steal them for their gardens.

Botanists studying sphagnum bogs in the Georgian Bay region only found the **twining screwstem** (*Bartonia paniculata*) growing there in 1973. Tiny scales appearing on the annual vine instead of leaves have led researchers to speculate that the plant may rely on soil fungi for its growth, as do orchids. The Ontario stand appears to be a fluke, as the next closest population occurs 600km (372mi) away.

Fauna

Mammals

Ontario is home to 84 different mammals, including beaver, bear (black bear and polar bear), cottontail rabbit, coyote, eastern chipmunk, eastern cougar, lynx, groundhog, mink, moose, muskrat, porcupine, raccoon, fox (red and grey), skunk, snowshoe hare, squirrel (gray, red and southern), timber wolf and white-tailed deer.

In the southern Carolinian Forest region, whitetail deer, coyotes, red foxes, eastern cottontails and more temperate species such as the least shrew and southern flying squirrel may be seen in parks. Specific places to observe the inhabitants of the Carolinian Forest include **Short Hills** (see p. 145), **Long Point** (see p. 95), and **Rondeau** (see p. 109) provincial parks.

The Chapleau Game Preserve, north of the town of Chapleau, is North America's largest moose and bear sanctuary. No firearms are allowed.

Rare mammals include eastern elk, opossums, woodland caribou, cougars, southern flying squirrels, grey foxes and wolverines. **Eastern elk** (*Cervus elaphus canadensis*) once ranged throughout Ontario, but became extinct in 1850. The species was hunted for its antlers and teeth, which were used in necklaces. The Ministry of Natural Resources is trying once again to re-introduce the species. Ministry officials successfully introduced elk from Manitoba in the 1930s but the herd had to be destroyed in 1949, when a deer parasite was found in cattle near one of the release sites.

The **opossum**, Canada's only marsupial, lives in the Carolinian forest of **Rondeau Provincial Park** (see p. 109) near Chatham.

About 20,000 **woodland caribou** (*Rangifer tarandus caribou*) live in Ontario's boreal forest. A small herd lives on the Coldwell Peninsula in Neys Provincial Park, on the north shore of Lake Superior near Marathon. This particular subspecies of caribou is the last of its kind in Ontario.

Cougars sighted in northwestern and central Ontario are assumed to be cougars from Western Canada (*Puma concolor*) rather than the original eastern cougar (*Puma concolor couguar*) subspecies which is presumed extinct, although it's possible that those spotted in the Far North could be the descendants of the original population. Those seen

Common Animals in Ontario

The **beaver**: Known as a skilful and tireless dam builder, the beaver is Canada's national symbol. European colonization of the country began with the beaver pelt trade. The beaver has a stout body, short, webbed hind feet and a large scaly tail, which the animal uses to steer as it swims. Its powerful lower incisors allow it to cut down the trees it uses to build its shelter.

The **European cormorant**: With its glistening black plumage, this bird can reach 1m in height. An excellent diver, it can hold its breath for up to 30 seconds, long enough to catch some food.

The **raccoon**: This small animal weighs about 12kg (7.5lbs) and is characterized by the black, mask-like stripe across its eyes, the six rings around its tail and its luxuriant fur. The raccoon is a nocturnal animal. It has a reputation for cleanliness because of the way it washes its food, though the real reason the raccoon does this is to ease swallowing.

The **coyote**: Smaller than the wolf, the coyote adapts easily to various surroundings. Depending on what is available, this carnivore can survive as a vegetarian.

in southern Ontario are thought to be escaped pets.

Southern flying squirrels (*Glaucomys volans*) live in southern deciduous forests, particularly in the Long Point area.

Grey fox (*Urocyon cinereoargenteus*) kits were born in Ontario for the first time in spring 1999 on Pelee Island.

Hundreds of **wolverines** (*Gulo gulo*) live in Ontario's boreal forest, where caribou, their favourite food, is in plentiful supply.

Birds

Ontario is home to more than 300 kinds of birds. Common species include black-crowned night herons, blue jays, cardinals, chickadees, egrets, great blue herons, great horned owls, green herons, house sparrows, loons, mallard ducks, red-tailed hawks, robins, ruffed grouse, woodpeckers (downy, hairy, pileated), and a wide variety of other waterfowl and songbirds. The common loon was adopted as Ontario's official bird on June 23, 1994.

Bird migrations can be seen along the shoreline of Lake Ontario, particularly at **Point Pelee National Park** (see p. 106) and at provincial parks such as Presqu'ile, **Long Point** (see p. 95) and **Rondeau** (see p. 109). Whistling swans can also be seen in Aylmer, Ontario in the spring, where they stop to rest on their way to the High Arctic. North America's oldest privately funded bird observatory is the Long Point Bird Observatory, which is located near the park entrance.

There are also many rare birds in Ontario, some of which—like the peregrine falcon and the wild turkey—have been successfully re-introduced into the wild.

Peregrine falcons (*Falco peregrinus*) were put back into the wild between 1977 and 2006, and are now considered stable in the province, although they remained threatened. **American white pelicans** (*Pelecanus erythrorhynchos*) can be seen on Lake Nipigon, on Rainy Lake, and in Lake of the Woods Provincial Park in northwestern Ontario. The white pelican remains on Ontario's Endangered Species Act.

The **barn owl** (*Tyto alba*), another endangered bird, also lives in Ontario, although fewer than 30 breeding pairs remain. This owl has a whitish heart-shaped face, black eyes, lightly speckled pale underside, and long legs. Thanks to the popular cartoon character Woody Woodpecker, most people would have no trouble identifying another southern Ontario favourite, the **red-headed woodpecker** (*Melanerpes erythrocephalus*). Unfortunately, the Ontario-based red-headed woodpecker population has declined by about two thirds in the last 10 years due to habitat destruction by forestry and agriculture and nest-site competition from European starlings. It is now considered rare.

Rare **trumpeter swans** can be seen in Central and Eastern Ontario.

The endangered **piping plover** (*Charadrius melodus*) no longer breeds on the shores of the Great Lakes, as it once did, although a recovery plan is in place.

Butterflies

Hikers used to be able to observe **Karner blue butterflies** (*Lycaeides melissa samuelis*) in **Pinery Provincial Park** (see p. 101), but the planting of pine trees in the 1940s helped destroy its habitat. It is now considered extirpated (extinct in Ontario, but continuing to exist elsewhere). The Ontario Karner Blue Recovery Team, formed in 1993, has been conducting prescribed burns in one of the butterfly's former habitats to encourage the growth of wild lupine. If the wild lupine returns, it will also benefit the endangered **frosted elfin** (*Incisalia irus*).

The first native butterfly of spring, the **West Virginia white** (*Pieris virginiensis*) is also vulnerable in Ontario. Only 50 sites throughout the province have been found.

Monarch butterflies migrating south to Mexico in September usually gather for rest stops at **Point Pelee National Park** (see p. 106) and at Presqu'ile and **Darlington** (see p. 125) provincial parks.

Species at Risk

Canada's law to protect indigenous plants and wildlife is known as the Species at Risk Act. This act requires the Canadian Government to publicize which species are threatened, endangered and extinct in each province. For a list of the various designated species in Ontario and throughout the country, consult the **Species at Risk Public Registry** *(351 St. Joseph Blvd., 4th Floor, Gatineau, Quebec K1A 0H3, www.sararegistry.gc.ca).*

Reptiles and Amphibians

Ontario is home to 24 reptile and 42 amphibian species, including garter snakes, leopard frogs, bull frogs, spring peepers, massasauga rattlesnakes and many turtles (Blanding's, painted, snapping, spotted and wood).

Ontario's only lizard, the **five-lined skink**, lives in **Awenda** (see p. 161), **Petroglyphs** (see p. 173), **Pinery** (see p. 101) and **Rondeau** (see p. 109) provincial parks and on the southern shores of Lake Huron. The Pinery is also home to the grey tree frog, red-backed salamanders, blue-spotted salamanders and the rare hog-nose snake.

The rare **eastern massasauga rattlesnake** (*Sistrurus catenatus*), Ontario's only remaining venomous snake, prefers habitats in wetlands and in rocky areas. It lives on the Bruce Peninsula and on Beausoleil Island, the largest island in Georgian Bay National Park. There are also sporadic populations on the Niagara Peninsula and in the Windsor area.

Only three populations of the **wood turtle** (*Clemmys insculpta*)—nicknamed "old redleg"—can be found in Ontario. One of these populations occurs in Bonnechere River Provincial Park near the Algonquin Park boundary. Wood turtles live in clear rivers, streams or creeks with a moderate current and a sandy or gravelly bottom, although they spend a great deal of time out of the water, preferably in wet meadows, swamps and fields. They overwinter on stream bottoms.

About 1,200 rare **Fowler's toads** (*Bufo fowleri*) live on the north shore of Lake Erie. This rare toad likes sandy beach habitats, although it breeds in the marshy shallows of lakes or permanent ponds. Threats to the toad include beach erosion, habitat alteration and pesticides in run-off from agriculture lands. It can be found at **Point Pelee National Park** (see p. 106) and **Long Point** (see p. 95, **Rondeau** (see p. 109) and Turkey Point provincial parks.

Bright yellow spots on a black shell make the **spotted turtle** (*Clemmys guttata*) a popular sight.

The small turtle is vulnerable, however, because it depends on aquatic vegetation growing in ponds, marshes and bogs, which are quickly disappearing or becoming contaminated.

Public Lands

Ontario has many types of publicly held lands accessible to hikers.

National Parks

There are 18 national parks and historic sites in Ontario, five of which feature hiking trails. The regional chapters of this guide cover the four best hiking locations: **Bruce Peninsula National Park** (see p. 86), **Georgian Bay Islands National Park** (see p. 164), **Point Pelee National Park** (see p. 106), which has become famous as a bird-watching and butterfly migration-viewing site, and **Pukaskwa National Park** (see p. 253), a wilderness park on the north shore of Lake Superior.

> Further Information

Parks Canada
25 Eddy St., Gatineau, QC K1A 0M5
☎ 819-997-0797 or 888-773-8888
www.parkscanada.pch.gc.ca

Provincial Parks

There are more than 270 provincial parks in Ontario, many with hiking trails. Some of the most interesting have been mentioned throughout this portrait. The ones with the best hiking trails are covered in the regional chapters of this guide.

> Further Information

Ontario Ministry of Natural Resources Information Centre
300 Water St., PO Box 7000
Peterborough, ON K9J 8M5
☎ 705-755-2000 or 800-667-1940
(Note: attendants at these numbers can also transfer you directly to the parks)
900 Bay St., Room M1-73
Toronto, ON M7A 2C1
☎ 416-314-2000
☎ 888-668-7275 (Ontario Parks reservations)
www.ontarioparks.com

Ontario Ministry of Tourism
900 Bay St. 9th floor
Toronto, ON M7A 2E1
☎ 416-326-9326 or 800-668-2746
www.tourism.gov.on.ca

Conservation Areas

Conservation authorities partner with the provincial government, member municipalities and local water experts in organizations that are mandated to protect and maintain all the public land within a single watershed. Ontario has 36 such authorities (see p. 45). Each one owns a group of conservation areas established to prevent floods and erosion and to protect the prime natural resources within each watershed. The areas offer a variety of opportunities for hikers and other recreational users to increase conservation awareness.

> Further Information

Conservation Ontario
PO Box 11, 120 Bayview Pkwy.
Newmarket ON L3Y 4W3
☎ 905-895-0716
www.conservation-ontario.on.ca

Botanical Gardens and Arboretums

Thanks to dedicated organizations and individuals, Ontario has 10 botanical gardens that make good hiking destinations. They are the Dominion Arboretum at the Central Experimental Farm in Ottawa, the Centennial Botanical Conservatory in Thunder Bay, the Claude E. Garton Herbarium and Arboretum at Lakehead University in Thunder Bay, the Humber College Arboretum in Rexdale, the Niagara Parks Botanical Gardens in Niagara Falls, the **Royal Botanical Gardens** (see p. 72, 121) in Hamilton, the Cedar Valley Arboretum and Botanic Gardens in Brighten, the Sherwood Fox Arboretum at the University of Western, Ontario, the Toronto Botanical Garden, and the J. J. Neilson Arboretum at the University of Guelph.

The Canadian Botanical Conservation Network
c/o The Royal Botanical Gardens,
PO Box 399
Hamilton, ON L8N 3H8
www.rbg.ca/cbcn

The Humber Arboretum has been open seven days a week year-round since it opened in 1982. **The Humber Valley Trail** (see p. 137) goes through the 96,237ha (237,705-acre) park. You'll also find a Nature Orientation Centre, a wooden viewing deck, and the Dunington Grubb Gardens. The 10ha (24.7-acre) fringe Woodlot and Meadow Garden contains Carolinian hardwood forests of ash, maple, beech and ironwood encircling a naturalized meadow of more than 5,000 plants.

The Humber Arboretum
205 Humber College Blvd.
Toronto, ON M9W 5L7
☎ 416-675-6622 x 4467
www.humberarboretum.on.ca

Ontario Nature

Formerly known as the Federation of Ontario Naturalists, Ontario Nautre started in 1961 what has become Ontario's largest non-government nature reserves system. So far, the program has preserved 21 properties covering a total of 1,600ha (4,000 acres) of imperiled and vulnerable habitats. Within these properties are countless rare and endangered species, including the spotted turtle, the blue racer snake, the ram's head lady slipper orchid, and the bald eagle.

Although the lands are primarily biological reserves, Bruce Alvar, Kinghurst Forest, Petrel Point and Stone Road Alvar nature reserves all have short interpretive trails suitable for hiking. These areas are very sensitive, and care must be taken to stay on the trails. Ontario Nature also sets up opportunities for volunteers. See their web site for details.

› Further Information

Ontario Nature
366 W. Adelaide St., Suite 201
Toronto, ON M5V 1R9
☎ 416-444-8419 or 800-440-2366 (within Ontario)
www.ontarionature.org

1. Ausable Bayfield
2. Cataraqui Region
3. Catfish Creek
4. Central Lake Ontario
5. Conservation Halton
6. Credit Valley
7. Crowe Valley
8. Essex Region
9. Ganaraska Region
10. Grand River
11. Grey Sauble
12. Hamilton
13. Kawartha
14. Kettle Creek
15. Lakehead Region
16. Lake Simcoe Region
17. Long Point Region
18. Lower Thames Valley
19. Lower Trent
20. Maitland Valley
21. Mattagami Region
22. Mississippi Valley
23. Niagara Peninsula
24. Nickel District
25. North Bay - Mattawa
26. Nottawasaga Valley
27. Otonabee
28. Quinte
29. Raisin Region
30. Rideau Valley
31. Saugeen
32. Sault Ste.Marie Region
33. South Nation
34. St. Clair Region
35. Toronto and Region
36. Upper Thames River

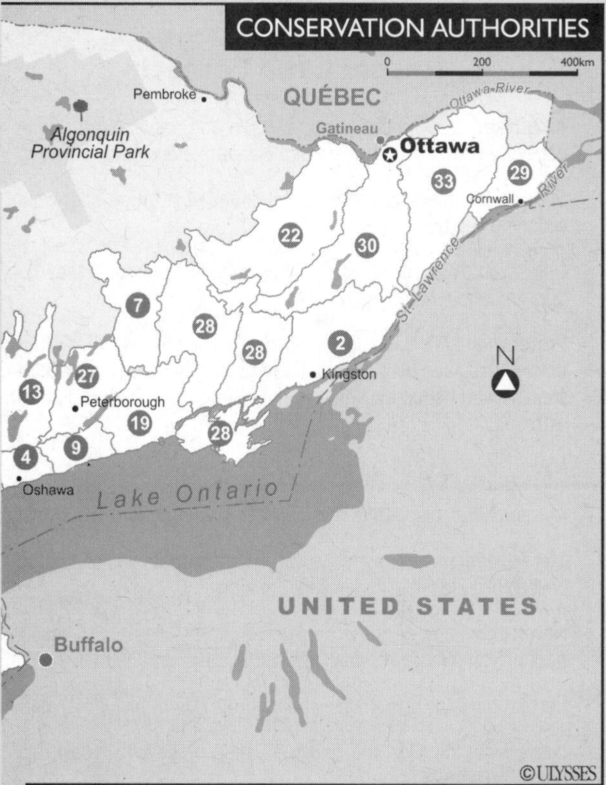
CONSERVATION AUTHORITIES
0
200
400km
QUÉBEC
Pembroke
Algonquin
Provincial Park
Gatineau
Ottawa
Ottawa River
River
Cornwall
St. Lawrence
33
29
22
30
7
28
28
2
Kingston
N
27
13
Peterborough
19
28
9
4
Oshawa
Lake Ontario
UNITED STATES
Buffalo
©ULYSSES

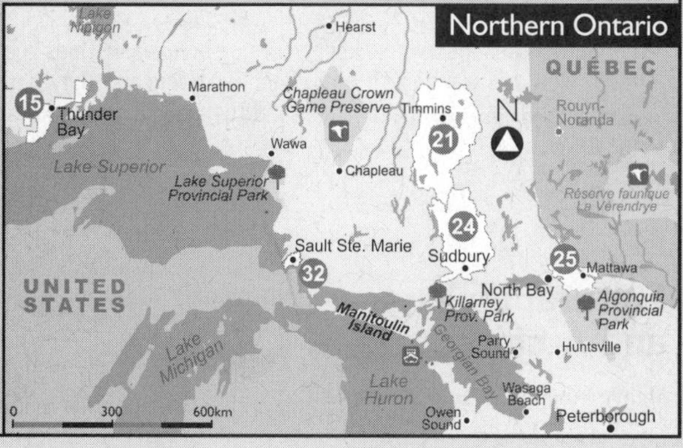
Northern Ontario
Lake Nipigon
Hearst
QUÉBEC
Marathon
Chapleau Crown
Game Preserve
Timmins
Rouyn-
Noranda
15
Thunder
Bay
Wawa
21
N
Lake Superior
Chapleau
Lake Superior
Provincial Park
Réserve faunique
La Vérendrye
24
Sault Ste. Marie
Sudbury
25
Mattawa
32
North Bay
UNITED
STATES
Killarney
Prov. Park
Algonquin
Provincial
Park
Manitoulin
Island
Lake
Michigan
Georgian Bay
Parry
Sound
Huntsville
Lake
Huron
Wasaga
Beach
0
300
600km
Owen
Sound
Peterborough

Respect the Forest!

As a hiker, it is important to preserve and respect the fragile ecosystem and limit your impact. Here are a few guidelines:

Stay on the trails to protect the ground vegetation and avoid widening the trail.

Unless on a long trek, wear lightweight hiking boots; they do less damage to the vegetation.

Protect waterways, bodies of water and the ground water when in forest regions by digging back-country latrines at least 30m from all water sources, and covering everything (paper included) with soil.

Never clean yourself with soap in lakes or streams.

At campsites, dispose of waste water only in designated areas.

The water in forest regions is not always potable and should be boiled for at least 10min before drinking.

Never leave any garbage behind. Bags are often provided at park offices, but bring your own just in case.

Certain types of flowers are endangered; do not pick anything.

Leave everything as you find it so that those who follow can enjoy the beauty of nature.

For safety reasons, always keep your dog on a leash. Dogs that roam free can wander off and chase wild animals. They have even been known to chase a bear and then lead it back to their master.

Cultural History and Architecture

Many of the trails that hikers now enjoy pass through previously settled areas or former industrial sites. This brief summary of the history of the province will help you identify these remnants of the past.

The history of Ontario falls into several distinct periods, outlined below.

Aboriginal Communities (prior to 1639)

Ontario had a population of about 60,000 Aboriginal people when the first European explorers arrived. They were divided into six nations: Huron, Petun (Tobacco), Neutrals, Ottawa, Ojibwa and Cree. Those living in southern Ontario were farmers, while those in the north—the Ojibwa and Cree—were mostly nomadic. They farmed where they could, but mainly lived by hunting and fishing. The Petun nation settled the area southwest of Lake Huron. A group of about 30,000 settlers from the Huron nation lived in the Georgian Bay area. The Ottawa nation lived in the eastern part of the province. The Neutrals lived on both sides of the Niagara River and to the west of Lake Ontario.

The Aboriginal community left a fascinating collection of outdoor art, much of which can be discovered while hiking or canoeing. Canada's largest concentration of Aboriginal rock carvings, for example, can be found in **Petroglyphs Provincial Park** (see p. 173). A building now protects the rocks, which were originally used by Aboriginal elders as teaching aids.

Aboriginal pictographs also appear on a granite cliff in **Bon Echo Provincial Park** (see p. 185) in Cloyne, on Agawa Rock in **Lake Superior Provincial Park** (see p. 231) near Sault St. Marie, in Death Valley Gorge on the **Casque-Isles Hiking Trail** (see p. 244), and at Fairy Point in Missinaibi Provincial Park near Chapleau.

Ojibwa paintings appear on Agawa Rock in **Lake Superior Provincial Park** (see p. 231). The region is also home to shallow rock basins created by Anishnabe locals. The purpose of the "Pukaskwa pits" is not certain, although they may have been used as either vision pits or shelters.

Images of moose, caribou, hunters in canoes and other mysterious pictographs appear on cliff faces in **Quetico Provincial Park** (see p. 255), but these are best seen from a canoe.

European Explorers (1611 to 1615)

Étienne Stephen Brûlé, a French explorer, was the first European to explore many parts of Ontario. Brûlé arrived even before English explorer Henry Hudson reached the shores of Hudson Bay in 1611 to lay claim to the area. Brûlé seems to have joined Samuel de Champlain on his 1608 voyage to Québec, but he later continued farther on his own. On his first trip, Brûlé travelled along the St. Lawrence River to the Great Lakes and into Pennsylvania. On his return, he met Champlain at the Lachine Rapids on June 13, 1611. Along the way, he learned to speak many Aboriginal languages and became an interpreter for the French. He then continued exploring Ontario and the eastern United States down to Florida until the Hurons killed him in 1633.

Christian Missions (1615 to 1649)

Christian missionaries followed directly in the explorer's footsteps; the first one, Father Joseph le Caron, arrived in Huron territory in 1615. The largest mission was a Jesuit settlement called St. Marie Among the Hurons, located on the Wye River near present-day Midland. It was also the site of Ontario's first hospital. Iroquois attacks forced the missionaries to burn down their creation in 1649.

Fur-Trading Posts (1671 to 1763)

By the time the Hudson's Bay Company opened a post in Moose Factory in 1671, the Revillon brothers were already established fur traders in the area, relying on the plentiful beaver that inhabited the region. One of their posts was established near present-day Marathon, in what is now Neys Provincial Park. Later, the Hudson's Bay Company replaced the French fur trading post with a fort of their own. The series of battles over beaver pelts faltered in 1713, when France ceded Hudson Bay, Nova Scotia and Newfoundland to the British, but didn't really end until 1763, when France gave Britain the entire Ontario area under the 1763 Treaty of Paris.

Military Forts (1673 to 1774)

Louis de Buade, Comte de Palluau et de Frontenac, built Ontario's first fort in 1673. Fort Frontenac stood on the site of the present day city of Kingston. It was abandoned during the French and Indian War, which began in 1754. The French also built Fort Assumption in today's Windsor (in 1749) and Fort Rouillé in today's Toronto. All this fort building ended in 1774, when southern Ontario was annexed to the British province of Québec.

For their part, the British built forts in Moose Factory (Moose Fort) and Fort Albany.

Although hikers today aren't likely to see many traces of this old fort-building era, some of the trails we currently use began as supply trails for the original forts.

American Revolution Settlers (1775-1784)

When the Treaty of Paris (Peace of Versailles) ended the American Revolution, American colonists who remained loyal to Great Britain moved into the British province of Québec and created three new settlements in what is now known as Ontario.

The first settlement was composed of 600,000 United Empire Loyalists who established homesteads along the northern shores of the St. Lawrence River and Lake Ontario and on the western side of the Niagara River. Hikers can see a pioneer cemetery dating from a family of United Empire Loyalist settlers along the Burk Trail in **Darlington Provincial Park** (see p. 125).

The second and third settlements were established by groups of Six Nations Iroquois who received land in exchange for the lands they lost in New York. One group created the Tyendinaga Reserve, near the Bay of Quinte in 1784. The other, led by Mohawk Chief Joseph Brant (Thayendanega), settled in the Grand River valley, near today's Brantford.

Simcoe and Talbot Settlements of the Georgian Period (1791 to 1812)

English-speaking United Empire Loyalists continued moving to Québec in the aftermath of the American Revolution. Eventually, they become so numerous that Britain decided to divide the British colony of Québec into Upper and Lower Canada. The former colony, now southern Ontario, was mainly settled by English-speaking colonists, while the latter, now southern Québec, was mainly French-speaking. Upper Canada was assigned a lieutenant governor named John Graves Simcoe, who built roads and offered land grants to encourage settlement of his vast territory. He also officially ended slavery in the province on May 21, 1793. One of the settlement officers Simcoe appointed was Colonel Thomas Talbot, who was largely responsible for settling the area of Ontario between Fort Erie and Windsor. Hikers will also encounter many Georgian structures outside of the Talbot settlement in Niagara-on-the-Lake, a town that was originally capital of Upper Canada. Some examples also remain in Port Credit, Port Hope and Sault Ste. Marie.

The War of 1812

The United States declared war on Britain on June 18, 1812 and surrendered by December 1814. Major battles included the Battles of Queenston Heights, Stoney Creek, Beaver Dams, Put-in-Bay, Moraviantown, Châteauguay, Crysler's Farm, Chippewa, Lundy's Lane and Lake Champlain.

Hikers in Ontario can see a grist mill that supplied flour to the British forces in **Ball's Falls Conservation Area** (see p. 119), or the sandbar that protected Canada in the Battle of Stoney Creek at **Cootes Paradise** (see p. 121).

Pioneer Wheat Settlements of the Victorian Era (1814 to 1850)

After the war of 1812, immigration from Britain increased dramatically. Also, in the early 1820s many refugee slaves escaped to Canada with the help of a network of people who hid them from authorities as they travelled. By 1851, southern Ontario had a population of more than a million people.

The rapid construction of settlements during this period has left many traces on hiking trails throughout the province. Trails at the **Dundas Valley Conservation Area** (see p. 129) lead past the ruins of an estate and gatehouse built by George Leith in 1855 and past the home of escaped slave Enerals Griffin. The remains of an 1840s homestead appears on the DeLaurier Trail in **Point Pelee National Park** (see p. 106). A visit to **Backus Heritage Conservation Area** (see p. 84) includes the 1843 Victoria Carriage Shop and an 1850 brick house hand-made from local clay. Many old homesteads, including the remains of the 1847 Hardwood Bay farm, can be seen on trails at **Frontenac Provincial Park** (see p. 191).

Oil and Railroads (1855 to 1885)

Heavy industrialization and the discovery of the world's first oil well on the southeastern border of Lake Huron led to a need for better transportation, including steam trains. By 1856, railway beds extended 2,200km (1,364mi) through the province. Two major east-west lines, the Grand Trunk and the Great Western, served Ontario by 1871. Railways crisscrossed the entire province. Today, these railway beds are being rediscovered as multi-use recreational paths within the **Trans Canada Trail** (see p. 55). The Dundas Valley Trail Centre, at **Dundas Valley Conservation Area** (see p. 129) in Hamilton, includes an authentic reproduction of a Victorian railway station, while hikers along the Peterborough section of the **Ganaraska Trail** (see p. 61) will see a Grand Trunk Railway Station dating from 1885.

Hikers can also see an 1859 grist mill and 1850s stone houses along the **Elora Gorge** (see p. 66), the 1865 Victoria Bridge made of stone on the **Avon Trail** (see p. 82), ruins of an 1868 woolen mill at Brook Conservation Area on the **Lynn Valley Trail** (see p. 99), and the 1885 hydroelectric mill at Cataract Falls on the **Bruce Trail** (see p. 57).

Logging (1886 to 1902)

Ontario's logging heyday began in the 1880s and continued through the beginning of the 20th century. This is evident from the fact that many hiking trails are old logging roads, and many of the rivers they pass include traces of old rock cribs and other signs of the days when logs were sent up- or down-river. Remains of what was the world's largest logging mill in 1894 can be seen along Booth's Rock Trail in **Algonquin Park** (see p. 152).

Main Streets and Mines (1903 to 1913)

While the urbanization of Southern Ontario led to more than half of its population living in cities, towns and villages by 1911, communities in eastern and northern Ontario continued to rely on logging for economic viability or they began opening mines.

Hikers interested in this period will want to visit **Murphys Point Provincial Park** (see p. 203) and **Frontenac Provincial Park** (see p. 191), both in Eastern Ontario.

World War I (1914 to 1918)

The First World War period attracted a million European immigrants to Canada, and many of them settled in Ontario, creating a rapid expansion in homesteads and trade.

Canada's busiest railway line during World War I was the Ottawa-Arnprior-Parry Sound Railway, part of wich forms today's **Seguin Trail** (see p. 176). Hikers can also view two wooden train trestles and the former location of a major hotel and train station on the Track and Tower Trail located in **Algonquin Park** (see p. 152).

Depression Era (1920s and 1930s)

When World War I ended, the return of soldiers to Canada created an unemployment crisis, particularly in Ontario. By the time the stock market collapsed in October 1929, families in Ontario were already in trouble. One group of 35 families worked together to create a Catholic colony. The church that served them can still be seen on the King East Section of the **Oak Ridges Trail** (see p. 66). You can also see a cabin dating from 1934 along the **Avon Trail** (see p. 82).

World War II (1939 to 1945)

Canada sent more than a million people to serve in Europe between September 10, 1939 and May 5, 1945. Hikers will see the occasional monument to these veterans on several trails, particularly those that go through small towns.

Post-War Era (1946 to 1970)

During the post-war era there was a growing understanding of conservation. This is the period when Ontario created its first conservation area, **Albion Hills** (see p. 118), worked to preserve some of its major marshes, including **Luther Marsh** (see p. 97), and established Mountsberg Reservoir at **Mountsberg Conservation Area** (see p. 139).

Today (1970 to 2010)

The period from 1970 to the present has seen the creation of several long-distance footpaths for hikers in Ontario, including the **Bruce Trail** (see p. 57), the **Ganaraska Trail** (see p. 61), the **Voyageur Trail** (see p. 70) and the **Rideau Trail** (see p. 211).

This brief overview has described only a few of the many wonders that hikers can spot along the trails included in this book. Read on for more.

MULTI-REGIONAL TRAILS

Multi-Provincial Trails - - - - - - - - -

1. National Trail (follows 4 trails in Ontario: Bruce, Ganaraska, Rideau and Voyageur)
2. Trans Canada Trail (links 78 different existing trails in Ontario)

Multi-Regional Trails ···············

3. Bruce Trail (Niagara to Tobermory)
4. Ganaraska Trail (Port Hope on Lake Ontario to Wasaga Beach and the Bruce Trail, near Collingwood)
5. Grand Valley Trail (Lake Erie to Alton)
6. Oak Ridges Trail (Caledon to Gores Landing)
7. Voyageur Trail (Thunder Bay to South Baymouth, Manitoulin Island)
8. Waterfront Trail (shore of Lake Ontario from Niagara-on-the-Lake to Brockville)

Multi-Regional Trails

Canada's first long-distance walking trail was completed in Ontario in 1967, just in time for the country's 100th birthday. Known as the **Bruce Trail** (see p. 57), this footpath followed the ridge of the Niagara Escarpment for 700km (434mi). It has been extended since then, and now runs 1,285km (771mi), including all the side trails.

The popularity of the Bruce Trail inspired several other Ontario groups to begin blazing trails in the early 1970s. Two of the trails—the **Ganaraska Trail** (see p. 61) and the **Grand Valley Trail** (see p. 64)—naturally link with the Bruce by following the routes of major rivers flowing from the Niagara Escarpment. A third, the **Oak Ridges Trail** (see p. 66) follows the Bruce Trail's example by leading hikers across the top of another major landform, the Oak Ridges Moraine, which fortuitously intersects with the Niagara Escarpment. A fourth—the **Voyageur Trail** (see p. 70)—follows the northern shoreline of Lake Superior. The landscape faced by these northern volunteers is much more rugged than that encountered by the southern trail blazers, but these dedicated souls are still at it. About half of Voyageur's anticipated 1,100km (682mi) has been completed so far, but it takes a lot of dedication from volunteers to keep the trail open.

The Bruce Trail also inspired like-minded folks in other provinces to try and develop ties across the nation. In 1971, efforts to blaze a footpath called the **National Trail** (see p. 55) began. The National Trail hasn't yet been completed and has been somewhat overshadowed by the cross-country **Trans Canada Trail** (see p. 55). This 16,000km (9,920mi) multi-use trail is open to cross-country skiers, cyclists, equestrians and snowmobilers, in addition to hikers. Some 9,000km (5,580mi) have thus far been completed.

The Trans Canada Trail has inspired further efforts in Ontario. A group of municipalities located along the shore of Lake Ontario, for instance, has been busy building a trail to link 41 different cities, towns and villages. So far, 780km (485mi) of the **Waterfront Trail**'s (see p. 71) potential 900km (560mi) has been completed. The Waterfront Trail already connects to Québec's *Route verte* (Green Trail) and in future may link with similar trails on the U.S. side so that ambitious hikers and cyclists will be able to circuit around Lake Ontario.

› Further Information

Hike Ontario
165 W. Dundas St., Suite 400
Mississauga, ON L5B 2N6
✆ 905-277-4453 or 800-894-7249
www.hikeontario.com

National Trail

Location *Canada–from the Atlantic Provinces to British Columbia*

Number of trails *4 in Ontario: Bruce, Ganaraska, Rideau and Voyageur*

Total distance *10,000km (6,200mi) when complete*

Markers *A stylized pedestrian logo*

Interesting features *Welcomes hikers, walkers, cross-country skiers and snowshoers along winding, rocky paths*

The National Trail is important for hikers because it does not allow motorized vehicles on its path and so follows the most scenic rugged journey across the country. It has existed since 1971, when National Trail visionary Doug Campbell and other activists met at a conference in Toronto. It took another six years before the National Trail Association of Canada (now run by Hike Canada En Marche) was officially registered, and some 10 years after that before the first national trail marker made it onto a post.

In Ontario, the trail includes the **Bruce** (see p. 57), **Ganaraska** (see p. 61), **Rideau** (see p. 211) and **Voyageur** (see p. 70) trails.

› Getting There

Although off-road hiking from one side of Ontario to the other is not yet possible, most of the province can be covered along the Bruce, Ganaraska, Rideau and Voyageur trails.

› Further Information

Hike Canada En Marche
16520 40th Ave.
Surrey, BC V3S 0L2
☎ 519-389-4101
www.nationaltrail.ca

Trans Canada Trail

Location *Newfoundland, Nova Scotia, P.E.I., New Brunswick, Québec, Ontario, Manitoba, Saskatchewan, Alberta, British Columbia, N.W.T., Yukon and Nunavut*

Total distance *16,000km (9,920mi), 3,500km (2,170mi) in Ontario*

Markers *Trans Canada logo*

Interesting features *Multi-use trail for walking, cycling, horseback riding, cross-country skiing and snowmobiling*

The Trans Canada Trail in Ontario links 78 different existing trails, including several trails that are ideal for hiking. These are each outlined in detail in the appropriate chapter in this guide. They are: the **Avon Trail** (see p. 82), the **Elgin Hiking Trail** (see p. 89), the **Georgian Trail** (see p. 166), the Elora section of the **Grand Valley Trail** (see p. 64), the **Gordon Glaves Memorial Pathway** (see p. 93) in Brantford, the Hamilton to Brantford Rail Trail in the **Dundas Valley Conservation Area** (see p. 129), the **Lynn Valley Trail** (see p. 99), the **Maitland Trail** (see p. 100), the **Old Nipissing Colonization Road** (see p. 172), the **Niagara Glen** (see p. 141), the **Seguin Trail** (see p. 176), the Tiny Trails section of the **Ganaraska Trail** (see p. 61), the **Voyageur Trail** (see p. 70), and the **Waterfront Trail** (see p. 71).

Many of the other trails that form part of the Trans Canada Trail are old railway beds, which means that they tend to be rather flat for hikers and more interesting for cyclists.

There are seven such rail trails in the Greater Toronto and Niagara Region: the Caledon Trailway, the Chippawa Rail Trail, the Elora Cataract Trailway, the Fort Erie Friendship Trail, the Hamilton to Brantford Rail Trail, the Niagara Parks Recreation Trail and the S.C. Johnson Trail.

Southern Ontario has 30: the Aylmer Kinsmen Trail, the Bayham Trans Canada Trail, the Blair Trail, the Brouwers Line, the CASO St. Thomas Trail, the Cambridge to Paris Rail Trail, the Central Frontenac Trailway, the Chatham-Kent Trans Canada Trail, the Chrysler Canada Greenway, the Delhi Rail Trail, the Dutton/Dunwich Trans Canada Trail, the Elgin Trans Canada Trail, the Goderich to Auburn Rail Trail, the Gord Harry Conservation Trail (formerly Wainfleet Rail Trail), the Grand Trunk Trail, the Health Valley Trail, the Homer Watson Trail, the Kissing Bridge Trailway, the Laurel Trail, the Living Levee Trail, the Schneider Creek Trail, the Simcoe to Delhi Rail Trail, the Thames Valley Trail, the TH&B Rail Trail in Brantford, the Tillsonburg Trans Canada Trail, the Walter Bean Grand River Trail, the Waterford Heritage Trail, the Wellesley Township Trans Canada Trail, the West Elgin Trans Canada Trail and the West End Recreation Way.

In Central Ontario, there are 13: the Beaver River Wetland Trail, the Gravenhurst Trans Canada Trail, the Innisfil Trail, the Iron Horse Trail, the Jackson Creek Kiwanis Trail, the Kaladar Trail, the Kawartha Trans Canada Trail, the Midland Rotary Waterfront Trail, the North Muskoka Trail, the North Simcoe Rail Trail, the Saugeen Rail Trail, the Simcoe Waterfront Trail, and the Uhtoff Trail.

In Eastern Ontario, five trails follow former railway lines. These are the Cataraqui Trail, the Hastings County Trail Network, the K&P Trail, the Ottawa to Carleton Railway and the Ottawa River Pathway.

In Northern Ontario, part of the Kate Pace Trailway and other trails in North Bay lie on old railway beds, but elsewhere they are still in use, so hikers will enjoy any of the trails. A few parts of the Trans Canada Trail are flat, such as when it follows old mining or logging roads or along the paths of hydro lines, gas lines and water lines, as it does near Ignace.

There are scenic attractions on all of these trails that are well worth visiting by hikers who happen to be nearby. History buffs will want to see the locks on the Welland Canal in Port Colborne and the Rideau Canal in Ottawa. Or they might want to follow the Kissing Bridge Trailway between Guelph and Elmira to go through a covered bridge in West Montrose. Other historical wonders include the huge wooden trestle bridges dating from the steam train railway era, such as the one between Emily Lake and Orange Corners roads in Omemee and two others over Innisfil Creek near Cookstown. Recent engineering feats are also worth a side trip. The Ramney Gorge Suspension Bridge over the Trent River in **Ferris Provincial Park** (see p. 163), for instance, is awe-inspiring. The new immense pedestrian bridges over highways are also remarkable. There's one over Highway 10 near Inglewood, and two others cross Highway 401, one in Kitchener and the other in Hamilton.

Natural wonders are important too. The stairs up the Niagara Escarpment between Hamilton and Burlington should be climbed at least once. The stunning waterfalls that begin and end the Elora to Cataract Trailway are beautiful, as are High Falls along the Muskoka Trail, which drop 14.6m (48ft).

This list doesn't even include the numerous geological and natural features that attract birdwatchers and other naturalists to just about any part of the Trans Canada Trail.

› Getting There

Most Ontario communities have a Trans Canada Trail or a spur trail to it somewhere nearby. Check with the local tourist information office or the contacts below.

› Further Information

Ontario Trails Council
556 O'Connor Dr., Suite 130
Kingston, ON K7P 1N3
877-668-7245
www.ontariotrails.on.ca

Trans Canada Trail Foundation
43 N. Westminster Ave.
Montréal, QC H4X 1Y8
514-485-3959 or 800-465-3636
www.tctrail.ca

Bruce Trail

Location *Niagara to Tobermory*

Number of sections *9*

Total distance *885km (531mi) plus 400km (240mi) of side trails*

Markers *White blazes for main trail, blue blazes for side trails*

Interesting features *Niagara Escarpment, 300 bird species*

Other *Dogs on leashes permitted*

Canada's oldest, longest marked trail began in 1960, when Raymond Lowes, a member of the Hamilton Naturalists Club, proposed that the Federation of Ontario Naturalists build a footpath along the entire Niagara Escarpment. Since then, the idea has become a reality. The main trail was established in 1967, four years after the incorporation of the Bruce Trail Association (now known as the Bruce Trail Conservancy). Today, the conservancy includes nine member clubs, with a total membership of 8,500. Members mark blazes, build bridges, stiles and boardwalks, negotiate with park administrators and landowners to maintain 1,285km (771mi) of trail, and work to add or replace more every year. Currently, 1,050 active volunteers maintain the trail; the other 7,400 provide the funding that helps make it possible.

Less than half of the Bruce Trail crosses public lands, including one national park, seven provincial parks, 40 conservation areas and 43 public parks or nature reserves. The Bruce Trail Conservancy itself owns more than 2,500ha (6,175 acres), but the rest of the trail crosses private property. Hikers should take great care to stay on the blazed trail, avoid littering and refrain from disturbing plants or wildlife.

Protecting the unusual beauty of the Niagara Escarpment itself has been an international priority since 1990, when the United Nations named it a UNESCO World Biosphere Reserve. The recognition came in part because the area is home to more than 300 bird species, 53 mammals, 35 reptiles and amphibians and 90 fish species. More than 37 species of ferns and 40 species of orchids grow on the escarpment.

An estimated 410,000 hikers use the trail every year. If you plan to hike this trail, the Bruce Trail Conservancy offers an excellent trail guide complete with colour maps and descriptions of camping areas along the trail. For day hikers, the Peninsula Bruce Trail Club has produced a mini-map guide to the Tobermory region.

› Getting There

A variety of conservation areas and nature reserves provide access to the trail. Please see trailheads for each section.

› Further Information

Bruce Trail Conservancy
PO Box 857
Hamilton, ON L8N 3N9
☎ 905-529-6821 or 800-665- 4453
www.brucetrail.org

Niagara Section

Location *Queenston to Grimsby*

Level of difficulty 🚶🚶

Distance *84km (52mi) linear plus 64km (40mi) along 10 side trails*

Approx. time *7 to 10 days each way*

Access points ***Ball's Falls Conservation Area*** *(see p. 119), Brock University, Decew House Park, Fireman's Park, Glendale Ave., Kinsmen Community Park, Louth Conservation Area, Morningstar Mill, Pelham Rd., Rockway Community Centre, Rockway Conservation Area,* ***Short Hills Provincial Park*** *(see p.145), Thorold Old Stone Rd., Quarry Rd., Woodend Conservation Area*

› Further Information

www.niagarabrucetrail.org

This part of the trail is covered with Carolinian forest. Look for ash, beech, crocus, coltsfoot, interrupted ferns, hepatica yellow lady's slipper, maple, ostrich ferns, sassafras, showy lady's slipper, sycamore, tulip and walking ferns.

Iroquoia Section

Location *Grimsby to Kelso*

Level of difficulty 🚶🚶

Distance *125km (75mi) linear plus 41km (25mi) along 35 side trails*

Approx. time *13 to 15 days each way*

Access points *Battlefield Park, Beamer Memorial Conservation Area,* ***Crawford Lake Conservation Area*** *(see p. 123), Devil's Punch Bowl Conservation Area,* ***Dundas Valley Conservation Area*** *(see p. 129), Felker's Falls Conservation Area, Kelso Conservation Area, Gage Park, Mount Nemo*

Conservation Area, Mountainview Conservation Area, Rattlesnake Point Conservation Area, Rock Chapel Sanctuary, Snake Rd. (Halton), Spencer Gorge Wilderness Area, ***Tiffany Falls Conservation Area*** *(see p. 129), Vinemount Conservation Area, Webster's Falls Park, Winona Conservation Area*

› Further Information

www.iroquoia.on.ca

This section of the trail begins just prior to Beamer's Point Bluff in Grimsby, an area known for spectacular hawk migrations in the fall. It then passes through Stoney Creek, Hamilton, Dundas, Burlington and Milton. You'll pass five waterfalls: Tiffany, Sherman, Webster's, Tews and Borer's. There's also a huge pothole, 34m (112.5ft) deep with a circumference of 180m (591ft), called Devil's Punch Bowl, just west of Battlefield Park.

Toronto Section

Location *Kelso Conservation Area to Cheltenham*

Level of difficulty

Distance *50km (30mi) linear plus 54km (33mi) along 13 side trails*

Approx. time *4 to 6 days each way*

Access points *Dufferin Quarry Bridge, Halton Country Inn, Hilton Falls Conservation Area, Limehouse Conservation Area, Scottsdale Farm, Terra Cotta Conservation Area*

› Further Information

416-763-9061

www.torontobrucetrailclub.org

This trail begins at Highway 401 near Campbellville Road and then travels along the edge of the Niagara Escarpment past small 500-year-old cedars and over the Dufferin Quarry Bridge.

Caledon Hills Section

Location *Cheltenham to Mono Centre*

Level of difficulty

Distance *68.9km (41mi) linear plus 63.1km (37.9mi) along 13 side trails*

Approx. time *8 to 10 days each way*

Access points ***Albion Hills Conservation Area*** *(see p. 118), Belfountain Conservation Area, Caledon Administration Centre, Forks of the Credit Provincial Park,* ***Glen Haffy Conservation Area*** *(see p. 136), Ken Whillans Resource Management Area (east side of Hwy. 10), Inglewood Arena, Resource Management parking lot in Alton Village*

› Further Information

www.caledonbrucetrail.org

This trail begins north of Creditview Road at the Cheltingham Badlands, a series of ridges of rock-hard red and grey soil that resembles the Alberta Badlands. From there, it passes the ruins of McLaren Castle, an 1864 Norman-style stone building that was destroyed in a fire in 1964, and a view of the 1885 hydroelectric mill at Cataract Falls. Part of the trail follows the Caledon Trailway through a sheep farm. After leaving the old railway bed, the path leads north past **Albion Hills** (see p. 118) and **Glen Haffy** (see p. 136) to the Hockley Valley.

Dufferin Hi-Land Section

Location *Mono Centre to Lavender*

Level of difficulty 🚶 🚶

Distance *51km (32mi) linear plus 12km (7.5mi) along 4 side trails*

Approx. time *5 to 6 days each way*

Access points *1st Line East Hurontario St. south of Dufferin Rd. 17,* ***Mono Cliffs Provincial Park*** *(see p. 169), Boyne Valley Provincial Park*

› Further Information

www.dufferinbrucetrailclub.org

This trail begins at Mono Centre, and continues through **Mono Cliffs Provincial Park** (see p. 169). It then turns north past Boyne Valley Provincial Park and Pine River Fishing Area and through an area of Honeywood loam known as one of Ontario's best farming regions.

Blue Mountains Section

Location *Lavender to Craigleith*

Level of difficulty 🚶 🚶

Distance *59km (37mi) linear plus 19km (12mi) along 13 side trails*

Approx. time *5 to 7 days each way*

Access points *Devil's Glen Provincial Park, Nottawasaga Bluffs Conservation Area, Petun Conservation Area*

› Further Information

www.bmbtc.org

This trail passes a series of drumlins, Best Caves, an old Petun Aboriginal settlement, Petun Conservation Area, Singhampton Caves (moss-covered crevices open to the sky), Nottawasaga Bluffs, the Blue Mountain Ski slopes and Scenic Caves.

Beaver Valley Section

Location *Craigleith to Blantyre*

Level of difficulty 🚶 🚶

Distance *113.1km (67mi) linear plus 50km (30mi) of side trails*

Approx. time *9 to 11 days each way*

Access points *Beaver Valley Lookout, Blantyre Community Hall, Duncan Crevice Caves Provincial Nature Reserve, Epping Lookout, Old Baldy Conservation Area*

› Further Information

www.beavervalleybrucetrail.org

This trail begins on Maple Lane and follows the Niagara Escarpment through many woods and pastures to the summit of Metcalfe Rock, which offers a good view over Kolapore Creek. It then descends through a rocky gorge to the valley and the base of Pinnacle Rock, a large chunk of limestone that has separated from the edge of the escarpment. The trail then leads along several side roads to Old Baldy Conservation Area. Old Baldy is the 152m-high (500ft) section of the escarpment that's known locally as Kimberley Rock. Expect to see soaring turkey vultures and red-tailed hawks. The trail then continues on to Epping Lookout, an area managed by the Grey Sauble Conservation Authority, and Anthea's Waterfall.

Sydenham Section

Location *Blantyre to Wiarton*

Level of difficulty 🚶 🚶

Distance *125km (75mi) linear plus 22km (14mi) along 13 side trails*

Approx. time *13 to 15 days each way*

Access points *Bruce Caves Conservation Area, Grey-Bruce Tourist Information Office (Hwys. 6 and 21), Harrison Park, Indian Falls Conservation Area, Ingis Falls Conservation Area, Pottawatomi Conservation Area, Skinner's Bluff Conservation Area, Walters Falls Conservation Area*

Other *Watch for Ontario's only venomous snake, the endangered Massasauga rattlesnake*

› Further Information

www.sydenhambrucetrail.org

This trail crosses and parallels Rocklyn Creek in Blantyre and then goes through the Bighead and North Spey river valleys, up to Centennial Tower and into Inglis Falls Conservation Area. From there, it travels alongside Owen Sound to the Pottawatomi Conservation Area for a look at Jones Falls. The trail then goes to the Glen Management Area, a horseshoe-shaped indentation in the escarpment. It continues north to Kemble Mountain and then up and down to Dodd's Hill. A beautiful green wetland south of you is known as the Slough of Despond, where cerulean warblers nest. The trail then continues to an overhanging lookout known as Skinner's Bluff and then past Bruce Caves Conservation Area. The final segment leads to Bluewater Park in Wiarton.

Peninsula Section

Location *Wiarton to Tobermory*

Level of difficulty 🚶 🚶 🚶

Distance *165km (99mi) linear plus 84.6km (50.1mi) on 29 side trails*

Approx. time *14 to 16 days each way*

Access points ***Bruce Peninsula National Park*** *(see p. 86), Cape Croker Park, Colpoy's Bluff, Hope Bay Forest Provincial Nature Reserve, Lion's Head Provincial Nature Reserve, Smokey Head-White Bluff Provincial Nature Reserve, Spirit Rock Conservation Area*

Other *Endangered Massasauga rattlesnake; home to home stays available in this region, see www.hometohomenetwork.ca*

› Further Information

www.pbtc.org

This section of the Bruce Trail is definitely the most difficult. It also features a variety of unusual rock formations that can't be seen elsewhere along the trail, including Devil's Monument, also known as Devil's Pulpit, a 14m (45.9ft) flowerpot-shaped pillar between Cape Chin and Dyer's Bay. You'll also see the ruins of the Corran, a 17-room mansion built by Alexander McNeil in 1882.

Ganaraska Trail

Location *Port Hope on Lake Ontario to Wasaga Beach and the **Bruce Trail** (see p. 57), near Collingwood*

Number of sections *9*

Total distance *500km (310mi)*

Markers *White blazes for main trail and blue blazes for side trails*

Interesting features *Copeland Forest, drumlin fields, Fenelon Falls, Fort Willow, Ganaraska River, Ganaraska Forest, Moore Falls, Peterborough Drumlin Field, Trent Canal (lock 33), Wasaga Beach,* ***Wye Marsh*** *(see p. 179)*

Other *Inn to Inn hiking available.*

Volunteers with nine different clubs maintain the Ganaraska Trail, which was started in 1967 to connect Port Hope with the Bruce Trail along what used to be the Port Hope to Lindsay and Beaverton Railway line.

Today, the trail goes through Lindsay and Orillia, passing the drumlin fields of Peterborough, the Oak Ridges Moraine, some of the Kawartha Lakes, the Minesing Swamp and a series of sand dunes, known as the Blueberry Hills, east of Wasaga Beach.

Another branch turns north from Copeland Forest to get to the **Wye Marsh** (see p. 179) in Midland.

› Getting There

Choose any of the trailheads or access points mentioned under each section.

› Further Information

Ganaraska Trail Association
PO Box 693
Orillia, ON L3V 6K7
www.ganaraska-hiking-trail.ca

Pine Ridge Section

Level of difficulty 🚶

Distance *63km (38mi) linear*

Approx. time *6 to 8 days each way*

Access points *Port Hope Townhall, Port Hope Conservation Area, Sylvan Glen Conservation Area, Fudge's Mill, Ganaraska Forest Centre, Hwy. 7 between Lindsay and Omemee*

This section leads from the Port Hope Town Hall along the west and then east bank of the Ganaraska River to Corbett's dam and a fish ladder near Highway 401. The trail passes through the Ganaraska Forest and past the Peterborough drumlin field.

Kawartha Section

Level of difficulty 🚶

Distance *77km (47.7mi) linear*

Approx. time *8 to 10 days each way*

Access points *Crosswinds Rd., Old Mill Rd., Post Rd., Hillhead Rd., Logie St., McDonnel Park, Carew Park and Boardwalk, Pottinger St., Victoria St., Lindsay St. in Fenelon Falls, Buller Rd., Moore Falls, Ken Reid Conservation Area*

Hikers who visit the Kawartha section of the Ganaraska Trail begin on the rail trail between Dranoel and Lindsay through the Peterborough drumlin field. They'll then travel along the shores of the Scugog River to King Street, then to Lindsay Street and south, past Lock 33 of the Trent Canal. They'll walk through McDonnel and Carew parks to the Victoria County Recreational Trail.

Wilderness Section

Level of difficulty 🚶🚶🚶

Distance *77km (48mi)*

Approx. time *10 days each way*

Access points *Devil's Lake, Moore Falls, Sadowa, Victoria Bridge*

Other *This trail should be hiked with an experienced leader the first time*

This rugged trail leads up and down the Canadian Shield for 19km (11.8mi) from Moore Falls to Devil's Lake, for 37km (22.9mi) from Devil's Lake to Victoria Bridge and 20km (12.4mi) from Victoria Bridge to Sadowa. If that's not enough for you, add one of two additional loops: the 16km (9.9mi) Ragged Rapids loop or the 12km (7.4mi) Montgomery Creek loop.

Orillia Section

Level of difficulty 🚶

Distance *70km (43mi) linear*

Approx. time *7 to 9 days each way*

Access points *Sadowa, Lake Couchiching, Lightfoot Trail, Tudhope Park, Leacock Estates, Sugerbush Estate Rd.*

Orillia-area volunteers maintain a trail that begins in Sadowa and continues along the shore of Lake Couchiching and through Scout Valley via the Lightfoot and Mariposa trails to the Sugarbush Estate, south of Horseshoe Valley Road.

Barrie Section

Level of difficulty 🚶

Distance *50km (31mi) linear*

Approx. time *3 to 6 days each way*

Access points *Sugarbush Estate, Huron Heights Rd., Copeland Forest, Craighurst, Midhurst Community Centre, Horseshoe Valley Ski Resort, Minesing Swamp, Hwy. 90*

The Barrie section starts at the Sugarbush Estate and continues through the Copeland Forest Resources Management Area. This mixed forest, swamp and meadow attracts songbirds and white-tailed deer. Hikers can then follow the markers through the villages of Craighurst and Midhurst, through the Simcoe County Forest to the Fort Willow Depot. The trail then travels through the east side of the Minesing Swamp to get to Highway 90.

Mad River Section

Level of difficulty 🚶

Distance *52km (31.2mi) linear*

Approx. time *20 to 28hrs each way*

Access points *Bruce Trail west of Glen Huron, Carruthers Memorial Conservation Area, New Lowell Conservation Area, Creemore*

This portion of the trail leads along the shores of the Mad River, where trout spawn in the spring. There are two lookouts, one from Ten Hill and the other from McKinney's Hill. The trail then leads through New Lowell and Carruthers Memorial conservation areas. It ends in the village of Creemore, home of Canada's smallest jail, which is no longer used.

Wasaga Beach Section

Level of difficulty 🚶

Distance *50km (31mi) linear*

Approx. time *4 to 6 days each way*

Access points *Allanwood Beach, Wasaga Stars Arena, 11th Concession*

Road in New Wasaga Beach, Wasaga Beach Provincial Park

This section connects Wasaga Beach and the Wasaga Beach Provincial Park with the Mad River section. Hikers will particularly enjoy the 13km (8mi) section through the Blueberry Trails, which pass through fields full of wild blueberries. You'll also travel along the Nottawasaga River and through many McIntyre Creek valleys.

Oro Medonte Section

Level of difficulty 🚶

Distance *18.5km (11.5mi) linear*

Approx. time *7hrs each way*

Access points *Copeland Forest, Vasey Road*

This section of the trail links the main Ganaraska trail with the Midland section. It begins in the Copeland Forest and leads north across the Highway 400 overpass. It continues through fields and then through the Sturgeon River Valley, known as "pretty valley" by the locals. The section ends at Vasey Road. The town of Vasey lies to the east.

Midland Section

Level of difficulty 🚶

Distance *35km (21.7mi) linear, plus 23.5km (14mi) linear Tiny Trails side trail*

Approx. time *2 to 3 days each way and 7 hrs each way*

Access points *Vasey Road, Wye Marsh and Balm Beach Road, Concession 12, Perkinsfield, Wyevale, Bluewater Beach*

The Midland section leads hikers north from Vasey Road along a rail trail to the **Wye Marsh** (see p. 179).

The Tiny Trails side trail leads south along the Tiny Railway Trail from Penetanguishene to just south of Wyeville and then west to Bluewater Beachleads hikers through the village of Perkinsfield, into Wyevale and on to Bluewater Beach.

Grand Valley Trail

Location *Lake Erie to Alton (to Luther Marsh in 2011)*

Number of sections *4*

Total distance *274.4km (163mi)*

Markers *White paint blazes for main trail, blue for side trails*

Interesting features *Grand River, monarch butterfly migration, spawning carp, migrating songbirds and waterfowl, Elora Gorge, Mennonite Pioneer Tower, Alexander Graham Bell Homestead, West Montrose covered bridge*

Other *Dogs on leashes permitted, except on a game farm between North and South Dumfries Townline and Sudden Tract Agreement Forest between Brantford and Paris*

The Grand Valley Trail began at a public meeting in Kitchener in January 1972. Since then, the trail has been extended along the Grand River several times, so that it now measures 271km (163mi).

The trail starts at the Haldimand County boat launch on Feeder Canal Road. The path follows the

Grand River through the Dunnville Marsh; along the **Gordon Glaves Memorial Pathway** (see p. 93) in Brantford; through the Walter Bean Grand River Trail in Cambridge, Kitchener and Waterloo; through Paris next to the Paris-Galt Moraine structure; past the covered bridge in West Montrose; along the Elora Gorge; and finally through Belwood Lake Conservation Area to the Pinnacle, a high hill overlooking the tiny community of Alton. By 2011, volunteers hope to extend the trail to reach **Luther Marsh** (see p. 97), with a side trail to the Pinnacle. Note that a portion of the Walter Bean Trail will be closed until 2011.

Members within four clubs organize volunteer work parties to maintain the trail, although some members have adopted sections of the trail that they maintain themselves. The club also organizes group outings and offers badges to any hiker who walks from one end of the trail to the other. As with any other long trail, members also deal with private landowners who graciously allow hikers to cross their land and others who ask that the trail be rerouted away from their properties.

› Getting There

Bellwood Lake Conservation Area, Bingeman Park, Brant Conservation Area, Byng Island Conservation Area, Churchill Park, Elora Gorge Park, Highland Pines Campground, La Fortune Campground, Laurel Creek Conservation Area, Pinehurst Conservation Area and Rock Point Provincial Park all have campgrounds close to the trail. The **Avon** (see p. 82), **Bruce** (see p. 57), Feeder Canal and Mill Run (Speed River) trails also connect to this trail. Refer to the Access points under each section.

› Further Information

Grand Valley Trails Association
PO Box 40068 RPO
Waterloo, ON N2J 4V1
519-576-6156
www.gvta.on.ca

Towpath Section

Level of difficulty

Distance *64.4km (39mi) linear*

Approx. time *3 days each way*

Access points *Haldimand County boat launch, Byng Island Conservation Area, County Rd. 54 in York, Caledonia Dam Riverside Park, Caledonia Dam, La Fortune Conservation Area*

Named after the water navigation route used in the 1830's, this flat section runs along a portion of the Welland Feeder Canal, before heading to the Grand River Marsh in Dunnville. It then continues through Cayugá, along the Grand River to York, past a sawmill to Sims Locks, then to Seneca Park and the Riverside park in Caledonia. After passing the Caledonia Dam, it follows County Road 54 to Mine Road where it turns into an open meadow. It finishes through a meandering path in La Fortune Conservation Area. Thanks to limited snowfall, this section of the trail often provides good winter hiking.

Carolinian Crest Section

Level of difficulty 🚶

Distance 68.9km (42.8mi) linear

Approx. time 3 days each way

Access points La Fortune Conservation Area, Onondaga Town Hall, McLellan Rd., Hamilton Rd., Brant Conservation Area, Hardy Rd., Curtis Ave. in Paris

The Carolinian section of the trail begins at the La Fortune Conservation Area. From there, it follows the Six Nations Reserve boundary to Onondaga. Hikers will enjoy travelling along the Grand River shore from Onondaga to Brantford, and then along the **Gordon Glaves Memorial Pathway** (see p. 93). The trail splits at Wilkes Dam and leads below Highway 403 on the way to Paris. It then follows the former Lake Erie and Northern rail line to Glen Morris, then local roads to the Brant-Waterloo Road.

Black Walnut Section

Level of difficulty 🚶

Distance 76km (45.6mi) linear

Approx. time 3 days each way

Access points Bingeman Park, Doon Conservation Area, Chicopee Hills Conservation Area, West Montrose Covered Bridge

The Black Walnut section of trail goes through Kitchener-Waterloo's Homer Watson Park, where Carolinian species grow, and through the white cedar swamps of Bingeman Park. It includes Hidden Valley and the Chicopee Hills Conservation Area through to Natchez Hill. From this point, it leads along gravel roads through Mennonite country and crosses Ontario's only remaining covered bridge at West Montrose.

Pinnacle Section

Level of difficulty 🚶

Distance 65.5km (39mi) linear

Approx. time 3 days each way

Access points Elora Gorge Conservation Area, Elora Bissel Park, Beatty Line in Fergus, Belwood Lake Conservation Area

After seeing the 24.4m (80ft) cliffs at Elora Gorge, you'll pass the picturesque town of Fergus and the smooth-surfaced reservoir of water at Belwood Lake Conservation Area. You'll then pass a gravel quarry, a fish hatchery, and a cedar swamp near Hillsburgh. The trail then crosses the Credit River and leads to the Pinnacle, a large hill overlooking Alton.

Oak Ridges Trail

Location Along the Oak Ridges Moraine between Caledon and Gores Landing on Rice Lake

Number of sections 10

Total distance 206km (127.7mi) so far, plus 51.4km (31.9mi) of side trails

Markers White blazes

Interesting features Warblers, red-shouldered hawks, witch hazel, black oak savanna, boreal and mixed forests, kettle lakes, swamps

Other *Dogs on leashes permitted, except in the Seneca College-King Campus Nature Preserve and on farms; no overnight camping allowed; beware of hunters between September and January and late-April until the end of May*

When finished, the Oak Ridges Trail will traverse the top of the Oak Ridges Moraine, a ridge running from the Niagara Escarpment in the west to Trent River in the east. High points along the moraine include the Caledon Hills, Mount Wolfe, Happy Valley Sandhills and Glenville Hills. The ridge is large enough to be seen from space and contains the headwaters of more than 30 rivers draining into Lake Simcoe and Lake Ontario. The most important of these include the Don, Duffin, Ganaraska, Holland, Humber, Nonquon, Nottawasaga, Pigeon and Rouge. Twenty-five percent of the Oak Ridges Moraine is forested, primarily by sugar maple and beech although white pine and red oak are also common. Black oak savanna also grows on the moraine, in a sandy area south of Rice Lake.

Volunteers have been working on a trail across the ridge since the Great Pine Ridge Trail was established in 1973, although efforts to blaze the current footpath officially began in 1992. Members are now divided into ten chapters: Aurora, Caledon, Clarington, Hope-Hamilton, King, Northumberland, Scugog, Uxbridge, Whitchurch-Stouffville and Richmond Hill, which hosted active members and includes some side trails. Together, chapters help build, maintain, promote and extend the trail. The Oak Ridges Trail connects to the **Bruce** (see p. 57), **Ganaraska** (see p. 61), **Humber** (see p. 137), **Rouge** (see p. 144) and **Trans Canada** (see p. 55) trails.

While on the trail, look for black-throated green warblers, bluebirds, hermit thrushes, northern goshawks, ovenbirds, pine siskins, pine warblers, purple finches, red-breasted nuthatches, red crossbills, red-shouldered hawks, scarlet tanagers, white-throated sparrows, whippoorwills, yellow-billed cuckoos and yellow-rumped warblers.

› Getting There

Several parking lots and conservation areas access the trail. Refer to the trailheads within each section.

› Further Information

Oak Ridges Trail Association
PO Box 28544
Aurora, ON L4G 6S6
☎ 905-833-6600 or 877-319-0285
www.oakridgestrail.org

Caledon Section

Level of difficulty 🚶

Distance *9.5km (5.9mi) linear*

Approx. time *4hrs*

Access points *Hall Lake Side Rd., 10th Concession at 18th Side Rd.*

This trail leads east from Palgrave for 4km along the Caledon Trailway and continues along roads and road allowances to the King/Caledon townline.

King Section

Level of difficulty 🚶

Distance *34.4km (21.3mi) linear*

Approx. time *14hrs*

Access points *8th Concession, 7th Concession, Weston Rd. at 16th Side Rd., Seneca College King Campus*

Other *Dogs not permitted on Seneca College's King Campus grounds*

This section leads from the King/Caledon townline past Pucks Farm, through Happy Valley Forest, the largest upland forest on the moraine. It then passes an orchard where apples are sold in the fall and Sacred Heart Church, the only remaining symbol of a Catholic colony, where 35 families worked together to survive the Depression. You'll also pass the Augustinian Monastery, located in a brick barn built by Sir Henry Pellatt in the early 1900s. You'll then pass through Seneca College, where you'll see Eaton Hall, a home built for Sir John and Lady Flora McCrae Eaton in the 1930s. This section ends at Bathurst Street.

Aurora Section

Level of difficulty 🚶

Distance *13.6km (8mi) linear*

Approx. time *8hrs*

Access points *16th Side Rd. east of Bathurst, Wellington St. East at Larmont, Sheppard's Bush Conservation Area, Vandorf Side Rd. at Bayview Ave., "Newmarket B" Go by bus from Finch subway station*

The Aurora section runs from Bathurst Street to Highway 404. It passes by Salamander Pond in a 17ha (42-acre) forest called Case Woodlot, Tamarac Green and Confederation Park. It also crosses Yonge Street and then passes through Sheppard's Bush Conservation Area and the Vandorf and Alliance woodlots. It goes south to Vandorf Road and then east to Highway 404.

Whitchurch-Stouffville Section

Level of difficulty 🚶

Distance *27.3km (16.9mi) linear*

Approx. time *11hrs*

Access points *Woodbine Ave. south of Aurora Rd., Whitchurch Conservation Area, Eldrid King on Hwy. 48*

This section of the trail passes by the 1947 Slaters Mill and through the Whitchurch Conservation Area. It also passes through six (Robinson, Clark, Patterson, Hall, Eldred King, Hollidge) of the 18 York Regional Forest Tracts that were planted in the 1920s to prevent soil erosion. The Whitchurch-Stouffville section ends at Musselman Lake, a kettle lake named after a Pennsylvanian family who settled nearby in 1807. The area became very popular with vacationers in the 1920s.

Uxbridge Section

Level of difficulty 🚶

Distance *21.6km (13.4mi) linear*

Approx. time *9hrs*

Access points *Hillsdale Rd., Secord Forest and Wildlife Area, Durham Regional Forest*

The Uxbridge section runs from the York Durham Boundary to Lakeridge Road. It begins at

Musselman Lake and continues through wetlands and forests to the Durham Regional Forest. Veterinarian Dr. Alan Secord once operated a pet cemetery in Secord Forest and Wildlife Area.

Scugog West Section

Level of difficulty 🚶

Distance *32km (19.8mi) linear*

Approx. time *12hrs*

Access points *Durham Regional Forest, Purple Woods Conservation Area*

The Scugog West section begins at the Durham Regional Forest and continues to Ocala Orchards Farm Winery along roads and road allowances. It passes the old rail bed of the "nip and tuck" railway that ran from Whitby to Port Perry in 1871 and on to Lindsay in 1876. (The railway was thus named because passengers had to jump off the train so it could climb the Oak Ridge Moraine.) A portion of the trail crosses Old Simcoe Road, an 18th-century route used by the Mississauga, who trapped beaver in Osler Marsh to trade with the French in current-day Oshawa. The trail also passes through Purple Woods Conservation Area, which is known for unusual spring wildflowers.

Clarington Section

Level of difficulty 🚶

Distance *35.5km (22mi) linear*

Approx. time *14hrs*

Access points *Long Sault Conservation Area, Ganaraska Forest Centre*

This trail begins at Long Sault Conservation Area, a 336ha (830-acre) forest, meadow and cedar swamp reserve. Look for interesting flora, including early buttercup, hoary vervain and tall white cinquefoil. It continues along road allowances and on private property to the Ganaraska Forest.

Hope-Hamilton Section

Level of difficulty 🚶 🚶

Distance *33km (20.1mi) linear*

Approx. time *13hrs*

Access points *Ganaraska Forest Centre, Bewdley, Gores Landing*

This trail begins at the Ganaraska Forest Centre and ends at the town of Gores Landing on Rice Lake. In between it passes along road and road allowances through the town of Bewdley and then past a memorial to Catherine Parr Traill before you reach the town of Gores Landing.

Northumberland Section

Level of difficulty 🚶 🚶

Distance *No established trail yet*

This chapter of the Oak Ridges Trail Association is examining the possibility of a trail from Gores Landing through Northumberland Forest to the eastern edge of the moraine.

Voyageur Trail

Location *Thunder Bay to South Baymouth, Manitoulin Island*

Level of difficulty 🚶 🚶 🚶

Number of trails *20*

Total distance *1,100km (682mi) when complete, currently 550km (372mi)*

Markers *White blazes for main trail, blue blazes for side trails, yellow blazes for loop trails*

Interesting features *Rolling terrain, coastal bluffs, secluded beaches and coves, wilderness camping*

Volunteers began planning the Voyageur Trail at a meeting in Sault Ste. Marie in March 1973. By late 1975, they had completed the Saulteaux section between Gros Cap and Mabel Lake. A year later, the Desbarats section between Tower Lake and Rydal Bank was completed, and additional sections were added as local volunteers were recruited. Volunteers from 24 clubs (eight currently inactive) have been maintaining and blazing trails for more than 30 years. They also organize hikes for local members, produce an excellent guidebook and liaise with the various Aboriginal communities, private landowners, public parks and municipalities along their proposed route, which traverses the north shores of Lake Superior and Georgian Bay.

There are currently 20 different trails that make up the route, including the **Nipigon River Recreation Trail** (see p. 250), the **Casque-Isles Hiking Trail** (see p. 244), the Marathon Peninsula Harbour Coastal Trail, the **Pukaskwa National Park Coastal Hiking Trail** (see p. 254), the Michipicoten Trail, the **Lake Superior Provincial Park Coastal Hiking Trail** (see p. 235), the Harmony Trail, the Stokely Creek Lodge Trail, the Goulais River Trail, the Saulteaux section, the Echo Ridges section, the Desbarats section, the Thessalon section, the Iron Bridge section, the Penewobikong section, the Elliot Lake section, the Spanish section, the Massey section, the Espanola section and Manitoulin Island.

Anyone interested in hiking the Voyageur Trail should obtain a copy of the *Voyageur Hiking Trail Guidebook*, and consider joining the Voyageur Association. Potential members are permitted to do one group hike with association members before membership is required.

› Getting There

Completed sections of the trail can be accessed in Nipigon, Terrace Bay, Marathon, Wawa, Goulais River, Elliott Lake or at **Pukaskwa National Park** (see p. 253), **Lake Superior Provincial Park** (see p. 231) and **Rainbow Falls Provincial Park** (see p. 257).

› Further Information

Voyageur Trail Association
PO Box 20040, 150 Churchill Blvd.
Sault Ste. Marie, ON P6A 6W3
☎ 877-393-4003
www3.sympatico.ca/voyageur.trail

Waterfront Trail

Location *Canadian shore of Lake Ontario*

Level of difficulty *🚶*

Total distance *900km (560mi) when complete, currently 780km (485mi)*

Markers *Stylized logo*

Other *In-line skating permitted; cycling permitted; dogs on leashes permitted*

The Waterfront Trail leads along the north shore of Lake Ontario from Niagara-on-the-Lake to Brockville. The trail links 41 communities, 182 parks and nature reserves and 170 marinas and yacht clubs.

Plans to build the trail began with a short section from Burlington to Trenton in 1995. Since then, additional communities have joined the trail, including the Seaway Trail in Western New York. It's hoped that one day the Waterfront Trail will loop around the coast of Lake Ontario.

› Getting There

Head to the water in any community on the trail and walk as far as you like.

› Further Information

Waterfront Regeneration Trust
372 W. Richmond St., Suite 308
Toronto, ON M5V 1X6
☎ 416-943-8080
www.waterfronttrail.org

Ajax

Distance *8.6km (5.3mi) linear*

Approx. time *3hrs each way*

Access points *Rotary Park, Pickering Beach*

This section leads from Liverpool Beachfront Park in Pickering to the Lynde Shores Conservation Area in Whitby. It passes through Duffins Marsh, a prime waterfowl viewing area.

Alnwick-Haldimand

Distance *27.8km (17.2mi) linear*

Approx. time *11hrs each way*

Access points *Lakeport, Nawautin Shores Nature Sanctuary, Wicklow Beach Boat Launch*

This section passes through some very rural areas. It also links to a series of trails at the Nawautin Shores Nature Sanctuary.

Augusta

Distance *12.8km (7.7mi) linear*

Approx. time *5hrs each way*

Access points *Anywhere along County Road 2*

This section follows County Road 2 from Fulford Street in Brockville, through Maitland, to Blue Church Road.

Belleville

Distance *4.2km (2.6mi) linear*

Approx. time *1.5hrs each way*

Access points *East and West Zwick Park, East Bayshore Park*

This section of the trail runs from East and West Zwick Park to East Bayshore Park.

Brighton

Distance *38km (23.6mi) linear*

Approx. time *15hrs each way*

Access points *Presqu'ile Provincial Park, downtown Brighton*

This section leads from Colborne village to Hanna Park in Trenton. It passes through Presqu'ile Provincial Park.

Brockville

Distance *6km (3.7mi) linear*

Approx. time *2hrs each way*

Access points *Henry and Water Streets, Blockhouse Island Parkway, Centeen Park*

The eastern extremity of the trail runs from east of Highway 46 to the Brockville Rowing Club just west of Blockhouse Island.

Burlington

Distance *23km (14mi) linear*

Approx. time *7hrs each way*

Access points *Beachway Park, Burloak Park, LaSalle Park, Royal Botanical Gardens*

This section runs from the canal/liftbridge to Shell Park in Oakville. It passes through Bayshore Park, Port Nelson Park, McNichol Park and the Sioux Lookout.

Clarington

Distance *37km (23mi) linear*

Approx. time *13hrs each way*

Access points ***Darlington Provincial Park*** *(see p. 125), Darlington Nuclear Information Centre, Bowmanville Harbour Conservation Area, Bond Head Parkette, Samuel Wilmot Nature Area*

This section runs from the General Motors of Canada Headquarters in Oshawa to downtown Port Hope. It passes through Darlington Provincial Park and the Samuel Wilmot Nature Area.

Cobourg

Distance *15km (9mi) linear*

Approx. time *6hrs each way*

Access points *Peace Park, Victoria Park*

This section of the trail begins on Rogers Road and continues through many parks and residential areas to the main street of Cobourg, along the boardwalk and then towards Colborne.

Cornwall

Distance *16.6km (10mi) linear*

Approx. time *7hrs each way*

Access points *Guindon Park, Second Street near Promenade Saunders, Grays Creek Conservation Area, Lamoureux Park*

This section follows the shore of the St. Lawrence River next to Cornwall and Pilon islands. Highlights include the old Cornwall Canal, Guindon and Lamoureux parks, the Eco-Gardens, the Cornwall Aquatic Centre and the grounds of St. Lawrence College.

Cramahe/Colborne

Distance *26km (16mi) linear*

Approx. time *10hrs each way*

Access points *Big Apple, Colborne Village Centre*

This section of the trail runs from Quinte West through the town of Colborne on Division and King Streets. It then follows Highway 2 through Salem to Union Road where it turns south to Lakeshore Road and into Brighton.

Deseronto

Distance *6.7km (4mi) linear*

Approx. time *2.5hrs each way*

Access points *Centennial Park*

This section of the trail begins on Bayshore Road and follows the waterfront through Centennial and Rathburn Parks to 4th Street. It then turns north to Dundas Street as it becomes Highway 2 west of the town.

Edwardsburgh/ Cardinal

Distance *12km (7.2mi) linear*

Approx. time *5hrs each way*

Access points *Cardinal Legion Waterfront Park*

This section follows County Road 2 through Johnstown and Cardinal and past the Galop Canal.

Gananoque

Distance *9km (6mi) linear*

Approx. time *3.6hrs each way*

Access points *Joel Stone Park*

This section begins on Highway 2 west of the golf club and passes through town to end up on the Thousand Islands Parkway.

Greater Napanee

Distance *38.8km (23.3mi) linear*

Approx. time *16hrs each way*

Access points *Lennox Generating Station, Rotary Park*

Greater Napanee is a junction. You can either take County Road 8 through the town of Napanee to Deseronto or you can follow the signed route along the Loyalist Parkway and travel between Glenora and Aldophstown via a ferry.

Grimsby

Distance *9.5km (5.9mi) linear*

Approx. time *4hrs each way*

Access points *Fifty Point Conservation Area, Forty Mile Creek Park*

This section begins at Fifty Point Conservation Area and follows Winston Road and the North Service Road to Lakeside Drive before reaching Forty Mile Creek Park. It then follows Lake Street past Grimsby Beach.

Hamilton

Distance *20.5km (12.7mi) linear*

Approx. time *8hrs each way*

Access points *Confederation Park, Van Wagner's Beach*

This trail leads from Beachway Park in Burlington to Campview Road in Fruitland.

Kingston

Distance *19km (11.8mi) linear*

Approx. time *7.5hrs each way*

Access points *Confederation Park, Lake Ontario Park*

This section leads through the city of Kingston, mainly along roads. Highlights include Fort Henry and the McLachlan Woodworking Museum.

Leeds and the Thousand Islands

Distance *37km (23mi) linear*

Approx. time *15hrs each way*

Access points *Ivy Lea Park, Rockport, Mallorytown Landing, Brown's Bay Provincial Park*

This section follows the St. Lawrence River along the Thousand Islands Parkway from Gananoque to Brown's Bay Park.

Lincoln

Distance *27km (16.7mi) linear*

Approx. time *11hrs each way*

Access points ***Ball's Falls Conservation Area*** *(see p. 119), Charles Daley Park, Lakehouse Restaurant in Vineland Station, Prudhommes Landing*

This section of trail follows roads around Jordan Harbour and then North Service Road to end at Tulford Road North. Ball's Falls is the only waterfall on the entire waterfront trail.

Loyalist

Distance *40km (24.8mi) linear*

Approx. time *16hrs each way*

Access points *Finkle Shores, Fairfield Park*

This section of trail leads from Greater Napanee to Loyalist along the Loyalist Parkway (Highway 33).

Mississauga

Distance *23.5km (14.6mi) linear*

Approx. time *9hrs each way*

Access points *Jack Darling Memorial, Lakefront Park, Lakeside Park, Port Credit Harbour, Marie Curtis Park, Rattray Marsh, Rhododendron Gardens*

Other *Rattray Marsh for pedestrians only*

This section leads from Gairlock Gardens in Oakville along the lake to Marie Curtis Park in Etobicoke, passing several waterfront parks, gardens, and Rattray Marsh.

Niagara-on-the-Lake

Distance *6km (3.7mi) linear*

Approx. time *2hrs each way*

Access points *Fort George, Nelson Park*

This section runs from Fort George to the intersection of Mary and Dorchester streets and then along Lakeshore Road from Town Line to Read Road. It also links with the Niagara River Recreational Trail, which leads to the **Niagara Glen** (see p. 141) and **Dufferin Islands** (see p. 128).

Oakville

Distance *22km (13.6mi)*

Approx. time *9hrs each way*

Access points *Coronation Park, Bronte Harbour, Gairloch Gardens, Oakville Harbour, Shell Park*

This section of the trail leads from Shell Park through Bronte and Hopedale to Oakville.

Oshawa

Distance *11.4km (7.1mi) linear*

Approx. time *4.6hrs each way*

Access points *Lakefront West Park*

This section leads from Heydenshore Kiwanis Park in Whitby to **Darlington Provincial Park** (see p. 125). It passes the Pumphouse Marsh Wildlife Reserve, Oshawa Harbour, the Second Marsh Wildlife Reserve and the Oshawa Community Museum.

Pickering

Distance *12.7km (7.9mi) linear*

Approx. time *5hrs each way*

Access points *Alex Robson Park, Millenium Square, Petticoat Creek Conservation Area, Rouge Beach Park*

This mostly off-road section leads from Rouge Beach Park in Scarborough to Rotary Park via charming boardwalks and over pedestrian bridges. It passes Frenchman's Bay and the Pickering Nuclear Generating Station.

Port Hope

Distance *18km (11mi) linear*

Approx. time *7hrs each way*

Access point *Lake or King streets parking lots, Port Hope*

This section leads through downtown Port Hope to Cobourg. Highlights include the Keith Richan Walkway bridge and the Alice King Sculthrope Memorial Woodland Marsh.

Prescott

Distance *7.1km (4.3mi) linear*

Approx. time *3hrs each way*

Access points *Centennial Park, municipal lot on Centre Street*

This section follows County Road 2 along the shore of the St. Lawrence River between Blue Church Road and Windmill Road. The highlight is the off-road Heritage River Trail in downtown Prescott.

Prince Edward County

Distance *15km (9.3mi) linear*

Approx. time *6hrs each way*

Access points *Bloomfield, Carrying Place, Glenora, Picton, Wellington*

This section of the trail follows the Loyalist Parkway (Highway 33) from Carrying Place Road to Glenora, where a ferry crossing can be taken to Adolphustown.

Quinte West

Distance 5km (3mi) linear

Approx. time 2hrs each way

Access points Bayshore Park, Centennial Park, downtown Quinte West, Hanna Park

This section of trail is asphalt and lit for easy travelling along the waterfront of Quinte West.

St. Catharines

Distance 9.8km (6mi) linear

Approx. time 4hrs each way

Access points Happy Rolph Bird Sanctuary, Charles Ansell Park, Port Dalhousie

This section runs along Lake Ontario between Port Dalhousie and the Happy Rolph Bird Sanctuary. It also connects with the **Bruce** (see p. 57) and **Merritt** (see p. 146) trails.

South Dundas

Distance 10.3km (6.2mi) linear

Approx. time 3hrs each way

Access points Morrisburg Golf Club, Riverside Park, Chrysler Park, Upper Canada Village, Morrisburg

This section follows Highway 2 from the Morrisburg Golf Club, through the Dupont Provincial Nature Reserve to Upper Canada Village.

South Glengarry

Distance 25.9km (155mi) linear

Approx. time 10 hrs each way

Access points Charlottenburgh Park and Cooper Marsh Conservation Area in Cornwall, and Glengarry Park in South Lancaster

This section follows the north shore of the St. Lawrence River south of Highway 2 from Cornwall to South Lancaster.

South Stormont

Distance 27.7km (16.6mi) linear

Approx. time 11hrs each way

Access points Upper Canada Village and the Upper Canada Migratory Bird Sanctuary in Morrisburg, Foran Park and Campground in Ingleside, McLaren Island south of West Gate, the Woodlands Day Use Park on Woodlands Island, the Lost Villages and Save Ontario Shipwrecks on Macdonell Island, the Milles Roches Day Use Area south of East Gate and the Long Sault Marina and Lost Villages Museum in Long Sault

This section follows Highway 2 from the Upper Canada Village in Morrisburg through Ingleside to Long Sault.

Toronto

Distance 46.5km (28.8mi) linear

Approx. time 23hrs each way

Access points Ashbridge's Bay Park, Balmy Beach, Cherry Beach, Colonel Samuel Smith Park, Coronation Park, Guildwood Park, Harbourfront, High Park, Humber Bay Park, Kew Beach, Sir Casimir Gzowski Park at the Humber Bridge, Marie Curtis Park, Ontario

Place, Rouge Beach Park, Scarborough Heights Garden Plots, Sunnyside Park, Sylvan Park, Tommy Thompson Park

This trail leads along Lake Ontario from Lakefront Promenade Park in Mississauga, through the Beaches area of Toronto, along the Scarborough Bluffs, through Guildwood Park and then through Rouge Beach Park. Each of the trailheads in this section leads to a different type of waterfront area, from beaches with boardwalks to amusement parks to wilderness bird and plant reserves. There's even a music garden development by Yo-Yo Ma and Toronto musicians.

Tyendinaga Township and Mohawks of the Bay of Quinte Tyendinaga Territory

Distance *28km (17mi) linear*

Approx. time *11hrs each way*

Access point *Tsitkerhododon Park*

The two sections of Tyendinaga Township and the Mohawks of the Bay of Quinte Territory begin at the edge of Belleville, continue through Shannonville and end at Bayshore. To get off the highway, trail users can go north to take Old Belleville Road through the township or south to take Bridge and Ridge roads through the only First Nations reserve on the Waterfront Trail.

Whitby

Distance *10.6km (6.6mi) linear*

Approx. time *4hrs each way*

Access points *Port Whitby Harbour, Rotary Sunrise Lake Park, Heydonshore Kiwanis Park and Pavillion, Lynde Shores Conservation Area*

This off-road section starts at the Ajax Waterfront Park and ends at Lakefront West Park in Oshawa. It passes the Iroquois Sports Centre, Rowe House, Station Gallery and Intrepid Park. Part of it travels through the last old growth white pine on the Lake Ontario shoreline in Thickson's Woods.

1. Avon Trail
2. Backus Heritage Conservation Area
3. Bruce Peninsula National Park
4. Elgin Trail
5. Fanshawe Conservation Area
6. Gordon Glaves Memorial Pathway, Brantford
7. Long Point World Biosphere Reserve
8. Luther Marsh Wildlife Management Area
9. Lynn Valley Trail
10. Maitland Trail
11. McKeough Conservation Area and Floodway
12. Pinery Provincial Park
13. Point Pelee National Park
14. Rondeau Provincial Park
15. Thames Valley Trail

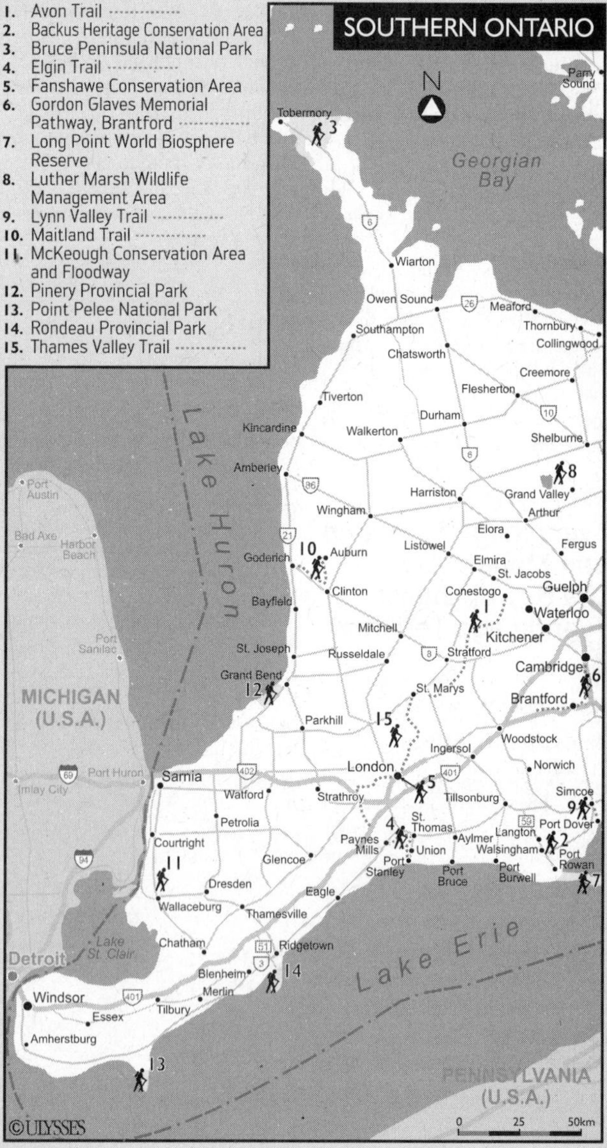

Southern Ontario

Southern Ontario falls between lakes Erie, Huron and St. Clair and stretches up to include the Bruce Peninsula, which is also bordered by Georgian Bay. It's probably not surprising, then, that water—whether in the form of large stunning lakes, misty waterfalls, meandering streams, rapidly flowing rivers, or various types of marsh—forms the most interesting landmarks in the area.

Hikers who are plant enthusiasts or bird-watchers should definitely visit all of the major landforms jutting out into the Great Lakes. They support important ecosystems, including freshwater marshes, dunes, and bogs. These characteristics combine with location to attract a wide variety of nesting and migrating bird species, including a great many warblers, ducks, swans and songbirds. Luckily, all of the landforms have been protected in provincially, nationally or internationally recognized parks. These include **Long Point World Biosphere Reserve** (see p. 95) and **Rondeau Provincial Park** (see p. 109), which jut eastward, **Point Pelee National Park** (see p. 106), which juts southward into Lake Erie, and the **Bruce Peninsula** (see p. 86), which juts into Lake Huron. The rivers in this region also attract a great many bird species and humans to their shores, a fact that has played an important role in the history of settlement. Two of them, the Thames and the Grand, have been so important to the development of the region that they have been nationally recognized as heritage rivers. Hikers are attracted to the many important trails that run beside each.

As its name implies, the **Thames Valley Trail** (see p. 112) follows the Thames River, as does part of the **Avon Trail** (see p. 82), although most of it borders the Avon River. The **Elgin Trail** (see p. 89) follows two Thames tributaries, the Kettle and Dodd creeks.

Other trails also border important rivers. The **Maitland Trail** (see p. 100) begins on a bridge over the Maitland River before following its banks. A trail following the shores of the Grand River in Brantford goes by the name of **Gordon Glaves Memorial Pathway** (see p. 93), while the **Lynn Valley Trail** (see p. 99) gets its charm from the Lynn River, which flows through the centre of the town of Simcoe.

Many of these large rivers had reputations for flooding in the spring and drying up in the summer. The **Luther Marsh** (see p. 97) at the headwaters of the Grand protects 75% of the river's flow, for instance. Wildwood Conservation Area on the **Thames Valley Trail** (see p. 112) on Trout Creek near St. Marys, and **Fanshawe Conservation Area** (see p. 90) on the Thames River in London, both feature large lakes created when dams were built. The **McKeough Conservation Area and Floodway** (see p. 101) was created in 1984 due to the traditional flooding of the Sydenham River, near the St. Clair River. Today, hikers enjoy walking through the more than 100,000 trees planted nearby.

Hikers interested in trees, however, should focus on the Carolinian forests and oak savanna for which Southern Ontario is famous. **Pinery Provincial Park** (see p. 101) protects one third of all the oak savanna remaining in the world, while **Backus Heritage Conservation Area** (see p. 84) preserves Canada's largest untouched tract of Carolinian forest. Those with a talent for close observation and an appreciation for subtle beauty will appreciate spending time in both of these locations, along with all the trails in Southern Ontario.

➤ Tourist Information

Bruce County Tourism
PO Box 129, 578 Brown St.
Wiarton, ON N0H 2T0
✆ 519-832-2020 or 800-268-3838
www.naturalretreat.com

Grey County Tourism
RR4, 102599 Grey Rd. 18
Owen Sound, ON N4K 5N6
✆ 519-376-2205 or 800-567-4739
www.greycounty.on.ca

Huronia Tourism Association
County of Simcoe Administration Centre
1110 Hwy. 26
Midhurst, ON L0L 1X0
✆ 705-726-9300 or 866-893-9300
www.county.simcoe.on.ca

Southern Georgian Bay Chamber of Commerce
208 King St.
Midland, ON L4R 3L9
✆ 705-526-7884
www.southerngeorgianbay.on.ca

Norfolk County Tourism & Economic Development
30 Peel St.
Simcoe, ON N3Y 1R9
✆ 519-426-9497 or 800-699-9038
www.norfolktourism.ca

Owen Sound City Hall
808 E. Second Ave.
Owen Sound, ON N4K 2H4
✆ 519-376-1440
www.city.owen-sound.on.ca

Economic Development & Tourism Haldimand
PO Box 400, 45 N. Munsee St.
Cayuga, ON N0A 1E0
✆ 905-318-5932 or 800-863-9607
www.haldimandcounty.on.ca

Brantford Visitor & Tourism Centre
399 Wayne Gretzky Pkwy.
Brantford, ON N3R 8B4
✆ 519-751-9900 or 800-265-6299
www.visitbrantford.ca

Tourism Services, City of Guelph
1 Carden St.
Guelph, ON N1H 3A1
✆ 519-837-5600 or 800-334-4519
www.visitguelphwellington.ca

The Hills of Headwaters Tourism Association
PO BOX 295, 200 Lakeview Court
Orangeville, ON L9W 2Z7
✆ 519-942-0314 or 800-332-9744
www.thehillsofheadwaters.com

Avon Trail

Location *St. Marys to Conestogo*

Number of sections *5*

Total distance *104km (64.5mi)*

Interesting features *Farmland, stiles, Wildwood Lake, Avon River, Waterloo County, Farmers Market, Waterloo moraine, Wildwood Conservation Area; links the Thames Valley and Grand Valley trails; connects to the Health Valley Trail from St. Jacobs*

Markers *White rectangular paint blazes, 15cm (6in) high and 5cm (2in) wide, offset top blaze indicates turn*

Facilities/services *Camping at the Wildwood Conservation Area*

Other *Dogs on leashes permitted*

Named after one of the rivers it follows, the Avon Trail passes over and by the glacier-created Waterloo moraine, along farmers' fields and through apple orchards, forests and tiny villages. Expect to have to climb up several stiles to get over farm fences and take several long and short footbridges over many creeks and rivers. Besides the Avon River, which flows through Stratford, you'll pass the Thames River in St. Marys, Trout Creek, Wildwood Lake, McCarthy Lake, Silver Creek, Bamburg Creek, Martin Creek, and the Conestogo River.

Just outside of the town of St. Marys, the trail passes through the Wildwood Conservation Area, a protected area surrounding Wildwood Lake. Great blue herons, double-crested cormorants, great egrets and eastern bluebirds frequent this park during the summer. (A reroute directs hikers to the north side of Wildwood Lake, rather than the south side).

Other interesting features along the way include the Waterloo County Farmers Market and the Brocksden School Museum. History buffs will also appreciate crossing the triple-arched Victoria Bridge in St. Marys, which was built in 1865 by Scottish stonemason Alexander McDonald. You'll also want to search for the old stone chimney–all that remains of a 1934 cabin–in the cedar stand on the trail between Perth Road 108 and Perth Line 40.

The Avon Trail began as a vision of Dr. Crosby Kirkpatrick in 1975 and was completed by volunteers by October 30, 1976. These volunteers now run the Avon Trail Association, which provides much-needed maps and a guidebook for the meandering trail.

› Getting There

Access the trail at the tennis courts on Thames Road in the town of St. Marys, at the intersection of Waterloo Regional Road 17 and Conestogo-Winterbourne Road in the town of Conestogo, in Wildwood Conservation Area, or at the Waterloo County Farmers Market on Weber Street in Waterloo.

› Further Information

The Avon Trail
PO Box 21148
Stratford, ON N5A 7V4
www.avontrail.ca

Section One: St. Marys and Wildwood Conservation Area

Level of difficulty 🚶 🚶

Distance *30km (18.6mi) linear*

Approx. time *12hrs each way*

Trailheads *St. Marys tennis courts, intersection of Perth Line 20 and Embro Rd. (Perth County Rd. 113)*

This section leads from the west side of the town of St. Marys through Wildwood Conservation Area and along Wildwood Lake. You'll pass or cross several creeks, climb through a couple of ravines and walk through a meadow.

Section Two: Flannigan Corners to Mennonite Corner

Level of difficulty 🚶 🚶

Distance *25.5km (15.8mi) linear*

Approx. time *10hrs each way*

Trailheads *Intersection of Perth Line 20 and Embro Rd. (Perth County Rd. 113), Perth Line 43 west of Mennonite Corner*

This section leads through several fields, with stiles allowing hikers to climb the fences between them. It then passes through a marshy area and past McCarthy Lake. After passing the junction for the Stratford Side Trail, leading west into the town of Stratford, you'll cross a creek. Climb the ravine to reach a road that leads to the Brocksden School Museum.

Section Three: Stratford Side Trail

Level of difficulty 🚶

Distance *9km (5.6mi) linear*

Approx. time *3.5hrs each way*

Trailheads *North of Hwy. 7/8 and east of Stratford on the main trail, 44km (27mi) from St. Marys or 62km (38mi) from Conestogo, Dunn's Bridge on O'Loane Ave. west of Stratford*

This trail follows the south shore of the Avon River into Stratford. You'll walk through Devon Street and Confederation Parks, past the Stratford Festival Theatre and through the Shakespearean Gardens. As the trail leads south of Lake Victoria, you'll see the island named after Stratford Festival founder Tom Patterson.

Section Four: Mennonite Corner to Farmers Market

Level of difficulty 🚶 🚶

Distance *42km (26mi) linear*

Approx. time *17hrs each way*

Trailheads *Perth Line 43 west of Mennonite Corner, Waterloo County Farmers Market on Weber St.*

This section leads through two deciduous forests, along the south shore of Silver Creek, through an area that can be quite wet and then through a marsh. It then follows trails groomed for cross-country skiing by the Musselman-Schneider family before reaching Conservation Drive, which is named for the Laurel Creek Conservation Area, to the east and south of the trail.

Section Five: Farmers Market to Conestogo

Level of difficulty *🚶*

Distance *8.5km (5.3mi) linear*

Approx. time *3hrs each way*

Trailheads *Waterloo County Farmers Market on Weber St., intersection of Waterloo Regional Rd. 17 and Woolwich Township Rd. 45*

This section follows the Trans Canada Trail from the Farmers Market in North Waterloo to the Conestogo River, then along the south bank past Martin's Creek to Country Squire Road. It then follows several different roads to get to the Grand Valley Trail.

Backus Heritage Conservation Area

Location *North of Port Rowan and south of Langton*

Number of trails *5*

Total distance *18.5km (11.5mi)*

Interesting features *John C. Backhouse Mill, Backus Homestead, Backus Woods Carolinian Forest, 3 mills, 2 barns, 2 shops, playhouse, herb garden and farm implements*

Facilities/services *Parking, toilets, Conservation Education Centre, shipwreck museum, restaurant, camping, swimming pool, showers, laundry*

Other *Dogs on leashes permitted*

A visit to Backus Heritage Conservation Area, a 502ha (1,240-acre) site, satisfies a curiosity for both natural and social history.

A heritage village that emulates southern Ontario life in the late 1800s and early 1900s forms the best-known section of the park. It includes four buildings that were on the site when the Backus (originally Backhouse) family sold the property in 1955, plus a variety of other period structures relocated here by the Long Point Region Conservation Authority. The most impressive of these is a hand-hewn beam structure now known as the John C. Backhouse Mill. Wheat has been stone ground into flour in this building since 1798, making it Ontario's oldest continuously operating grist mill. It is also one of the few mills close to the U.S. border that survived the War of 1812. Another structure worth noticing is the large brick house, which was built by the Backus family in 1850 from clay found on the property. Restoration efforts have included repainting the interior in its original colours and reconstructing the veranda in 1996.

Backus Heritage Conservation Area also contains Canada's best stand of untouched Carolinian forest. Inspired by an interest in trees, original owner John C. Backhouse preserved the 283ha (700-acre) woodlot, and his descendants respected his vision. Now referred to as Backus Woods, the forest includes black gum, pawpaw, shagbark hickory, sweet chestnut, sycamore, swamp white oak and tulip trees among the maple, beech, yellow birch, red maple and red oak trees typical of an Ontario deciduous forest. Stands of white pine, yellow birch and hemlock also appear. The interesting flora includes flowering dogwood and southern beech fern. Eighty species of birds—including hooded mergansers, Louisiana water thrushes, orioles, pileated woodpeckers, prothonotary warblers, winter wrens, vireos, and yellow-bellied sapsuckers—nest in the trees, while flying squirrels leap from branch to branch. The woods are also home to opossums, Ontario's only marsupial, and six species of bats, including rare eastern pipistrelles. Concession 4 divides the woodland into a northern swamp and southern forest.

The Charles Sauriol Carolinian Forest, a 60ha (148-acre) tract of re-generated farmland that was planted with red oak, sycamore and green ash in 1991, lies next to the property north of Concession 3.

➤ Getting There

Take Regional Road 59 north from Long Point or south from Langton. Turn east on Regional Road 42 for the Heritage Village and Backus Woods or Highway 24 for Backus Woods only.

➤ Further Information

Long Point Region Conservation Authority
RR3, 146 Radical Rd.
Simcoe, ON N3Y 4K2
519-428-4623
www.lprca.on.ca

Heritage Village Tour

Level of difficulty 🚶

Distance *5km (3mi) multi-loop trail*

Approx. time *2.5hrs return*

Trailhead *Conservation Education Centre*

Pick up a visitor's guide at the Conservation Education Centre and tour past 19 restored and reconstructed buildings, through the heritage herb and vegetable garden and past a variety of old-fashioned farm implements. Besides the mill and homestead, items of interest include a Baptist church dating from 1869, a log house, a Vittoria Carriage Shop dating from 1843, an octagonal schoolhouse, a horse-drawn treadmill and drag saw, a tripod stump puller, a cider press, a corn crib, an ice house and an outdoor bake oven.

Flood Plain Trail

Level of difficulty 🚶

Distance *3km (1.9mi) semicircle*

Approx. time *2.5hrs each way*

Trailhead *The millpond on the opposite side of the mill, the road that leads past the Teeterville Baptist Church and Campground E, the road around Campground E, or the Sugarbush Trail*

This trail leads alongside the millpond, through a forest and along Dedrich Creek, the reason for the original placement of the John C. Backhouse Mill in 1798. Look for pileated woodpeckers, black-throated green warblers and barred owls.

Sugar Bush Trail

Level of difficulty 🚶

Distance *4km (2.5mi) loop*

Approx. time *1.5hrs return*

Trailhead *Concession 4, Flood Plain Trail, the road that leads past the Teeterville Baptist Church and Campground E*

Although named for the sugar maples that still produce delicious maple syrup every March, this loop is also the best way to view 200-year-old beech trees and tulip trees that grow to heights of 40m (131ft).

Sassafras Trail

Level of difficulty *🚶*

Distance *.5km (.3mi) linear*

Approx. time *30min return*

Trailhead *Sugar Bush Trail*

This woodland trail highlights the sassafras tree, a deciduous tree that grows in dry sandy soil. Children enjoy collecting the lobed leaves of the sassafras, which resemble mittens.

Wetlands Trail

Level of difficulty *🚶*

Distance *6km (3.7mi) loop and linear extension to Hwy. 24*

Approx. time *2.5hrs return*

Trailhead *Hwy. 24 parking lot, Concession 4 or the Sugar Bush Trail*

This trail provides a good view of the swamp, where 400-year-old black gum trees grow. Look for Louisiana water thrushes and golden-winged and blue-winged warblers. In August, you'll see lots of stalked water horehound growing on the logs.

Bruce Peninsula National Park

Location *East and west side of Hwy. 6*

Number of trails *7*

Total distance *26.1km (16.2mi)*

Interesting features *Niagara Escarpment, orchids, Eastern massasauga rattlesnakes, ferns*

Facilities/services *Parking, toilets, telephones, camping, outdoor amphitheatre, swimming beach, Tobermory Visitor Centre, Tobermory Diver Registration Centre*

Bruce Peninsula National Park is actually three parks in one. Hikers who like sandy, flat beach walks will appreciate Dorcas Bay, on the shores of Lake Huron to the west of Highway 6. Those who prefer walks along limestone cliffs, through a mixed forest of aspen, birch, cedar, fir and spruce, will prefer Cyprus Lake on the shores of Georgian Bay, to the east of Highway 6. Park staff offers guided walks and other programs during the summer. Those who prefer a more rustic, backcountry experience, or like walking along boulder beaches, will prefer to access the Bruce Trail via the Halfway Log Dump Trail.

Star-gazers will appreciate the visible night sky in the area because artificial lighting is actively limited. In fact, the Royal Astronomical Society of Canada designated Bruce Peninsula National Park and Fathom Five National Marine Park as Canada's 8th Dark Sky Preserve in March 2009.

BRUCE PENINSULA NATIONAL PARK

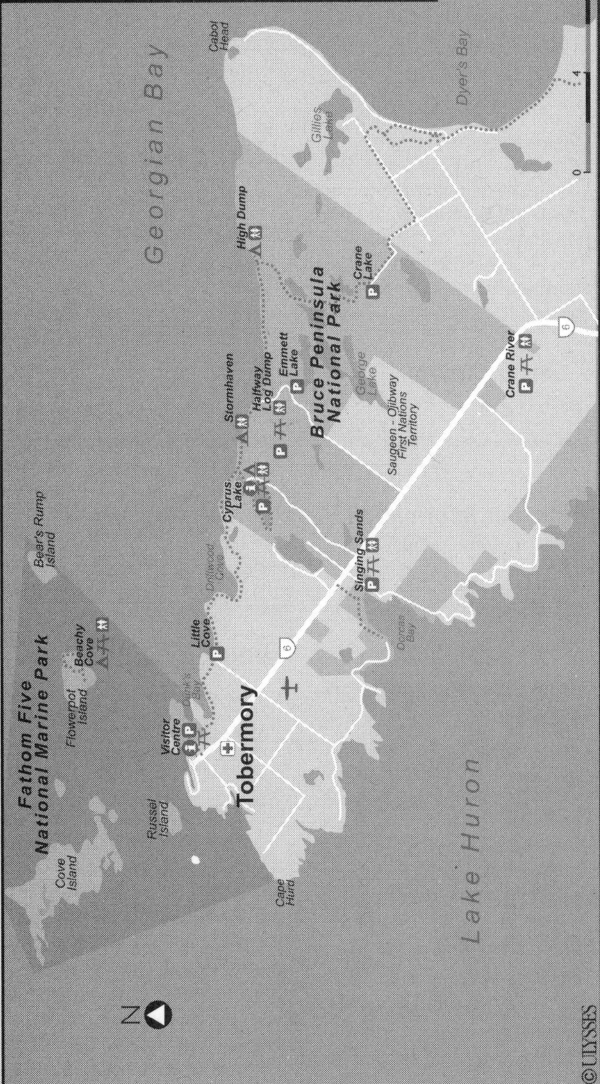

Georgian Bay
Lake Huron
Fathom Five National Marine Park
Bruce Peninsula National Park
Tobermory
Cabot Head
Dyer's Bay
Gillies Lake
High Dump
Crane Lake
Emmett Lake
Halfway Log Dump
Stormhaven
George Lake
Saugeen - Ojibway First Nations Territory
Crane River
Cyprus Lake
Driftwood Cove
Singing Sands
Dorcas Bay
Little Cove
Bear's Rump Island
Beachy Cove
Flowerpot Island
Dunk's Bay
Visitor Centre
Russel Island
Cove Island
Cape Hurd
6
0
4
8km
N
©ULYSSES

Plant enthusiasts can spot up to 43 species of orchids, 20 species of ferns, Canada's best stand of Indian plantain and half the world's dwarf lake iris on the trails on the Dorcas Bay side (which used to be a reserve owned by Ontario Nature).

Eastern massasauga rattlesnakes, deer, snowshoe hares, raccoons, porcupines, skunks, black bears, fishers, red squirrels, beavers, chipmunks and red fox live in the area.

› Getting There

Take Highway 6 north from Wiarton or south from Tobermory.

› Further Information

Bruce Peninsula National Park
PO Box 189
Tobermory, ON N0H 2R0
☎ 519-596-2233
www.pc.gc.ca

Friends of the Bruce District Parks Association
PO Box 66
Tobermory, ON N0H 2R0
☎ 519-596-8181
www.castlebluff.com

Georgian Bay Trail

Level of difficulty 🚶

Distance *1.5km (.9mi) linear*

Approx. time *1hr each way*

Trailhead *Head of trails parking lot*

This trail is the most popular in the area. It leads to the east of Marr Lake along the easiest path to Halfway Rock Point and Indian Head Cove on the shore of Georgian Bay. Continue north on the Bruce Trail to get to the natural arch and the Grotto sea cave or return to the parking lot via the Marr Lake Trail.

Marr Lake Trail

Level of difficulty 🚶🚶

Distance *1.5km (.9mi) linear*

Approx. time *2hrs each way*

Trailhead *Head of trails parking lot*

This trail leads along the western shore of Marr Lake to the Bruce Trail on the shore of Georgian Bay. Take the Bruce Trail south to get to Halfway Rock Point and Indian Head Cove and return to the parking lot or the Georgian Bay Trail. Continue north for the natural arch and Grotto sea cave.

Singing Sands Trail

Level of difficulty 🚶

Distance *1.6km (1mi) loop*

Approx. time *1hr return*

Trailhead *Singing Sands day use area*

This trail leads from the parking lot to Dorcas Bay Beach, dune and alvar, an area of soft sand, quiet water and a wide diversity of plants, including pitcher plants, orchids and jack pine. It then returns along a path that used to be known as the Old Dorcas Bay Road. This whole area has recently been allowed to regenerate and is still very fragile, so please stay on the trails.

Cyprus Lake Trail

Level of difficulty 🚶

Distance *5km (3mi) loop*

Approx. time *2.5hrs return*

Trailhead *Head of trails parking lot or the Cyprus campground*

This trail circles Cyprus Lake, past the Birches, Poplars and Tamarack campgrounds and along marshland and beaches. This is a great opportunity to see some of the ferns, orchids and marsh wildflowers that have made the park famous.

Half Way Log Dump Trail

Level of difficulty 🚶

Distance *1km (.6mi) linear*

Approx. time *15min each way*

Trailhead *Head of trails at Cyprus Lake or Halfway Log Dump parking lot, on Halfway Log Dump Rd., off Emmett Lake Rd.*

This trail leads to the Bruce Trail about 5km (3mi) south of Indian Head Cove.

Horse Lake Trail, Cyprus Lake

Level of difficulty 🚶 🚶

Distance *1km (.6mi) linear*

Approx. time *30min each way*

Trailhead *Head of trails parking lot*

This trail leads from the parking lot along the eastern side of Horse Lake, past a marsh and through woodland to a boulder beach on Georgian Bay, where it connects with the Bruce Trail.

Bruce Trail

Level of difficulty 🚶 🚶 🚶

Distance *14.5km (9mi) linear*

Approx. time *8hrs each way*

Trailhead *Head of trails at Cyprus Lake or Halfway Log Dump parking lot, on Halfway Log Dump Rd., off Emmett Lake Rd.*

A short portion of the 800km (496mi) Bruce Trail lies within the national park, following the shoreline of Georgian Bay. This very challenging walk leads through a maple birch forest and marshland, across boulder beaches and along the edge of the Niagara Escarpment. Longer hikes along this trail are possible by continuing north or south of the park.

Elgin Trail

Level of difficulty 🚶 🚶

Location *Southdel Bourne Road through Paynes Mills, Union and St. Thomas to Port Stanley*

Number of trails *1*

Total distance *41km (24.6mi)*

Approx. time *16hrs*

Markers *White blazes*

Interesting features *Kettle Creek, Dodd's Creek, Mackie's Restaurant, trestle bridge, deciduous and Carolinian forests, McCaig and McCoogan bushes; connects to the* ***Thames Valley Trail*** *(see p. 112)*

Facilities/services *Parking*

Other *Dogs on leashes permitted*

The Elgin Trail follows Dodd's and Kettle creeks between Lake Erie and the Thames River. The trail passes through former agricultural lands, red pine plantations, private and publicly owned forests, and past wetlands and bogs. As a result, many species of flora and fauna can be seen. Squirrels are the most common fauna, but there are also plenty of rabbits and deer. Some coyotes can also be seen. Some parts of the trail feature ferns and moss, while others feature field species, like milkweed and jewelweed. It also passes past and under an operating railways.

› Getting There

In Port Stanley, parking lots are available on the shore of Lake Erie near Mackie's Restaurant and on Carlow Road south of Warren Street.

In Union, there's a parking lot on County Road 4, just south of Fingal Line.

In Paynes Mills, the parking lot is on Talbot Line, just northwest of Dodd Creek.

The trail follows Fourth Line between McGoogan Bush and Parson Road.

The trail ends at McCaig Bush on County Road 17 (Southdel Bourne Road) east of County Road 15. Parking is along County Road 17 (Southdel Bourne Road).

› Further Information

Elgin Hiking Trail Club
c/o Kettle Creek Conservation Authority
RR8
St. Thomas, ON N5P 3T3
www.elginhikingtrail.org

Fanshawe Conservation Area

Level of difficulty 🚶

Location *London*

Number of trails *5*

Total distance *30.5km (18.3mi)*

Interesting features *Fanshawe Reservoir, Fanshawe Pioneer Village, Fanshawe Dam; links to the **Thames Valley Trail** (see p. 112)*

Facilities/services *Parking, toilets, telephones, camping, laundry, showers, swimming pool, fishing, boat launch, yacht club and sailing school*

Other *Dogs on leashes permitted*

Fanshawe Conservation Area was created in 1952, when the Upper Thames River Conservation Authority built the massive structure for $5 million. The 1200ha (2,964-acre) site now serves as a centre for boating recreation and camping. The nature reserve also protects typical flora and fauna, such as skunks and raccoons, as well as several rare reptiles, including threatened spiny softshell turtles and threatened queen snakes.

A highlight on the site is the Fanshawe Pioneer Village. The replica village was founded by W. Wilfred Jury and his wife Elsie McLeod Murray Jury in 1953 and run by Wilfred for almost three decades. Both Jurys were archaeologists and journalists and donated many items to the village, including Jury's boyhood farmhouse. Today's Pioneer Village is much larger than it was then and includes regional buildings from four periods between 1820 and 1920.

FANSHAWE CONSERVATION AREA

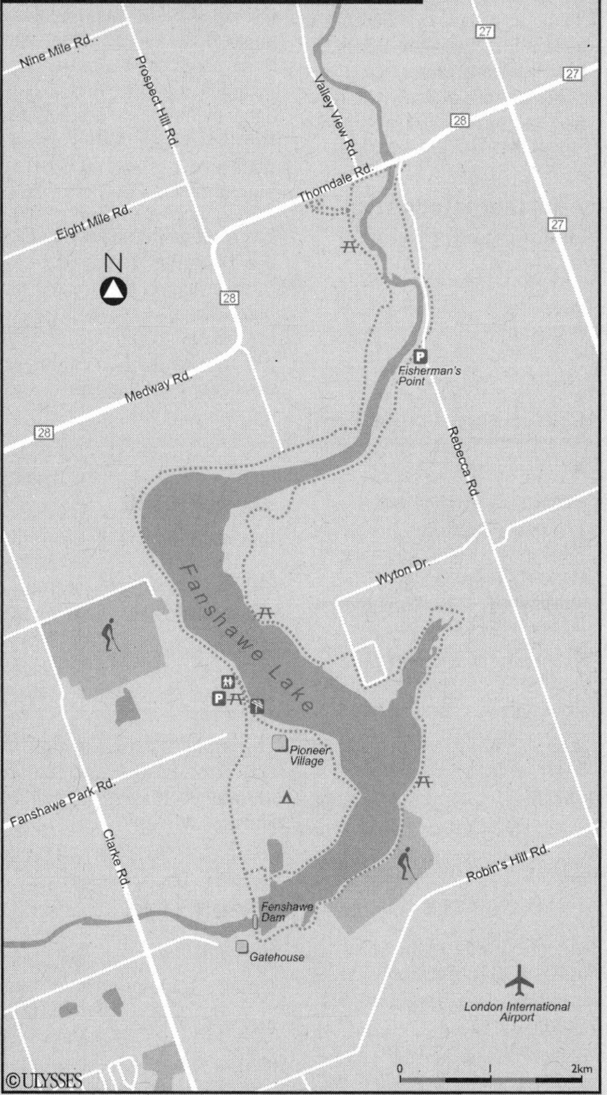
Nine Mile Rd.
Prospect Hill Rd.
Valley View Rd.
27
27
28
Thorndale Rd.
Eight Mile Rd.
27
N
28
Fisherman's Point
Medway Rd.
28
Rebecca Rd.
Fanshawe Lake
Wyton Dr.
Pioneer Village
Fanshawe Park Rd.
Clarke Rd.
Robin's Hill Rd.
Fenshawe Dam
Gatehouse
London International Airport
0
1
2km
©ULYSSES

> Getting There

The entrance to Fanshawe Conservation Area is on Clarke Road in London, between Fanshawe Park Road and Huron Street. Veterans Memorial Parkway leads directly from exit 194 on Highway 401 to the park entrance.

> Further Information

Fanshawe Conservation Area
1424 Clarke Rd.
London, ON N5V 5B9
519-451-2800
www.thamesriver.on.ca

Fanshawe Lake Trail

Level of difficulty

Distance 20km (12mi) loop

Approx. time 4hrs return

Markers White and blue blazes (to indicate the main and secondary Thames Valley Trails)

Trailheads Fanshawe Park Day Use Area and Beach, Thorndale Road, Fanshawe Dam

Other The west side of the trail forms part of the Thames Valley Trail

This trail travels all the way around the Fanshawe Lake Reservoir. It uses the bridge on Thorndale Road and the Fanshawe Dam to cross the Thames River.

The west side of the trail features views of the pioneer village buildings, a maple and black cherry forest and a steep floodplain forest with hackberry, sycamore and white ash trees, along with the dam and campground. One highlight is the well-marked George Furtney Memorial Forest.

The east side of the trail goes through two pine plantations, dense shrubs, the Fanshawe Sugar Bush and a mature hardwood forest. It also passes some cottages and Wye Creek. Highlights include two lookouts over Fanshawe Lake, both furnished with picnic tables and garbage bins, and decks over Wye Creek.

The route from the Rowing facilities over the dam and to the campground is not marked with blazes, so it's easy to get mixed up and try to follow the park's red trail instead of taking the main road over the dam and past the campground.

Yellow Trail

Level of difficulty

Distance 4km (2.4mi) loop

Approx. time 1.5hrs return

Markers Yellow

Trailheads Day use area, park office, campground

This trail circuits through the conservation area and features the waterfront, historic buildings and groundhogs.

Green Trail

Level of difficulty

Distance 3km (1.8mi) loop

Approx. time 1hr return

Markers Green

Trailheads Junctions of main conservation entrance road with the dam road or the park office

This trail leads through a pine plantation, a spruce plantation, a small deciduous forest and an open meadow to the north of the campground.

Red Trail

Level of difficulty 🚶

Distance *2km (1.2mi) loop*

Approx. time *1hr return*

Markers *Red*

Trailhead *Fanshawe Dam Road to the east of the dam*

This trail travels along the shore of the Fanshawe Reservoir to pass the rowing centre and the Fanshawe Lake Trail.

Blue Trail

Level of difficulty 🚶

Distance *1.5km (.9mi) loop*

Approx. time *45min return*

Markers *Blue*

Trailhead *Parking lot just north of the front gate*

This short trail loops through plantations of pine, spruce and larch.

Gordon Glaves Memorial Pathway, Brantford

Location *South of Brantford*

Number of trails *5*

Total distance *25km (15.5mi)*

Interesting features *Alexander Graham Bell Homestead, Gilkison Flats, Lions Park, Brant Conservation Area; connects to the* ***Grand Valley Trail*** *(see p. 64) and the Brantford/Hamilton Rail Trail*

Facilities/services *Parking, toilets, telephones, camping at Brant Conservation Area*

Other *Dogs on leashes permitted*

The Gordon Glaves Memorial Pathway is a network of trails along the south and north shores of the Grand River in Brantford. On the south side, the trails connect the Grand Valley Trail, Alexander Graham Bell Homestead, Gilkison Flats, Lions Park, Brants Crossing Park and Lorne Park. To the north, they connect the Brantford/Hamilton Rail Trail, Waterworks Park and the Brant Conservation Area, and the other side of the Grand Valley Trail. The northern side is also part of the Trans Canada Trail.

The area is an important migration route, particularly for geese, swallows and warblers.

Three of the trails, the Grand River Ramble, the Old Field Path and the Pond Loop, are in Lions Park.

➤ Getting There

Access points are available along Ballantyne Drive, Erie Avenue, Gilkison Street, Grand River Avenue, Greenwich Street, Hardy Road, Heights Road, Market Street South, Parkside Drive, Water Street, and through Bellview Park, Brant Conservation Area, Cockshutt Park, D'Aubigny Creek Park, Fordview Park, Lions Park and Waterworks Park.

› Further Information

City of Brantford Parks and Recreation
1 Sherwood Dr.
Brantford, ON N3T 1N3
519-756-1500
www.brantford.ca

Gordon Glaves Memorial Pathway, Trans Canada Trail

Level of difficulty

Distance *12.5km (7.8mi) linear*

Approx. time *5hrs each way*

Trailhead *Parking lot at the locks and canal on Locks Rd. or the parking lot on Oak Park Rd.*

This trail travels along either side of Mohawk Street and Birkett Lane until reaching the Grand River at River Road. It then continues along the north side of the River through Brantford and finishes along Oak Park Road at Highway 403. Interesting features along the way include Her Majesty's Royal Chapel of the Mohawks, Kanata Iroquois Village and Wilkes Dam.

Gordon Glaves Memorial Pathway, South of the Grand River

Level of difficulty

Distance *7.5km (4.7mi) linear*

Approx. time *3hrs each way*

Trailhead *D'Aubigny Creek Park or the Bell Homestead*

This section of the Gordon Glaves Memorial Pathway travels along the south side of the Grand River, starting at the Bell Homestead and then through the Mary Welsh Nature area in Lions Park, then Fordview, Cockshutt and D'Aubigny Creek parks. Bridges cross the river at Brantford Southern Access Road (BSAR) and Wharf Street. The major feature is the Gilkison Flats, a prime wetland area.

The Grand River Ramble, Lions Park

Level of difficulty

Distance *2km (1.2mi) linear*

Approx. time *1hr each way*

Trailhead *"The Valley Wall" escarpment on the south side of Gilkison St. in Lions Park*

Other *Wheelchair accessible*

This hike travels from the escarpment that marks the edge of the Grand River flood plain and along the shores of the Grand River, past a pickerel spawning area known locally as "green waters." Look for smallmouth bass, catfish, carp, pike and brown trout in these waters. You may also see some kingfishers, herons, gulls, geese and muskrats. Wood ducks, woodpeckers, squirrels and raccoons live in the silver and Manitoba maples, and cottonwoods and willows grow along the shore.

The Old Field Path, Lions Park

Level of difficulty 🚶

Distance *1.8km (1mi) loop*

Approx. time *30min return*

Trailhead *"The Valley Wall" escarpment on the south side of Gilkison St., in Lions Park*

This loop circles through a Carolinian forest growing in a flood plain between the Valley Wall and the Grand River. You'll see ash, basswood, black walnut, elm, hackberry, mulberry, red oak, sycamore and white pine trees. Opossums, white-tailed deer and chipmunks live in this forest.

Pond Loop, Lions Park

Level of difficulty 🚶

Distance *1.2km (.7mi) loop*

Approx. time *30min return*

Trailhead *"The Valley Wall" escarpment on the south side of Gilkison St., near the pond in Lions Park*

This trail loops along a small pond on a spot where the Grand River used to meander. Fed by flooding, storm water and perhaps a spring or two, the pond now shelters water striders, dragonflies, four species of amphibians, two species of turtles and a variety of garter and water snakes. Cattails, purple loosestrife, crinkle leaf, duckweed and reeds grow in the murky depths.

Long Point World Biosphere Reserve

Location *At the end of Hwy. 59, south of Walsingham*

Number of trails *2*

Total distance *3.2km (2mi)*

Interesting features *Dunes, migrating butterflies and birds, rare plants, seven species of turtles, black garter snakes*

Facilities/services *Parking, toilets, telephones, convenience store, camping, fishing, playgrounds, swimming, laundry area, showers, boat launch*

Other *Dogs on leashes permitted*

The Long Point Peninsula, a 32km-long (19.8mi) sand spit jutting into Lake Erie, is one of Canada's most fragile ecosystems. The United Nations Education, Scientific and Cultural Organization (UNESCO) recognized the area as a prime example of a Great Lakes coastal ecosystem in 1986. The Long Point World Biosphere Reserve includes a protected core, a buffer zone and a zone of cooperation. The protected core includes the 3,250ha (8,000-acre) Long Point Wildlife Area and a private sanctuary that's been owned by the Long Point Company since 1866. The buffer zone, which begins at the 100-year flood line of Lake Erie and Long Point Bay, includes the Long Point Peninsula and Turkey Point. The zone of cooperation includes the Big Creek and Dedrich Creek flood plains, **Backus Woods** (see p. 84) and the St. Williams Crown Forest.

Although there are no actual hiking trails anywhere on the spit yet, this region is too important to be missed. Currently, hikers can best explore the area by walking along the beach at Long Point Provincial Park and along the Canadian Wildlife Service's South Beach, between the provincial park and the border of the privately owned Long Point Company lands. The rest of the peninsula is off-limits to humans, thanks to the wildlife reserve and private lands already mentioned.

A visit to Long Point also gives you a chance to drive across the causeway between Lake Erie and the inner bay, a spine-tingling experience that's going to be even better by 2012 or so. A causeway improvement project to protect frog, reptile and other species' migration includes plans for a 3.5km (2mi) multi-use pathway along this route.

Monarch butterflies already congregate along the spit during their migration in September. The area is also a prime location for 273 species of migratory birds, including buffleheads, canvasbacks, kinglets, mallards, mergansers, pintails, redheads, scaup, sparrows, teals, thrushes, warblers and wigeons; 131 of these, including bald eagles, Forster's tern and piping plovers, have been known to nest on the sand spit. The Long Point Bird Observatory, North America's oldest private bird observatory, is located near the entrance to the provincial park.

If you visit the area in June, you'll see seven types of turtles making their way from the marshes to the sand dunes, where they lay their eggs. The spit is one of the last areas that is home to large, intact breeding populations of many rare and endangered reptiles and amphibians, including Blanding's turtles, eastern spiny softshell turtles, Fowler's toads, hognose snakes and spotted turtles. Chipmunks, coyotes, deer mice, eastern foxes, meadow voles, melanistic (black) garter snakes, mink, muskrats, raccoons, skunks and white-tailed deer also live here. Meadow crayfish, one of Canada's rarest invertebrates, have been spotted at the very tip of the spit, near the lighthouse.

Hikers who are interested in plants should look for bottle gentians, fringed gentians, grass-of-Parnassus, ladies-tresses orchids and sneezeweed. Carolinian species such as tulip trees and sassafras also grow here.

› Getting There

Take Regional Road 59 south from Walsingham to the causeway.

› Further Information

The Long Point World Biosphere Reserve Foundation
PO Box 338
Port Rowan, ON N0E 1M0
☎ 519-410-8878
www.longpointbiosphere.org

Long Point Provincial Park
PO Box 99
Port Rowan, ON N0E 1M0
☎ 519-586-2133, 800-667-1940 or 888-668-7275
www.ontarioparks.com

Long Point Provincial Park Beach

Level of difficulty 🚶

Distance *2.2km (1.4mi) linear*

Approx. time *1hr each way*

Trailhead *Day use area or at one of the second vehicle parking lots*

This long beach is a wonderful walk along a flat expanse of sand edged with brush and tree-covered sand dunes.

South Beach, Canadian Wildlife Service

Level of difficulty 🚶

Distance *1km (.6mi) linear*

Approx. time *1hr return*

Trailhead *The second vehicle parking lot at the east end of Long Point Provincial Park*

Hikers who carefully avoid walking on dunes are permitted to walk along the sandy beach between Long Point Provincial Park and the land owned by the Long Point Company. Please do not pass the sign indicating the boundary of the Long Point Company property.

Luther Marsh Wildlife Management Area

Location *On the 6th concession, north of Grand Valley*

Number of trails *3*

Total distance *24km (14.9mi)*

Interesting features *Luther Lake, Townsend Cairn, heron nests, double-crested cormorants, Windmill Island, Tovell Farm House, ruffed grouse, magnificent sunsets from the lookout tower on the east side of the lake*

Facilities/services *Parking, two rental buildings available for groups, canoe or kayak launch, cycling trail, hunting*

Note *Autumn visitors should call ahead to make sure not to plan visits on days when hunting is permitted*

Named after the leader of the Protestant Reformation by a frustrated Catholic farmer, Luther Marsh's 5,261ha (12,995 acres) make it one of southern Ontario's largest wetlands. Bogs, fens, marshes and swamps encircle both 1,400ha (3,500-acre) Luther Lake, which was created in 1952 by the Grand River Conservation Authority. The dam that created Luther Lake from Black Creek enables the authority to supply up to 75% of the water that flows along the upper Grand River during the summer.

An additional 35ha (86.5 acres) were flooded by Ducks Unlimited in 1985 to create Mallard, Pintail, Wood Duck and Blue-winged Teal ponds. The organization flooded another 182ha (408 acres) in the year 2000 as part of the Monticello Project. A visit to Luther Marsh provides an extraordinarily rich and varied experience for bird-watchers and other naturalists. The area is a prime location for viewing butterflies, especially swallowtails, and a variety of plants, including asters, broad-lipped twayblades, dogwoods, irises, leatherleaf, goldenrod, one-flowered pyrolas, pale laurels, pitcher plants, sensitive ferns, showy lady's slippers, swamp birches, swamp valerians, sundews, water shields, water stargrasses and wild garlic.

Bird-watchers have spotted 237 species in the area, including bitterns, bobolinks, black-crowned night herons, black terns, blue-winged teals, canvasbacks, common flickers, common loons, double-crested cormorants, gadwalls, great blue herons, green-winged teals, killdeer, hooded mergansers, least bitterns, lesser scaups, mallards, marsh wrens, northern pintails, northern shoveler, ospreys, redheads, red-necked grebes, red-winged blackbirds, ring-necked ducks, ruddy ducks, sedge wrens, sparrows, wigeons, Wilson's phalaropes, white egrets, wood ducks and yellow warblers.

You also have a good chance of spotting beavers, porcupines, raccoons and white-tailed deer. Butler's garter snakes, coyotes, ermines, green snakes, leopard frogs, mink frogs, mink, muskrats, northern brown snakes, northern ribbon snakes, red foxes, turtles of all types, and weasels also live in the area.

› Getting There

Take Highway 25 north from Grand Valley or south from Highway 89. Turn west onto Concession Road 6-7 and then continue to the main gate on Side Road 21. Please drive slowly along the dirt side road.

The black spots you may see on the road are turtles that would appreciate a helping hand to cross. If you decide to be a good Samaritan, pull over as far as you can and put on your flashers. Locals have a habit of driving quickly along this road.

› Further Information

Luther Marsh Area Superintendent
☎ 519-928-2832

Grand River Conservation Authority
PO Box 729, 400 Clyde Rd.
Cambridge, ON N1R 5W6
☎ 519-621-2761
www.grandriver.ca

Shoreline Trail

Level of difficulty 🚶🚶

Distance *5km (3mi) loop*

Approx. time *2hrs return*

Trailhead *Main parking lot*

This very wet, grassy trail begins at the observation tower and then leads along the shores of Luther Lake, through meadows where you may see ant mounds and signs of crayfish burrowing. Depending on the season, this part of the trail can be under 60cm (2ft) of water in spots. At the boat launch, you can look out over the lake towards Windmill Island with its farmhouse and windmill ruins. The path then leads through a coniferous plantation and into a mixed forest. Look for an old wellhead and foundation stones in the clearing in the middle of the forest. Continue towards the large beaver pond, cross the bridge and take the interior road back to the parking lot.

Bootlegger Trail

Level of difficulty 🚶

Distance *16km (9.9mi) each way*

Approx. time *13hrs return*

Trailhead *Main parking lot*

Other *Wheelchair accessible, mountain bikes permitted*

This trail, named after a bootlegger's drop-off spot, was actually designed as a mountain bike trail, but it's little used and interesting enough to be worthwhile for hikers. It passes by the 1954 dam, through coniferous plantations and then along an interior road. Hikers will definitely want to walk the first 2.5km (1.5mi) to the Townsend Cairn, a stone marker erected by the ancestors of a pioneer family in 1992. You'll also pass waterfowl sanctuaries, a view of Windmill Island and lots of beaver baffles (paved hollows in the road that replace culverts). Notice the wood duck nesting boxes in the trees, the messy-looking heron nests along the shore, and the white and yellow water lilies.

Mallard Pond Trail

Level of difficulty 🚶

Distance *3km (1.9mi) loop plus two 1km (.9mi) side trails*

Approx. time *2hrs return*

Trailhead *Side Road 21, just south of the Luther Centre about 3km (1.9mi) south of the main entrance*

This grassy loop circles Mallard Pond, a waterfowl shelter. Even in years when water in the pond is lowered (every seven years) to allow the sedges and water plants to regenerate, you'll still see lots of waterfowl nesting on islands and in wood boxes. Part of this trail offers a good view of Luther Lake and later, a good view of the South Bog, where loons and mergansers live. If you don't choose to take the shortcut extension that cuts this loop in half, you'll see the stone ruins of the Tovell Farm House surrounded by–depending on the season–domestic daylilies, lilacs, roses and sweet peas.

Lynn Valley Trail

Level of difficulty 🚶

Location *Between Simcoe and Port Dover*

Number of trails *1*

Total distance *10km (6mi)*

Approx. time *3hrs each way*

Trailheads *Memorial Park, Simcoe; Silver Lake Fountain, Port Dover*

Interesting features *Lynn River, tundra swans, four trestle bridges, Brook Conservation Area, links to Waterford Heritage Trail*

Facilities/services *Parking, toilets*

Other *Dogs on leashes permitted*

The Lynn Valley Trail follows the Lynn River along the bed of the former Lake Huron and Port Dover Railway. (It was founded by Chris Lee, who died at the age of 77 in 2008.) Highlights include four original wooden trestle bridges, which have all been repaired and reinforced. Another key feature along the way are the ruins of an old woollen mill.

Several sections of the trail lead through mixed forests containing some Carolinian species, particularly beech, cherry, ash and mulberry. Others pass wildflower meadows containing pink smartweed, scotch thistle, sedge and skunk cabbage. Birders will appreciate the tundra swans and the abundance of chickadees, blackbirds, blue jays, eastern wood pewees, juncos and mallards that you're bound to see in the area. Look for beds of white, pink, burgundy and red trilliums in the spring; raspberries, blackberries and grapes in the summer; and scarlet sumac in the fall.

› Getting There

To get to Simcoe, take Highway 3 east from Tilsonburg or west from Jarvis and turn south onto Highway 24, or take Highway 24 south from Brantford or north from Long Point.

› Further Information

Brook Conservation Area
c/o Long Point Region Conservation Authority
RR3, 146 Radical Rd.
Simcoe, ON N3Y 4K2
519-428-4623
www.lprca.on.ca

Lynne Valley Trail Association
PO Box 993
Simcoe, ON N3Y 5B3
519-428-3292
www.lynnvalleytrail.ca

Maitland Trail

Level of difficulty 🚶🚶

Location *Between Goderich and Auburn*

Number of trails *1*

Total distance *48km (28.8mi) linear*

Approx. time *19hrs each way*

Markers *White blazes and identification plates*

Interesting features *Lake Huron, Menesetung Bridge, od growth oak tree, Colborne Riverside Park, Robertson Tract, Ball's Bridge, Morris Tract, Benmiller Inn, Falls Reserve Conservation Area*

Facilities/services *Parking, toilets, swimming, camping, fishing*

Other *Dogs on leashes permitted*

The Maitland Trail follows the shores of the Maitland River from Auburn to Lake Huron, near the Menesetung Trestle Bridge (which is shared with the Goderich to Auburn Rail Trail). Trail maintenance and promotion are handled by a volunteer association originally created in 1975.

Three important wooded areas form part of this trail: the Morris Tract, the Robertson Tract and a section of trail that goes through the Goud Property, which the Nature Conservancy of Canada wants to purchase. All three forests offer habitat for wood thrushes, Philadelphia vireos and pileated woodpeckers.

One of the scenic highlights is the section that goes through the Falls Reserve Conservation Area, which allows camping and swimming.

› Getting There

Take Regional Road 8/Base Line to get to Blyth Road 25 in Auburn. Turn left (west) and cross the Auburn Bridge. Turn left (south) onto Bridge Road and park without blocking bridge access.

In Goderich, start on the Menesetung Bridge and divert towards the river. (The Goderich to Auburn Rail Trail continues straight.)

➤ Further Information

Maitland Trail Association
PO Box 443
Goderich, ON N7A 4C7
www.maitlandtrail.ca

McKeough Conservation Area and Floodway

Location *North of Wallaceburg*

Number of trails *2*

Total distance *10km (6mi)*

Interesting features *Floodway control, Carolinian forest*

Facilities/services *Parking*

Other *Dogs on leashes permitted*

The Town of Wallaceburg is protected from the flooding of the Sydenham River by Ontario's largest floodway project, which was constructed in 1984. Known as the W. Darcy McKeough Floodway, the structure includes an earth fill dam embankment and two sluice gates between the Sydenham River and the St. Clair River. More than 100,000 trees have been planted to naturalize the structure.

For hikers, the dam consists of three possible walks along the 7km-long embankment—along both sides and down the middle. The middle is kept neat through mowing, but the grass is longer on top, so lots of butterflies can be seen. Trails lead for 3km (1.8mi) through the Carolinian forest between Holt Line and the dam.

A 3-km trail winds through a Carolinian forest just south of the McKeough Dam. Look for the rare blue ash and Kentucky coffee trees.

➤ Getting There

Take Highway 40 north from Wallaceburg or south from Sarnia. Turn east at Holt Line to get to the entrance.

➤ Further Information

St. Clair Region Conservation Authority (SCRCA)
205 Mill Pond Cr.
Strathroy, ON N7G 3P9
☎ 519-245-3710
www.srca.on.ca

Pinery Provincial Park

Location *Hwy. 21, south of Grand Bend*

Number of trails *10*

Total distance *17.5km (10.9mi)*

Interesting features *Oak savanna, sand dunes, Old Ausable Channel*

Facilities/services *Parking, toilets, telephones, visitor information centre, convenience store, canoe and kayak rental, bicycle rental, playground, fishing, swimming beaches, camping, 12 yurts (furnished year-round tents), laundry area, showers, boat launch*

Two hundred years ago, North America was covered in grassland, forest and a transition habitat called "oak savanna" that grew between the two. Oak savanna consisted primarily of huge black oaks and red cedars spaced widely and separated by vast meadows of grasses, wild-flowers and shrubs such as cherry, witch-hazel and serviceberry. This once prevalent ecosystem was found on the margin between forests and the drier areas prevailing over the prairies. It provided sustenance for a wide range of interesting species, including rare prairie plants such as blue heart, dense blazing star, and wild lupine, the only food of the nationally rare Karner blue butterfly.

Today, the world's largest intact example of an oak savanna ecosystem, one third of all that exists, can be found at Pinery Provincial Park. Unfortunately, a misguided white pine planting program in the late 1950s almost destroyed it. Officials have been working since 1981 to remove the 3.5 million white pines that were planted, thereby restoring oak savanna within the park. A program of controlled fires and hand cuts is beginning to show positive effects. Interested hikers will notice vast differences between rejuvenated savanna with oaks separated by large shrubs and grasses, recently burned wild-flower carpeted savanna and recently cut areas where rotting white pines carpet the forest floor. Park officials are also planting wild lupine in hopes that Karner blues will soon reappear in the park.

Only 60% of the 2,400ha (3,871 acres) in the park is oak savanna, much of which covers parallel dunes left behind by glaciers and since built up by wave action from Lake Huron. The rest is made up of Carolinian forests, natural red pine forests, cedar savanna, 10km (6.2mi) of sandy beach, and a river that no longer flows (the Old Ausable Channel). A vast wetland called the Thedford bog is located next to the park.

These diverse habitats support 29 species of mammals, 757 species of plants, 325 species of birds, 50 species of butterflies and 1,241 species of moths. Some of the rare species hikers might see include southern flying squirrels, eastern hognose snakes, five-lined skinks, Olympia marble wing butterflies and red-backed salamanders. Chipmunks are common, as are bats, beavers, coyotes, deer, frogs, muskrats, raccoons, red squirrels, frogs and toads. Birds that nest or migrate through the area include Baltimore orioles, buffleheads, common mergansers, eastern kingbirds, great horned owls, hooded mergansers, old squaws, nighthawks, pintails, rare prairie warblers, red-bellied woodpeckers, scarlet tanagers, scaups, spring warblers, tundra swans, turkey vultures and whippoorwills. Monarchs migrate through the park in September.

The trails at this park are quite short, but ambitious hikers can walk for a good 9hrs, 23km (14.3mi), by beginning at the Cedar Trail parking lot, walking about 1.5km (.9mi) to the beach, then walking along the 10km (6.2mi) beach past the day use area to the end, where an entrance leads to the end of the Wilderness Trail. You can either turn around or continue along the Wilderness Trail. It's another 1.5km (.9mi) to the road and another 10km (6.2mi) back to the visitor parking lot, if that's where you left your car. Careful to stay on the beach between Dunes Beach and the

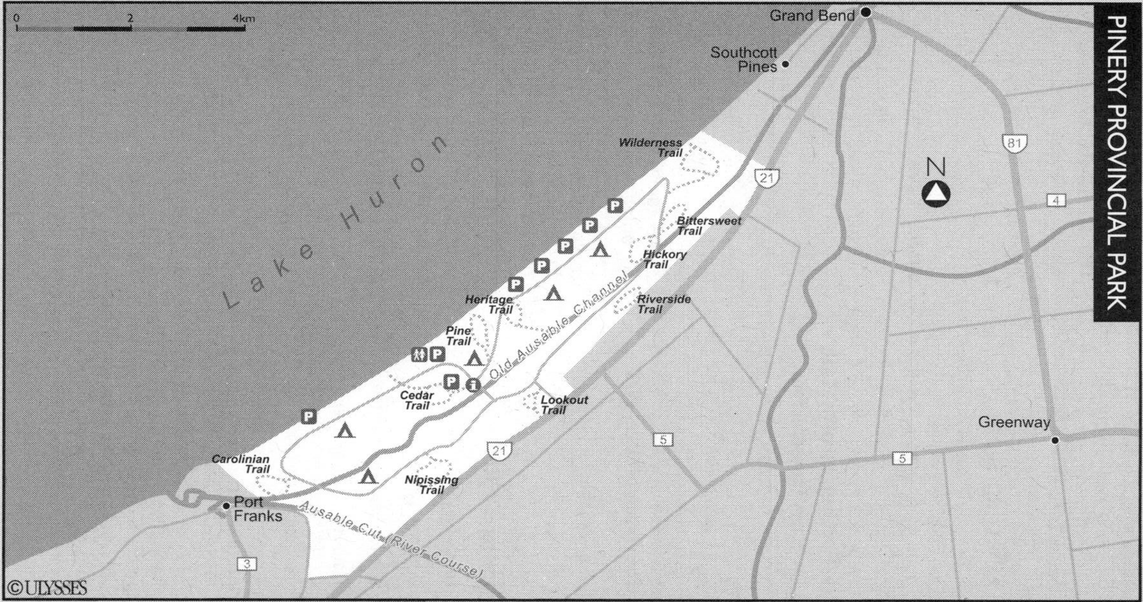
PINERY PROVINCIAL PARK
0
2
4km
Grand Bend
Southcott Pines
Lake Huron
Wilderness Trail
Bittersweet Trail
Hickory Trail
Riverside Trail
Heritage Trail
Pine Trail
Old Ausable Channel
Cedar Trail
Lookout Trail
Carolinian Trail
Nipissing Trail
Port Franks
Ausable Cut (River Course)
Greenway
N
21
81
4
5
3
©ULYSSES

day use area; the area between the first dune ridge and the road is a nature reserve and remains out of bounds to hikers.

› Getting There

Take Highway 21 north from Northville or south from Grand Bend. The park is on the west side of the highway.

› Further Information

The Pinery Provincial Park
RR2
Grand Bend, ON N0M 1T0
519-243-2220, 800-667-1940 or 888-668-7275
www.ontarioparks.com

The Friends of Pinery Park
519-243-1521
www.pinerypark.on.ca

Pine Trail

Level of difficulty

Distance *.8km (.5mi) loop*

Approx. time *30min return*

Trailhead *Along the Dunes Beach Rd., behind the park office just before the campground gatehouse*

A major fire in the late 1800s permanently marked the oak savanna with an area that has since been replaced by this natural red pine forest. Most of the surface is a woodland path, although two boardwalks along the way protect the dunes from erosion.

Riverside Trail

Level of difficulty

Distance *1km (.6mi) loop*

Approx. time *30min return*

Trailhead *A parking lot along the road east of the traffic circle*

Other *Wheelchair-accessible*

This trail loops from the road through an oak and pine forest to a floodplain forest on the south shore of the Ausable Channel. A large viewing deck and benches enable hikers to sit and watch the river. This spring-fed river is really more like a large, narrow pond. Thanks to ancient floods of the Ausable River, the soil surrounding the channel contains lots of silt, enabling some trees to grow higher here than elsewhere in the park, and others–such as the basswood, sycamore and ash–to grow here and nowhere else in the vicinity. The clear Ausable Channel supports a variety of rare fish, including pugnose shiners, lake chubsuckers and longear sunfish.

Lookout Trail

Level of difficulty

Distance *1km (.6mi) loop*

Approx. time *30min return*

Trailhead *Along the road just after the park entrance across from the sanitation station*

This loop leads to the top of one of the largest dunes in the park, allowing for a view of a lush oak savanna canopy.

Hickory Trail

Level of difficulty 🚶

Distance *1km (.6mi) loop*

Approx. time *30min return*

Trailhead *A parking lot along the road east of the traffic circle, after the Riverside Trail and across from the Bittersweet Trail*

Follow this trail from the road along the north shore of the Ausable Channel and return through a natural red pine and oak forest. Carolinian trees along the route include shagbark hickory, bladdernut and tulip tree.

Bittersweet Trail

Level of difficulty 🚶

Distance *1.5km (.9mi) loop*

Approx. time *1hr return*

Trailhead *The Hickory Trail parking lot*

Like the Hickory Trail, this trail leads from the road and then along the north shore of the Old Ausable Channel. This trail, however, leads up and down a dune ridge covered by a mature oak and pine forest. The corresponding trail guide highlights the various mammal species inhabiting the park.

Carolinian Trail

Level of difficulty 🚶

Distance *1.8km (1mi) loop*

Approx. time *1hr return*

Trailhead *Parking lot on the east side of the road adjacent to the trail, south of the park store and past the riverside campground, over the Old Ausable Channel*

This trail leads up and down the dunes through a rich Carolinian forest and an oak savanna towards the Ausable River. It's a good place to compare the two types of forest ecosystems. Along the path, you'll reach two lookouts, one over a small pond and another which reveals a tulip tree and oak forest canopy. You'll also walk along three boardwalks that lead across the dunes. (Footsteps can damage the roots of fragile plants growing in the sand.) Common southern species found along this trail include chinquapin oaks, tulip trees, basswoods, climbing grapes and Virginia creepers.

Nipissing Trail

Level of difficulty 🚶🚶

Distance *2km (1.2mi) loop*

Approx. time *1hr return*

Trailhead *A parking lot on the south side of the road, south of the park store and past the wood yard*

This trail leads you up the park's oldest and largest dune ridge past an area of oak savanna that was subjected to a controlled burn in 1993. A lookout provides a good view of Lake Huron and the Thedford bog to the east of Pinery.

Cedar Trail

Level of difficulty 🚶

Distance *2.3km (1.4mi) loop plus 1km (.6mi) extension to the beach*

Approx. time *2hrs return*

Trailhead *Visitor centre*

Other *The loop is wheelchair accessible, although the extension is not*

This trail leads over and past several dune ridges, many covered in oak savanna, others in cedar savanna. Notice the juniper, white cedar, sumac and chokecherry undergrowth. An extension leads to a huge lookout deck overlooking the beach and the shores of Lake Huron. On the trail, you'll pass a deer exclosure, built to keep deer out so that wildflowers and other plants can be monitored for the effects of browsing.

Heritage Trail

Level of difficulty 🚶

Distance *2.5km (1.6mi) loop, plus .5km (.4mi) extension*

Approx. time *1hr return*

Trailhead *A parking lot along the road next to day use area 9 and beside group campsite 3*

Other *Wheelchair accessible*

This trail leads through a stand of oak savanna that was burned in 1990. The corresponding trail guide highlights the unique history of Pinery and the surrounding area. A .6km (.4mi) extension leads to a viewing platform on the northern shore of the Old Ausable Channel.

Wilderness Trail

Level of difficulty 🚶

Distance *3km (1.9mi) extension plus loop*

Approx. time *2hrs return*

Trailhead *A parking lot on the east side of the road, east of the traffic circle and past the Hickory and Bittersweet trails*

This path leads through a red pine and mixed oak and pine forest, some of the oldest growth in the park, to a lookout over the shore of Lake Huron. You'll see pine specimens that are more than 250 years old. It's estimated that these larger trees have survived at least 11 different forest fires, thanks to their thick, strong bark. You'll also see black, white and red oak specimens. Closer to the beach, you will pass through cedar glades and open areas with grasses on newer dunes.

Point Pelee National Park

Location *On County Rd. 33, south of Leamington*

Number of trails *7*

Total distance *15.9km (9.5mi)*

Interesting features *Birds, butterflies, marsh boardwalk, restored 1840s homestead*

Facilities/services *Parking, toilets, telephones, visitor information centre, gift shop, trail guides, Marshville aquarium and observation deck, bicycle rental, canoe rental ,swimming beaches, 10-person freighter canoe, canoe launch, fishing, group camping*

Other *Dogs on leashes permitted*

At about 42 degrees of latitude, this 1,575ha (3,890-acre) park at the southern tip of Ontario lies at the same latitude as the border between Oregon and California, which explains the great variety of plants, including

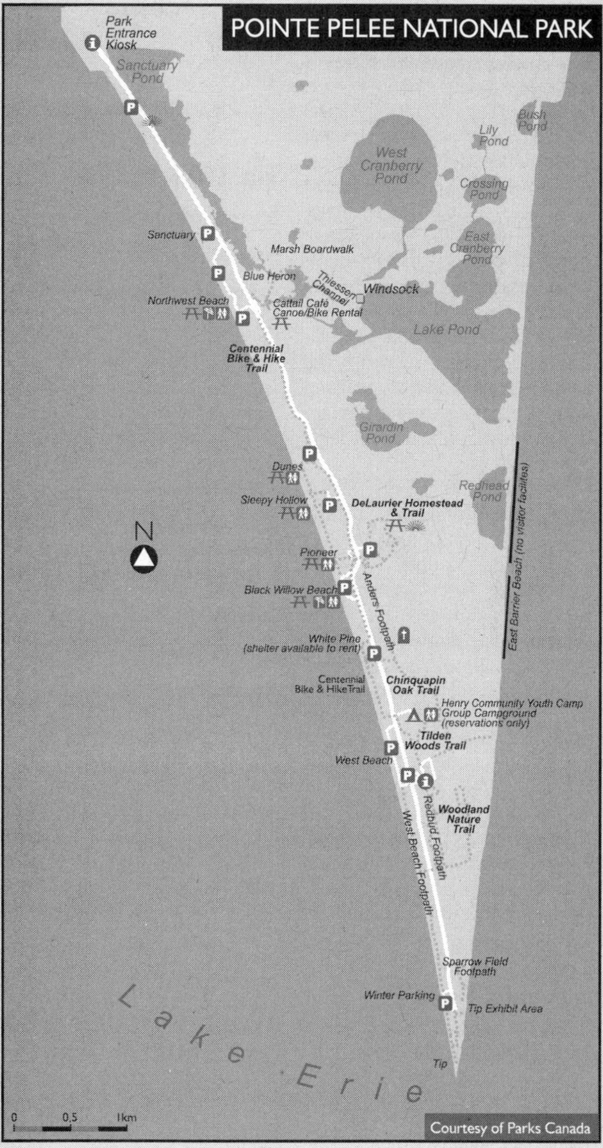
POINTE PELEE NATIONAL PARK
Park Entrance Kiosk
Sanctuary Pond
Bush Pond
Lily Pond
West Cranberry Pond
Crossing Pond
East Cranberry Pond
Sanctuary
Marsh Boardwalk
Blue Heron
Thiessen Channel
Windsock
Northwest Beach
Cattail Café
Canoe/Bike Rental
Lake Pond
Centennial Bike & Hike Trail
Girardin Pond
Dunes
Redhead Pond
Sleepy Hollow
DeLaurier Homestead & Trail
East Barrier Beach (no visitor facilites)
N
Pioneer
Black Willow Beach
Anders Footpath
White Pine (shelter available to rent)
Centennial Bike & Hike Trail
Chinquapin Oak Trail
Henry Community Youth Camp Group Campground (reservations only)
Tilden Woods Trail
West Beach
Woodland Nature Trail
Redbud Footpath
West Beach Footpath
Sparrow Field Footpath
Winter Parking
Tip Exhibit Area
Tip
Lake Erie
0
0,5
1km
Courtesy of Parks Canada

the usual Carolinian species such as pawpaw, as well as cacti, Kentucky coffee trees and 747 other plant species.

Point Pelee's real claim to fame is as a bird-watching mecca. The number of bird species sighted here has reached 370. So many warblers—42 of the 55 species of American wood warblers—have been seen so far, and at least 36 of those are seen every year, that the park is known as the "warbler capital of North America." The spring migration, which peaks in mid-May,. begins in late January or February, when horned larks appear, followed by ducks, blackbirds, geese and swans. In the fall, species often seen include buff-breasted sandpipers, golden eagles, merlins, northern saw-whet owls, peregrine falcons and red-necked phalaropes. The birding season is so important to the park that staff open an additional 12km (7.4mi) of temporary trails for the spring migration, which are allowed to grow over after May.

In the summer, butterflies take centre stage. Every July and August, visitors participate in an annual butterfly count, which has reached 36 species so far. Hackberry, buckeye and giant swallowtail butterflies are all included.

› Getting There

From Leamington, take County Road 33 south to the park.

› Further Information

Point Pelee National Park
RR1, 407 Monarch Lane
Leamington, ON N8H 3V4
✆ 519-322-2365 or 888-773-8888
www.pc.gc.ca

Friends of Point Pelee
1118 Point Pelee Dr.
Leamington, ON N8H 3V4
✆ 519-326-6173

Tip Trail

Level of difficulty 🚶

Distance *1km (.6mi) loop*

Approx. time *30min return*

Trailhead *Tip–reached via a free transit service from the visitor centre*

This tiny trail leads to and along a frequently changing sandy beach to mainland Canada's southernmost point, which varies as waves add sand to the point.

Chinquapin OakTrail

Level of difficulty 🚶

Distance *4km (2.4mi) loop*

Approx. time *2hrs return*

Trailhead *Tilden's Woods or White Pine Picnic Area*

This trail weaves through a dry mixed forest. The highlights are the oaks that give it its name, because these trees grow as far south as Mexico and in this park they are at the northern point of their range.

Tilden's Woods and Shuster Trail

Level of difficulty 🚶

Distance *1.5km (.9mi) loop*

Approx. time *30min return*

Trailhead *North of the visitor centre*

This trail leads past the cactus viewing area and through mature swamp forest and red cedar savanna. A short extension, known as the Shuster Trail, leads to the East Barrier Beach.

Marsh Boardwalk

Level of difficulty 🚶

Distance *1.4km (1mi) loop*

Approx. time *2hrs return*

Trailhead *Marsh parking lot, just after the park entrance*

This looped boardwalk leads straight into the marsh, which covers more than two thirds of the park. Part of the boardwalk floats, while the other leads through waist-high cattails. When you're not enjoying a marsh-side view, you're on one of two observation towers looking over one of the Great Lakes' largest freshwater marshes. Definitely not to be missed!

DeLaurier Trail

Level of difficulty 🚶

Distance *1.2km (.8mi) loop*

Approx. time *1hr return*

Trailhead *Parking lot between the marsh boardwalk and the visitor centre*

This trail, which leads through meadows, red cedar savanna and a swamp forest and past old canals, includes a visit to two restored buildings that were once part of an 1840s homestead. You'll also enjoy the observation platform.

Woodland Nature Trail

Level of difficulty 🚶

Distance *2.75km (1.7mi) loop*

Approx. time *1hr return*

Trailhead *1km (.6mi) south of the visitor centre*

This trail combines many of the best natural features of the other trails. It leads through a dry Carolinian forest, through a swamp, past a red cedar savanna and over grassland.

Centennial Trail

Level of difficulty 🚶

Distance *4km (2.5mi) linear*

Approx. time *2hrs each way*

Trailheads *Marsh boardwalk and visitor centre*

Other *Cycling also permitted on this trail*

This slightly sloping trail leads through dry hackberry forest and along the West Beach from the marsh boardwalk to the visitor centre.

Rondeau Provincial Park

Location *At the end of Hwy. 51, south of Hwy. 3*

Number of trails *6*

Total distance *27.1km (16.8mi)*

Interesting features *Cuspate sand spit, Carolinian forest, oak savanna, sand dunes, sloughs, marsh, prothonotary warblers, migrating waterfowl, rare plants including tall bellflowers, nodding pogonia, showy orchids and swamp rose mallow*

Facilities/services *Parking, toilets, telephones, potable water, visitor information centre, convenience store, canoe and kayak rental, bicycle rental, playground, fishing equipment loans, swimming beaches, camping, laundry area, showers, boat launch*

Other *. Dogs on leashes permitted*

Eleven kilometres (6.8mi) of sandy beach bordered by dunes and long, parallel ridges divided by long, parallel valleys called sloughs are just two of the many fascinating features of Rondeau, a park located on one of the world's best examples of a cuspate sand spit.

About a third of the park is made up of marsh, where cattails, wild rice and water lilies grow. It's an ideal place to see Carolinian species such as pumpkin ash, red mulberry, shagbark hickory, sassafras, sycamore, and tulip trees. The park also contains three areas of oak savanna that officials would like to enlarge.

All these different habitats make Rondeau a bird-watching mecca. About 134 bird species nest in the park, including the largest number of breeding prothonotary warblers in Canada. Another 200 species stop by during migration. Among those sited in the area are Acadian flycatchers, bald eagles, Baltimore orioles, black terns, brown thrashers, eastern kingbirds, indigo buntings, marsh wrens, northern mockingbirds, red-headed woodpeckers, savanna sparrows, tundra swans, yellow-breasted chats and yellow warblers.

Rondeau is also a must-visit location for plant enthusiasts. You'll see bluejoint, clammyweed, false mermaid, fox grape, four-angled spike-rush, green milkweed, little bluestem, muhly grass, nodding pogonia, Oswego tea, panicgrass, sand cherry, sandreed, sea rocket, spike rush, tall bellflower, showy orchid, swamp rose mallow, three birds orchid, wedge grass, wild yam root, yellow mandarin, yellow pond lily and yellow puccoon.

Mammals and reptiles are numerous and include Blanding turtles, bullfrogs, coyotes, white-tailed deer, eastern bluebirds, eastern hognose snakes, eastern spiny softshell turtles, five-lined skinks, fox snakes, Fowler's toads, grey foxes, raccoons, southern flying squirrels, spotted turtles, spring peepers and Virginia opossums.

› Getting There

Take exit 101 from Highway 401 to get onto County Road 15, which becomes Highway 51 after Highway 3. Continue driving straight into the park.

› Further Information

Rondeau Provincial Park
RR1 (Hwy. 15)
Morpeth, ON N0P 1X0
☎ 519-674-1750, 800-667-1940 or 888-668-7275
www.ontarioparks.com

Friends of Rondeau
RR1 (Hwy. 15)
Morpeth, ON N0P 1X0
☎ 519-674-1777
www.rondeauprovincialpark.com

Black Oak Trail

Level of difficulty 🚶

Distance *1.4km (.9mi) linear*

Approx. time *30min each way*

Trailhead *Bennett Rd.*

A packed-earth trail leads through a strip of pine and oak and past two meadow-like clearings, where you'll see a variety of plants including wild columbine, wood lily and woodland sunflower.

Spice Bush Trail

Level of difficulty 🚶

Distance *1.5km (.9mi) loop*

Approx. time *1hr return*

Trailhead *Rondeau Rd. at Bennett Rd.*

A path of compacted limestone leads through a Carolinian forest, where sassafras and oak trees grow, to and from a boardwalk leading across a cattail marsh.

Tulip Tree Trail

Level of difficulty 🚶

Distance *1km (.6mi) loop*

Approx. time *30min return*

Trailhead *Visitor centre*

Other *Wheelchair accessible*

Named after the huge tulip trees growing along its path, this compacted limestone and boardwalk trail leads over sloughs and through Carolinian deciduous forests. You'll see tulip trees, oak and other Carolinian favourites scattered throughout the maple and beech forest. This is the best trail from which to view prothonotary warblers.

Harrison Trail

Level of difficulty 🚶

Distance *8km (5mi) linear*

Approx. time *3hrs each way*

Trailhead *Rondeau Ave., the entrance of South Point Trail*

Other *Cycling permitted, watch for cars going to and from the group campground*

This gravel roadway leads through the centre of the park, providing a view of one of the three areas of oak savanna.

Marsh Trail

Level of difficulty 🚶

Distance *7.2km (4.5mi) linear*

Approx. time *6hrs return*

Trailhead *Rondeau Rd., near the store*

Other *Wheelchair-accessible boardwalk leads to observation deck in the marsh mid-way along the trail, cycling permitted*

A gravel roadway, and then a grass path leads along Rondeau Bay into the heart of the marsh towards the end of the spit. This trail provides a view of one of the three areas of oak savanna.

South Point Trail

Level of difficulty 🚶

Distance *8km (5mi) loop*

Approx. time *3hrs return*

Trailhead *South end of Lakeshore Rd. and Gardiner Ave.*

Other *Cycling permitted*

This old road leads through forests and along the shoreline of Lake Erie to the tip of the spit, providing a view of one of the three areas of oak savanna.

Thames Valley Trail

Location *Southdel Road to Saint Marys*

Number of trails *5*

Total distance *110km (66mi)*

Markers *White blazes on main trail, blue blazes on side trails*

Interesting features *Thames River, Sharon Creek Conservation Area, Delaware Conservation Area, Carolinian forests, Komoka Provincial Park, Warbler Woods, Springbank Park,Storybook Gardens, Greenway Park, Gibbons Park, University of Western Ontario, Kilally Meadows,* ***Fanshawe Conservation Area*** *(see p. 90), agricultural fields; connects to the* ***Elgin Trail*** *(see p. 89) and the* ***Avon Trail*** *(see p. 82)*

Facilities/services *Parking; toilets; telephones; camping at* ***Fanshawe Conservation Area*** *(see p. 90), Riverview Campground and Wildwood Conservation Area*

Other *Dogs on leashes permitted*

The Thames Valley Trail connects the **Elgin Trail** (see p. 89) from near Southdel with the **Avon Trail** (see p. 82) in St. Marys. Highlights include Komoka Provincial Park, several natural reserves and various parks in the city of London.

Conversations about the trail began when students at the University of Western Ontario began speaking with the London Chamber of Commerce. The non-profit volunteer association that currently maintains and promotes the trail was formed in 1971 and incorporated five years later, just as the St. Marys link in the trail was constructed. Expansions continued over the years with the current form of the trail completed in 1995.

› Getting There

The southern entrance to the trail is the junction of Carriage and Southdel roads. Parking is available on Southdel Road, just east of Carriage Road.

Parking is also available on Springer Road, south of Healy Drive; in Delaware, just north and south of Longwoods Road; in Komoka Provincial Park on Komoka and Carriage roads; in Kilworth Reserve on Oxford Street west, in Warbler Woods on Gideon Drive; in London on Westdel Bourne Road north of Oxford St. W., on Oxford Street west of Kains Road and another east of Boler Road; in Greenway Park, in Harris Park, in Gibbons Park, in Kilally Meadows ESA, in Fanshawe Conservation Area, on Thorndale Road; in Plover Mills; on Ebenezer Drive; on Elginfield Road (Highway 7); on Road 127; and on Perth Road 123.

The northern entrance to the trail is in St. Marys at the junction of Water and Queen streets. Parking is available.

› Further Information

Thames Valley Trail Association Inc.
Grosvenor Lodge
1017 Western Rd.
London, ON N6G 1G5
✆ 519-645-2845
www.thamesvalleytrail.org

Sharon Creek

Level of difficulty 🚶

Distance *27km (16.3mi) linear*

Approx. time *11hrs each way*

This trail travels on various roads and through Sharon Creek Conservation Area. The small meandering Thames River tributary was dammed in 1966. The current reservoir is 35.6ha (83 acres) and attracts many people for fishing, canoeing and swimming.

The trail then goes through the town of Delaware and then through the Delaware Conservation Area on the floodplain of the Thames River.

Komoka Provincial Park

Level of difficulty 🚶 🚶

Distance *19km (11.5mi) linear*

Approx. time *8hrs each way*

This portion of the trail leads along Gideon Drive and into Komoka Provincial Park. The main trail continues through the park, along wooden boardwalks and footbridges. After a short walk on Oxford Street, the trail leads through the Kains Road Forest, which was named the Roy Kerr section after the member who developed it.

Warbler Woods to Kilally Meadows

Level of difficulty 🚶

Distance *20km (12mi) linear*

Approx. time *4.5hrs each way*

This trail travels through Warbler Woods and into Springbank Park, where it passes Storybook Gardens. It then goes through Greenway Park and River Forks Park before passing the entrance to Harris Park to get to Gibbons Park. After going through the University of Western Ontario, the trail follows the North Thames River branch and passes Ross Park to get onto the grounds of St. Peter's Seminary. After passing under the Adelaide Street Bridge, it enters the Kilally Meadows Environmentally Significant Area.

Fanshawe Park

Level of difficulty 🚶

Distance *19km (11.4mi) linear*

Approx. time *6.5hrs each way*

This trail leads through Killally Meadows and along various roads and into the **Fanshawe Conservation Area** (see p. 90). It then follows the **Fanshawe Lake Trail** (see p. 92) along the western border of Fanshawe Lake to Thorndale Road.

Thorndale to St. Marys

Level of difficulty 🚶

Distance *20km (12mi) linear*

Approx. time *6.5hrs each way*

The northern part of the Thames Valley Trail follows Valley View Road past the Riverview Campground to the former water mill raceway for the mill that gave Plover Mills its name. It then follows the Thames River through private property, over some hilly terrain and to the River Valley Golf & Country Club property. It then continues along a short section on Perth Road 123 and to the roads near the tennis courts in St. Marys.

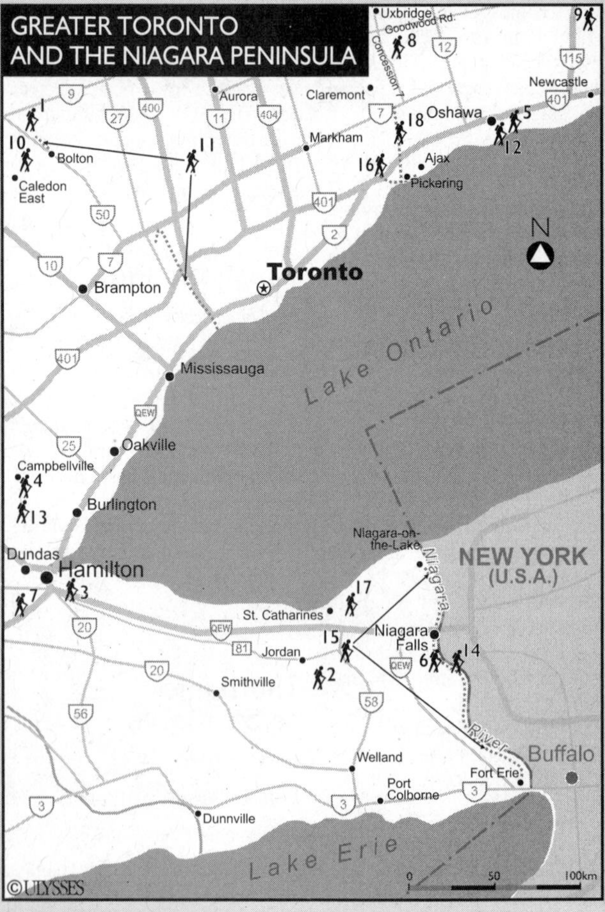

1. Albion Hills Conservation Area
2. Ball's Falls Conservation Area
3. Cootes Paradise, Royal Botanical Gardens
4. Crawford Lake Conservation Area and Iroquoian Village
5. Darlington Provincial Park
6. Dufferin Islands, Niagara Falls
7. Dundas Valley and Tiffany Falls Conservation Areas
8. Durham Regional Forest
9. Ganaraska Forest
10. Glen Haffy Conservation Area
11. Humber Valley Trail
12. McLaughlin Bay Wildlife Reserve and Second Marsh Wildlife Area
13. Mountsberg Conservation Area
14. Niagara Glen
15. Niagara River Recreation Trail
16. Rouge Trail
17. St. Catharines Trail System
18. Seaton Hiking Trail

Greater Toronto and the Niagara Peninsula

The Toronto and Niagara areas of Ontario wrap around the corner of Lake Ontario, following and extending from the most visible landmark in the area, a ridge of glacier-deposited rock known as the Niagara Escarpment. They extend north as far as the Ontario Greenbelt, a 728,745ha (1.8 million-acre) region that encompasses the Oak Ridges Moraine and the Niagara Escarpment.

Lake Ontario and the Niagara Escarpment combine to moderate the climate so that pawpaws, sassafras, tulip trees and other Carolinian species flourish in the area, even though it's more than five degrees of latitude north of their usual range, around the 36th parallel. The Greater Toronto–Niagara Peninsula region supports 64% of Ontario's native flora and 72% of all the migrating and nesting birds in the province.

Many of these species rely on the important warm-water marshes in the area for food, including **McLaughlin Bay Wildlife Reserve and Second Marsh Wildlife Area** (see p. 138) in Oshawa, **Cootes Paradise** (see p. 121) in Hamilton, and the huge 202ha (499-acre) water reservoir that was constructed in **Mountsberg Conservation Area** (see p. 139) during the 1960s. These areas are of primary importance to a wide range of migrating waterfowl, warblers, tundra swans and blue herons.

Trails along other important waterways, such as the **Humber Valley Trail** (see p. 137), the **Rouge Trail** (see p. 144) and the **Seaton Hiking Trail** (see p. 147), also provide a good place for viewing birds and other wildlife.

Many birds rely just as heavily on the Niagara Escarpment and the Oak Ridges Moraine, which is why the Niagara-Toronto region is the best area for viewing hawks, kestrels, turkey vultures and other raptors. In fact, Mountsberg has made a specialty of rescuing and training injured raptors from the area. Other good places to see such specimens include **Crawford Lake Conservation Area** (see p. 123), **Albion Hills** (see p. 118), the oldest conservation area in Ontario, and **Glen Haffy** (see p. 136). The last two are located on the Oak Ridges Moraine, where broad-winged and red-shouldered hawks make their home.

Other good places to view birds include the large tracts of reserved land in the region, such as the **Durham** (see p. 134) and **Ganaraska** (see p. 135) forests.

The ultimate place for bird-watching in the region, however, is Niagara Falls, between Lake Ontario and Lake Erie. The location alone attracts birds crossing the large bodies of water, but combine this convenient location with the Niagara Escarpment's sheltering effect, and the plentiful food living in the fast-flowing body of water that never freezes, and you get bird heaven. Birders now keep a close watch on the area from the vantage point of the **Dufferin Islands** (see p. 128), a close-by wetland and birding paradise. They also spend time scoping the gorge from below on the trails of the **Niagara Glen** (see p. 141) near the whirlpool rapids. Both of these trail systems can be easily accessed from the **Niagara River Recreation Trail** (see p. 143), a paved pathway between Niagara-on-the-Lake and Fort Erie.

Bird-watching and botany aren't the only reasons to visit the Niagara-Toronto region of Ontario. The area is also historically significant, having played a major role in four important episodes of Canadian history: the War of 1812, the settlement of United Empire Loyalists after the American Revolution, the freeing of black slaves via the underground railway from the United States to Canada and the expansion of train and canal transportation routes in the 1850s. Many of the major battles during the War of 1812 helped change the face of the Niagara region. You can still see signs of the war today, in the traces of grist mills that once existed on the **Dufferin Islands** (see p. 128), and the still-operating grist mill in **Ball's Falls Conservation Area** (see p. 119) that supplied flour to the British forces. The two brothers who built the mill were United Empire Loyalists, as were the pioneer farmers now buried in a cemetery in **Darlington Provincial Park** (see p. 125). Enerals Griffin, an escaped slave from the United States, built his home in what is now the **Dundas Valley Conservation Area** (see p. 129). Remnants of old canals also provide good features on hiking trails. The city of **St. Catharines** (see p. 145) has designed one of its trails, the Merritt Trail, around the first of the four Welland canals and named it after the canal's original engineer, William Hamilton Merritt.

> Tourist Information

Toronto Convention & Visitors Association
PO Box 126, 207 Queens Quay
Toronto, ON M5J 1A7
☎ 416-203-2500 or 800-499-2514
www.torontotourism.com

Tourism Niagara
PO Box 1042, 3550 Schmon Pkwy., 2nd floor
Thorold, ON L2V 4T7
☎ 905-984-3626 or 800-263-2988
www.tourismniagara.com

Albion Hills Conservation Area

Location Hwy. 50, between Hwy. 9 and Bolton

Number of trails 6

Total distance 24km (14.9mi)

Interesting features Wildflowers, rolling hills of grass

Other Dogs on leashes permitted

Facilities/services Parking, toilets, telephones, visitor information centre, convenience store, canoe and kayak rental and launch, playgrounds, fishing, swimming beach, cycling, camping, laundry area, showers

Albion Hills was created in 1954, which makes it the oldest conservation area in Ontario. Its location on a part of the Oak Ridges Moraine, locally known as the Caledon Hills, means that hikers can expect hilly terrain. Children particularly enjoy the three trails named after animals because of the many chipmunks and birds they can see. The other trails, which are maintained as cross-country ski trails in the winter and are used by mountain bikers in the summer, begin behind the chalet. Parts of the Red Trail parallel the **Bruce Trail** (see p. 57), which crosses the northwest portion of the 450ha (1,116-acre) park.

› Getting There

Take Highway 50 north from Bolton or south from Highway 9.

› Further Information

Toronto and Region Conservation Authority
5 Shoreham Dr.
Downsview, ON M3N 1S4
905-880-4855 or 416-661-6600
www.trca.on.ca

Green

Level of difficulty 🚶

Distance 2km (1.2mi) loop

Approx. time 1hr return

Trailhead A signpost behind the chalet

The Green Trail is a very easy walk through a meadow and part of a cedar bush. This is a good spot to see butterflies and moths in the summer and asters and goldenrod in the fall.

Yellow

Level of difficulty 🚶

Distance 2.5km (1.6mi) loop

Approx. time 1hr return

Trailhead A signpost behind the chalet

The Yellow Trail loops through a maple, beech and hemlock forest directly behind the chalet. It also leads through part of a swamp. You have a good chance of seeing porcupines and white-tailed deer.

Red

Level of difficulty 🚶

Distance 9km (5.6mi) loop

Approx. time 4hrs return

Trailhead A signpost behind the chalet

The Red Trail begins in the same maple, beech and hemlock forest as the Yellow Trail and joins the Yellow Trail for a short portion.

It then continues past a sugar shack and into a coniferous forest of pine, spruce and hemlock. It twice crosses Centreville Creek, which flows into the Humber

River. Your walk will pass by a farm and two education centres and will parallel the **Bruce Trail** (see p. 57).

Turtle

Level of difficulty 🚶 🚶

Distance *1.3km (.8mi) loop*

Approx. time *45min return*

Trailhead *Nature trailhead near Elmview picnic area*

Other *Equestrian trail shares sections*

This trail leads up and down several hills along a mown path lined with lilac trees and daylilies. It then goes into a mixed forest of American beech, ash, basswood and sugar maple. You'll also notice wild grapes and lilacs growing at the edges of the trail.

Squirrel

Level of difficulty 🚶 🚶

Distance *3km (1.9mi) loop*

Approx. time *1.5hrs return*

Trailhead *Nature trailhead near Elmview picnic area*

Other *Equestrian trail shares sections*

This trail leads along a wide grassy path, with a deciduous forest on one side and a coniferous plantation on the other. A lookout at the top of one of the larger hills provides a good view of the rolling hills through spruce trees.

After the lookout, the path is lined with lilac bushes until it reaches the deciduous forest.

Rabbit

Level of difficulty 🚶 🚶

Distance *5.8km (3.6mi) loop*

Approx. time *3hrs return*

Trailhead *Nature trailhead near Elmview picnic area*

Other *Equestrian trail shares sections*

The Rabbit Trail combines the Squirrel Trail with an additional forest trail and lookout.

Ball's Falls Conservation Area

Location *Regional Rd. 81 near Jordan*

Number of trails *3*

Total distance *7.6km (4.7mi)*

Interesting features *Historic village, circa 1810 grist mill, ruins of an old mill, four different waterfalls*

Facilities/services *Parking, toilets, telephones, visitor centre, building rentals*

Other *Dogs on leashes permitted*

Today's 88ha (218-acre) Ball's Falls Conservation Area contains less than half of the original 480ha (1,200 acres) purchased by the Ball brothers on October 13, 1807. Still, the area is big enough to protect 471 plant species, 212 migrating and nesting bird species, and several rare amphibians and reptiles, including the pickerel frog and the eastern spiny softshell turtle.

The area also offers vistors a brand new Centre for Conservation, along with a grist mill that supplied flour to the British forces during the War of 1812 and still continues to grind flour today. The 1810 building rests in a restored heritage village. The village houses a home dating from 1846, a barn, a lime kiln, an apple-drying shed, a carriage shed, an outdoor oven for baking, the Fairchild cabin, the Furry cabin and a blacksmith shop. There's also a wonderful relocated church (1864) that is popular for weddings.

The entire operation sits next to two large waterfalls on the Twenty Mile Creek that attracted United Empire Loyalists John and George Ball when they were looking for a good place to settle.

George Ball also built a second major business upriver, near the lower falls. Today, only the foundation of the 1824 five-storey woollen mill survives, although it provides a pleasant point of interest for hikers as they meander along the Cataract Trail.

› Getting There

Take Regional Road 24 (Victoria Avenue) south from the Queen Elizabeth Way or north from Highway 3. You'll pass two intersections and Vineland in the town of Lincoln. The entrance to Ball's Falls is on Regional Road 75, on the left side after the Vineland Quarry.

› Further Information

Niagara Peninsula Conservation Authority
250 W. Thorold Rd., 3rd floor
Welland, ON L3C 3W2
✆ 905-788-3135
www.conservation-niagara.on.ca

Cataract Trail

Level of difficulty 🚶

Distance *2.5km (1.6mi) loop*

Approx. time *1hr return*

Trailhead *Main parking lot*

This trail leads along the edge of Twenty Mile Creek, past the foundation of a five-storey woollen mill and factory built by George Ball in 1824, to the 10.7m-high (35ft) Upper Falls. The cap rock of grey-brown dolomite is supported by a base of dark grey shale. There are lilacs and apple trees all along the path. On the way back, you'll take a mown path that meanders at the edge of a Carolinian forest beside farm fields.

Twenty Mile Creek Valley Trail

Level of difficulty 🚶🚶

Distance *2km (1.6mi) linear*

Approx. time *1.5hrs return*

Trailhead *Between the Fairchild cabin and the Furry cabin on the opposite side of the road from the main parking lot*

The Twenty Mile Creek Valley Trail leads past most of the heritage buildings, which are located near the Lower Falls on the opposite side of Regional Road 75 from the main parking lot. Continue through the Bert Miller Arboretum, then down 62 steps along the side of the escarpment, through a Carolinian forest, full of moss, lichens, grapes and ferns. From here, the rocky, slippery path leads up and down the gorge, widening and thinning as the landscape allows. Views include a small waterfall and towering spruce and maple trees. The path ends on 21st Street (Glen Road) in Jordan.

Bruce Trail Side Trail

Level of difficulty 🚶🚶

Distance *3.1km (1.9mi) linear*

Approx. time *1.5hrs each way*

Trailhead *Arboretum, private laneway across the street from the Ball's Falls entrance gate*

A section of the **Bruce Trail** (see p. 57) goes through the northern end of Ball's Falls Conservation Area, through the arboretum, along the Twenty Mile Creek Valley Trail and then across the bridge to Fifth Avenue in the town of Louth.

Cootes Paradise, Royal Botanical Gardens

Location *Hamilton*

Number of trails *6*

Total distance *16.5km (10mi)*

Interesting features *Marsh boardwalk, Carolinian forest, Burlington Heights; links to **Bruce Trail** (see p. 57)*

Facilities/services *Parking, toilets, telephones, nature interpretive Centre, Rasberry House gift shop*

Other *Dogs on leashes permitted; no cycling permitted*

Cootes Paradise, formerly known as Dundas Marsh, is 840ha (2,075 acres) of marsh and forest at the mouth of Spencer Creek near the Dundas Valley on the west end of Lake Ontario, just off Hamilton Harbour (Burlington Bay). Much of the marsh itself is open water less than 1m (3.3ft) deep, although manna grass and cattails grow at the edges.

The Royal Botanical Gardens has several different properties, one of which is located on the north shore and one on the south shore of Cootes Paradise. The property on the north shore, the larger of the two, is also the location of the Nature Interpretive Centre and Rasberry House. Access points to the **Bruce Trail** (see p. 57) lead from here. The property on the south shore runs behind McMaster University and the Hamilton Aviary.

There are plans for a trail to circumvent the Cootes Paradise marsh and link to the **Bruce** (see p. 57) and **Waterfront** (see p. 71) trails by 2020.

› Getting There

Take Highway 403 east from Hamilton or west from Burlington.

To get to the north shore, get off at Highway 6 northbound. Turn left on York Road and then left again on Old Guelph Road, where the Royal Botanical Garden's Nature Interpretive Centre is located.

To get to the south shore aviary location from Hamilton, get off at the Main Street West/Longwood exit and continue to Longwood. If you're coming from Burlington, get off at the Main Street West exit, turn right on Main Street West and then left on Longwood.

Follow Longwood to King Street West and turn left. Then turn right on Marion Avenue, where the Hamilton Aviary is located.

To get to McMaster University, get off at either the Main Street West/Longwood or the Main Street West exit and turn left onto Main Street West, where McMaster is located.

› Further Information

Royal Botanical Gardens
680 W. Plains Rd.
Hamilton/Burlington, ON L7T 4H4
905-527-1158
www.rbg.ca

Captain Cootes, Marshwalk, Macdonell, Pinetum Trails, North Shore

Level of difficulty 🚶

Distance *5.4km (3.3mi) loop*

Approx. time *3hrs return*

Trailhead *nature interpretive centre*

This hike follows a well-trodden path from the nature interpretive centre to the north shore of Cootes Paradise. It then follows the shoreline past Hickory Island to Bull's Point and the marsh boardwalk, where one of the only remaining cattail coves on Cootes Paradise is located. A long walk into the cattails and a climb up a rather rickety observation tower are the highlights. The path continues past a marsh, a meadow with hydro lines and tree swallow boxes and into the Pinetum, an arboretum of marked coniferous species. The trail ends at a two-storey stucco house built in 1860. After housing three generations of descendants of the Earl of Roseberry, Rasberry House now shelters the headquarters of the **Bruce Trail Conservancy** (see p. 58).

Hopkins Trail, North Shore

Level of difficulty 🚶

Distance *3km (1.9mi) loop*

Approx. time *1.5hrs return*

Trailhead *Pinetum, west of the Macdonell junction*

This trail leads through three plantations: the Hopkins Creek Reforestation Area, a stand of hybrid poplars planted in 1985 and 1986, and a demonstration forest management area.

Arnotts Walk and Chegwin Trails, South Shore

Level of difficulty 🚶

Distance *5.8km (3.6mi) loop*

Approx. time *3hrs return*

Trailhead *McMaster University*

This trail leads from McMaster University around to Kingfisher and Arnott's points, back towards University Landing to Chegwin Point and then around to the tower at Paradise Point. It ends with a walk along Spencer Creek. You'll see stands of hemlocks, white pines and some 400-year-old oaks.

Ravine Road and Calebs Walk, South Shore

Level of difficulty 🚶

Distance *5.8km (3.6mi) loop*

Approx. time *3hrs return*

Trailhead *Hamilton Aviary parking lot*

This hike circles an old teaching garden and continues to the south shore of Cootes Paradise.

Ginger Valley Trail, South Shore

Level of difficulty 🚶

Distance *1.3km (.8mi) linear*

Approx. time *30min return*

Trailhead *Ravine Rd.*

This trail leads along escarpment hills and then along the south shore of the marsh towards Princess Point. You'll look out towards Cockpit Island in the marsh and Sassafras Point.

Sassafras Point Trail, South Shore

Level of difficulty 🚶

Distance *1km (.6mi) linear*

Approx. time *30min return*

Trailhead *Ravine Rd.*

This hike leads along Westdale Inlet to Sassafras Point, where the popular mitten-leaved tree still grows. This is a good place to look for bank swallows and belted kingfishers, which live in holes on Cockpit Island.

Crawford Lake Conservation Area and Iroquoian Village

Location *South of Campbellville*

Number of trails *5*

Total distance *19km (11.4mi)*

Interesting features *Reconstructed Iroquoian village, meromictic lake, elevated boardwalk, Niagara Escarpment, turkey vultures*

Facilities/services *Parking, toilets, telephones, visitor information centre, soft drinks*

Other *Dogs on leashes permitted, as long as they are kept away from the lake; links to **Bruce Trail** (see p. 57)*

Visitors to Crawford Lake will probably begin with a short tour through the reconstructed Iroquoian Village. A palisade wall encircles four longhouses—two of which are complete and two others which are only exterior frames—burial platforms, a grinding stone, a central fire pit, a sacred plant garden, a "three-sisters" (corn, beans and squash) garden, and a games field.

Hikes begin behind the visitor centre. The smallest trail is actually an elevated boardwalk that leads around Crawford Lake, a rare meromictic lake. Limited circulation and oxygen at depths below 15m (49ft) of the 24m-deep (79ft) lake have protected annual deposits of sediment (varves) that go back about 1,000 years. The natural process benefits archaeologists who analyse and date varves to confirm previous settlement patterns. They used the process to date the nearby Iroquoian village site to a period lasting from 1434 to 1459.

Other trails lead up and along the Niagara Escarpment, through woodlands and along rocky outcrops. At the edge of the Nassagaweya Canyon, you'll see turkey vultures soaring. Other possible bird sightings include black-throated warblers, blue warblers, blue-gray gnatcatchers, hermit thrushes, red-breasted nuthatches, woodpeckers, yellow-bellied sapsuckers and yellow-throated vireos. You may also spot some of the chipmunks, ermines, porcupines, raccoons, red squirrels, stinkpot turtles, white-tailed deer and woodland voles that also live near Crawford Lake.

Plant enthusiasts will appreciate the many marsh species that grow here, including blunt-leaved pondweed, buckbean, round-leaved sundews and small bladderwort. Green violets, maidenhair spleenwort, walking ferns, spicebush and small-flowered leafcups grow on the rocky plains of the Niagara Escarpment.

› Getting There

Take Highway 1, also known as Guelph Line, south from Campbellville or north from Lowville.

› Further Information

Conservation Halton
RR2 , 2596 W. Britannia Rd.
Milton, ON L9T 2X6
☎ 905-854-0234 or 905-336-1158
www.hrca.on.ca

Crawford Lake Trail

Level of difficulty 🚶

Distance *1.4km (.9mi) loop*

Approx. time *30min return*

Markers *Blue*

Trailhead *"Start of trails" sign behind the visitor centre*

Other *Wheelchair accessible*

This trail loops around a lake that was either created when an underground cavern collapsed or by hydraulic mining. You'll pass an old trail, two corkscrew cedars that mark the front porch site of Lloyd Crawford's family cottage, and a huge beech tree with eyes.

Woodland Trail

Level of difficulty 🚶

Distance *1.5km (.9mi) loop*

Approx. time *45min return*

Markers *Red*

Trailhead *"Start of trails" sign behind the visitor centre, Crawford Lake Trail, Escarpment Trail or Pine Ridge Trail*

Other *Wheelchair accessible*

This trail loops between the Crawford Lake Trail, the Escarpment Trail and the Pine Ridge Trail. This is the best wheelchair accessible trail to view woods, marsh and the edge of the escarpment.

Pine Ridge Trail

Level of difficulty 🚶

Distance *3.6km (2.2mi) loop*

Approx. time *1.5hrs return*

Markers Green

Trailhead Woodland or Bruce trails

This trail leads through deciduous and pine forests and open meadows to the edge of the Niagara Escarpment. Anyone who appreciates wildflowers will enjoy this trail in the spring, summer and fall.

Escarpment Trail

Level of difficulty 🚶 🚶

Distance 2.4km (1.5mi) loop

Approx. time 1hr return

Markers Yellow

Trailhead "Start of trails" sign behind the visitor centre, Woodland Trail or Pine Ridge Trail

This trail leads along a limestone plain to a lookout at the edge of the Nassagaweya Canyon. There are several benches along the way, one of which honours Professor J. Percy-Smith, a Crawford Lake researcher who died in 1999.

Nassagaweya Trail

Level of difficulty 🚶

Distance 7.2km (4.5mi) linear

Approx. time 3hrs each way

Markers Orange

Trailhead Escarpment Trail

This packed-dirt path leads down the Niagara Escarpment, through the Nassagaweya Canyon, along a footbridge across Limestone Creek and then up and along the other side of the Escarpment to Rattlesnake Point Conservation Area. You'll pass several lookouts over the canyon.

Snowshoe Trail

Level of difficulty 🚶 🚶

Distance 3.4km (2mi) loop

Approx. time 1.5hrs return

Trailhead Start of trails or Nassagaweya Trail

This trail through the forest behind the Iroquoian Village was designed for snowshoeing in the winter.

Bruce Trail

Level of difficulty 🚶 🚶

Distance 725m (.4mi) linear

Approx. time 30min each way

Markers White

Trailheads Guelph Line, southeast of Steeles or Walkers Line

The **Bruce Trail** (see p. 57) makes its own way through the park parallel to the ridges and Limestone Creek.

Darlington Provincial Park

Location Oshawa

Number of trails 4

Total distance 6.3km (3.8mi)

Interesting features Stints, stilts, plovers, spotted sandpipers, killdeers, monarch butterfly migration

Facilities/services Parking, toilets, telephones, visitor information centre, convenience store, canoe and paddleboat rentals, fishing, camping, showers, boat launch, laundry

Other Dogs on leashes permitted

After the American Revolution, the families of Roger Conant, John Burk and John W. Trull decided to leave their homes on the shore of the Susquehanna River in New York to resettle on British soil. Known as United Empire Loyalists, they arrived on the shores of Lake Ontario on October 2, 1794, ready to start clearing land for farming.

Although John Burk eventually returned to the United States, three of his sons stayed in Ontario. His son Samuel bought a parcel of land in what now forms Darlington in 1918, and settled and farmed it until his death in 1933. His remains, along with those of his wife Mary Van Camp, their sons Sylvester, Harvey and Peter, Peter's wife Barbara Barberg, and their daughter Sara are buried in a pioneer cemetery along the Burk trail.

Roger Conant made a fortune as a fur-trader and then, according to local legend, buried it near the mouth of Robinson's Creek. It has never been found.

Today, the area is a natural refuge. Forests and meadows have taken over the old farmers' fields, attracting butterflies and moths. In fact, the park is known as a resting spot for migrating monarch butterflies, which rely on the park's fields of goldenrod during their fall migration in late September. In 1999, three of the 500 monarchs tagged in Darlington were found in Mexico.

Lake Ontario, Robinson Creek and the McLaughlin Bay marsh attract a variety of migrating shorebirds in April and October, including Canada geese, dunlins, least sandpipers, pectoral sandpipers, plovers, sanderlings, semipalmated sandpipers, stilts and swans. The rest of the year, look for the American woodcocks, killdeers and spotted sandpipers that nest in the park. You may also spot one of nine different species of owls, including barred, common barn, eastern screech, great horned, long-eared, northern saw-whet and short-eared owls. The area is also known for the wide variety of songbirds, great blue herons and Coopers hawks that soar around the entrance of the park at dusk. You'll also notice several tree sparrow boxes along the trails.

The **Waterfront Trail** (see p. 71) links Darlington to the McLaughlin Bay Wildlife Reserve and the Second Marsh Wildlife Reserve to the west. Together, the three marshes are among the largest lakeshore reserves in Greater Toronto.

➤ Getting There

Take Highway 401 to Courtice Road South at Exit 425. Drive west for 2km (1.2mi) to Darlington Park Road.

➤ Further Information

Darlington Provincial Park
1600 Darlington Park Rd.
Bowmanville, ON L1C 3K3
☎ 905-436-2036 or 800-667-1940
www.ontarioparks.com

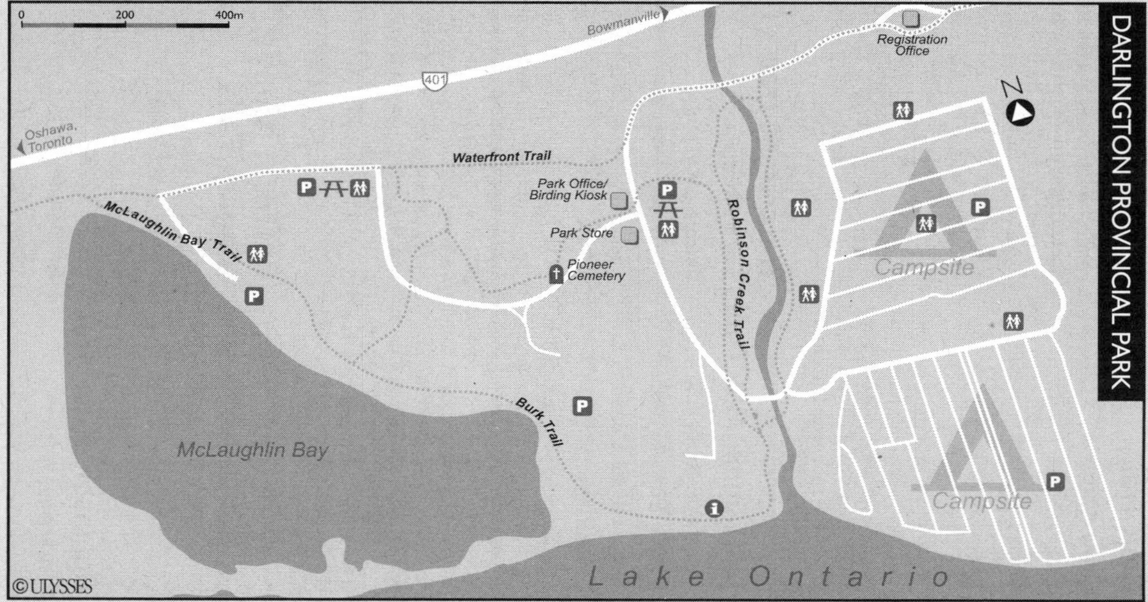
DARLINGTON PROVINCIAL PARK
0
200
400m
Bowmanville
Oshawa, Toronto
401
Registration Office
N
Waterfront Trail
Park Office/ Birding Kiosk
Park Store
Pioneer Cemetery
Robinson Creek Trail
Campsite
Campsite
McLaughlin Bay Trail
Burk Trail
McLaughlin Bay
Lake Ontario
©ULYSSES

Burk Trail

Level of difficulty 🚶

Distance *1.25km (.75mi) linear*

Approx. time *30 min each way*

Trailheads *Just south of the birding kiosk, the park store parking lot*

This trail follows the park road through a white birch forest to the pioneer cemetery. It then leads to a large picnic platform with a great view over Lake Ontario.

McLaughlin Bay Trail

Level of difficulty 🚶

Distance *1.5km (.9mi) linear*

Approx. time *1hr return*

Trailhead *Burk Trail*

This short mowed trail follows the shoreline of McLaughlin Bay, a warm, shallow marsh protected from the colder Lake Ontario waters by a barrier beach. You'll see asters, daisies, jewelweed and wild morning glories framed by giant willows growing in the field. It then continues past park borders to the McLaughlin Bay Wildlife Reserve. You're very likely to see great blue herons and nesting waterfowl along this trail. Walk along the Lake Ontario beach to see sand dunes and make a loop to the Robinson Creek Trail.

Robinson Creek Trail

Level of difficulty 🚶

Distance *1.6km (.9mi) loop*

Approx. time *1hr return*

Markers *Orange*

Trailhead *Visitor centre*

This trail begins on the shore of Lake Ontario at the visitor centre, which is an original log home dating from the 1830s and restored in 1967. It then loops around the Robinson Creek ravine through a mature forest of maple, willow, staghorn and sumac. Wooden bridges enable hikers to cross over to the east side of the creek and continue on past the group camping area.

Waterfront Trail

Level of difficulty 🚶

Distance *2.6km linear*

Approx. time *1hr each way*

Trailhead *Registration Office, or McLaughlin Bay Wildlife Reserve*

Other *Wheelchair accessible*

The portion of the **Waterfront Trail** (see p. 71) within Darlington parallels the Robertson Creek Trail and links with the Burk Trail along the shores of Lake Ontario and McLaughlin Bay. It then continues through the McLaughlin Bay Wildlife Reserve.

Dufferin Islands, Niagara Falls

Location *500m (.3mi) south of Horseshoe Falls in Niagara Falls*

Number of trails *One trail made up of seven inter-connecting sections*

Total distance *2km (1.2mi)*

Approx. time *1hr*

Level of difficulty 🚶

Trailheads *Niagara Pkwy. entrance, Portage Rd. entrance, public parking lots on the islands*

Interesting features *Fluctuating water levels, 21 bridges, warbler migration in May, peregrine falcons*

Facilities/services *Parking, toilets, picnic tables*

Other *Wheelchair accessible*

The Dufferin Islands, a 16.2ha (28-acre) park made up of eleven islands, are a stunningly beautiful area across the road from Horseshoe Falls. Although it takes only an hour to walk through the entire park, add at least another hour to your visit to enable frequent stops. You'll want to spend some time gazing at the scenery from one of the 22 tiny bridges that connect the islands, admiring the cattails in the marsh, or relaxing in the shade of the large poplars and oaks in the wooded areas.

The creek that gives the area its charm is actually the fast-flowing Niagara River, which is pushed into the area by a tilting of the Horseshoe Falls rock shelf.

Frequent hikers to the area will notice fluctuating water levels, a situation that has created good growing conditions for a variety of rare plants and trees, all of which like to get their feet wet. Some of the more interesting examples include dogwood, joe-pye weed, goldenrod, skunk cabbage, spicebush, swamp milkweed and viburnum.

The Dufferin Islands also attract many bird species, including Baltimore orioles, purple martins and yellow warblers.

› Getting There

Take the Niagara Parkway or Portage Road north from Upper Rapids Boulevard or south from Fraser Hill Road.

› Further Information

The Niagara Parks Commission
PO Box 150
Niagara Falls, ON L2E 6T2
905-371-0254 or 877-642-7275
www.niagaraparks.com

Dundas Valley and Tiffany Falls Conservation Areas

Location *On Hwy. 99 as it becomes Governor's Rd. in Dundas*

Number of trails *8 main trails and 11 side trails*

Total distance *77.3km (46mi)*

Interesting features *Niagara Escarpment, sulphur springs, the Hermitage ruins, Griffin House, replica railway station trail centre*

Facilities/services *Parking, toilets, telephones, visitor information centre, snack bar, gift shop*

Other *Dogs on leashes permitted; cycling and horseback riding permitted*

Any hiker interested in history should definitely visit one of two conservation areas within the Dundas Valley. Begin at the large Dundas Valley Conservation Area, which includes 1,200ha (2,964 acres), and hike towards the smaller Tiffany Falls Conservation Area as time permits.

A visit to the Dundas Valley Conservation Area provides a unique view on the Victorian era—a period when train travel was just beginning, when grand estates were fashionable, and when Harriet Beecher Stowe wrote her antislavery novel *Uncle Tom's Cabin,* which highlighted Canada's role in the Underground Railroad.

Start at the replica Victorian-era train station trail centre, which has interpretive natural history displays, a snack bar and gift shop, and a miniature exhibit highlighting old-fashioned station lore. From there, you'll hike along the Main Loop. The Main Loop allows you to see the ruins of an 1855 stone estate called the Hermitage, a small stone gatehouse with waterfalls called the "gatehouse cascade" and an old apple orchard. You can also take a short detour across Sulphur Springs Road to see a sulphur spring with a fountain built in 1972 that replicates an 1850 model located on this spot. Another short detour along the Headwaters Trail, just south of the fountain, leads to the restored home of escaped slave Enerals Griffin.

After hiking the Main Loop, add a short detour along the Carolinian Woodlands side trail, which is maintained by the **Bruce Trail Conservancy** (see p. 58). Here, you'll see many of the interesting plants that attract all the bluebirds, butterflies and hawks in the area.

For a more active day, four big trails (Headwaters, Heritage, McCormack, Monarch and Spring Creek) lead off the Main Loop—and a multitude of side trails lead off each of them—enabling you to explore a good part of the Dundas Valley. The Headwaters Trail passes the Griffin House towards the headwaters of Sulphur Creek to the west of the trail centre. The Heritage Trail leads up the Niagara Escarpment to Old Dundas Road. The Spring Creek Trail leads east of the trail centre to Sanctuary and Warren parks in Dundas.

Avid hikers will want to hike along the trails that lead up and along the Niagara Escarpment, which surrounds the Dundas Valley. The Lookout and Hilltop side trails and the Tiffany Falls Trail in the Tiffany Falls Conservation Area run through prime viewing regions. You might also prefer to follow the white and blue blazes of the **Bruce Trail** (see p. 57), that cross all three conservation areas.

If you prefer to head even farther away, the West Hamilton to Brantford Rail Trail behind the trail centre leads east to Ewen Road, near the north shore of Cootes Paradise or west to Brantford.

› Getting There

Take Governors Road, known as Regional Road 299, from Ancaster or Regional Road 399 from Dundas, to the entrance of the Dundas Valley Conservation Area.

› Further Information

Hamilton Region Conservation Authority
PO Box 7099, 838 Mineral Springs Rd.
Ancaster, ON L9G 3L3
✆ 905-627-1233, 905-648-4427, 905-525-2181 or 888-319-4722
www.conservationhamilton.ca

South of the Visitor Centre

Hamilton-Brantford Rail Trail

Level of difficulty 🚶

Distance *32km (19.8mi) linear*

Approx. time *12hrs each way*

Trailhead *Directly south of the visitor centre*

This trail runs along the old Toronto, Hamilton and Buffalo railway line. Head east towards Ewen Road near McMaster University in Hamilton or west towards Gordon Glaves Memorial Pathway in Brantford. The trail can also be used within the conservation area itself to provide a loop with the **Spring Creek Trail** (see p. 134).

Main Loop

Level of difficulty 🚶

Distance *3.3km (2mi) loop*

Approx. time *2hrs return*

Markers *Posts with red arrows*

Trailhead *South of the visitor centre, past the West Hamilton to Brantford Rail Trail*

Other *Wheelchair accessible*

This trail enables visitors to see the Hermitage, gatehouse and orchard all in one short hike. A short detour part way along the trail leads to Sulphur Springs Road. Cross the road and walk a bit to the north to see the replica Victorian fountain. (If you have a good sense of smell, the scent of rotten eggs will help lead the way.) Then come south again past your detour point to an entrance to the Headwaters Trail on the same side. Griffin House is about 500m (1,640ft) along this trail. Retrace your steps to the Main Loop to continue to the stone gatehouse. Be sure to take the short trail at the end of the small wall in back of the gatehouse and gatehouse garage, which leads to a small but beautiful waterfall known as the Gatehouse Cascade.

Orchard Side Trail

Level of difficulty 🚶

Distance *2km (1.2mi) loop*

Approx. time *45min return*

Markers *None*

Trailhead *Main Loop, Monarch Trail*

This trail loops around the old Merritt orchard, between the Main Loop and the Monarch Trail. A 150-year-old white oak marks the beginning of the orchard. A cider shack is located in the north corner.

Sulphur Creek Side Trail

Level of difficulty 🚶

Distance *1.5km (.9mi) linear*

Approx. time *1hr return*

Trailhead *Main Loop, Monarch Trail*

This trail leads along the north side of Sulphur Creek to Turnball Road.

Carolinian Woodlands Side Trail

Level of difficulty 🚶🚶

Distance *1.4km (0.9mi) loop*

Approx. time *1hr return*

Markers *Blue blazes*

Trailhead *Main Loop, Heritage Trail*

This steep **Bruce Trail** (see p. 57) side trail climbs up through Carolinian forest along a portion of the Niagara Escarpment. It's a great spot to see green violets, American chestnut trees and spicebushes. If you take this trail from the Main Loop, be careful: the trail ends on the Heritage Trail, and you have to retrace your steps back to the Main Loop.

Heritage Trail

Level of difficulty 🚶 🚶

Distance *1.8km (1.1mi) linear*

Approx. time *1.5hrs return*

Trailhead *South side of the Main Loop*

This trail leads into a mixed forest and up the escarpment, following the route of nomadic Aboriginals. The trail comes out at the parking lot of the historic old Ancaster mill, which is now a gourmet restaurant.

Tiffany Falls Side Trail

Level of difficulty 🚶 🚶 🚶

Distance *1km (.6mi) linear*

Approx. time *1hr return*

Trailhead *Heritage Trail, Wilson St.*

The Tiffany Falls Side Trail leads along Tiffany Creek to a 24.5m-high (80.3ft) waterfall. To get there from Dundas Valley, take the **Heritage Trail** (see above) to Old Dundas Road. From there, walk north on Old Dundas Road past Montgomery Drive, where you can start looking for the white blazes of the **Bruce Trail** (see p. 57). This main trail leads to the Tiffany Falls Side Trail. Follow the blue blazes up to the edge of Wilson Street, a major roadway connecting Ancaster and Hamilton. Cross the road carefully to get to the Tiffany Falls Conservation Area parking lot where a sign directs you to the Tiffany Falls Side Trail and towards the lower waterfall. Another trail leads to the upper waterfall, which is about a third of the height of the lower one, but still worth seeing.

Monarch Trail

Level of difficulty 🚶

Distance *7.1km (4.5mi) linear plus loop*

Approx. time *3hrs return*

Access points *North side of Main Loop, parking lot on Old Dundas Rd.*

This trail leads from the **Main Loop** (see p. 131), north past the Resource Management Centre and a maple sugar shack and then along the south side of Sulphur Creek to Old Dundas Road. The trail proceeds past the parking lot on Old Dundas Road into a loop to the west. A side extension enables you to climb Groundhog Hill for a panoramic view of the valley.

Headwaters Trail

Level of difficulty 🚶

Distance *10.2km (3mi) linear*

Approx. time *6hrs return*

Trailhead *Main Loop, Sulphur Springs Rd.*

The Headwaters Trail begins on the **Main Loop** (see p. 131) and continues on the west side of Sulphur Springs Road, just south of the fountain. It then leads past several sulphur springs and up and down many steep hills to the headwaters of Sulphur Creek, where it loops around a cattail marsh.

Homestead Side Trail

Level of difficulty 🚶

Distance *1km (.6mi) loop*

Approx. time *30min return*

Trailhead *Headwaters Trail*

This trail loops from the **Headwaters Trail** (see previous trail) on Sulphur Springs Road and is a good spot to see migrating turkey vultures in September.

Reforestation Side Trail

Level of difficulty 🚶

Distance *1km (.6mi) loop*

Approx. time *30min return*

Trailhead *North from the Headwaters Trail*

This trail loops through a plantation next to a section of Martin's Road that's closed to vehicles. Warblers and songbirds breed in the vicinity.

G. Donald Side Trail

Level of difficulty 🚶

Distance *1km (.6mi) loop*

Approx. time *30min return*

Trailhead *North from the Headwaters Trail*

This trail loops through the Donald farm property to Woodend, an 1860s home that was renovated in the 1980s to house the conservation authority main offices.

Clear View Side Trail

Level of difficulty 🚶

Distance *.7km (.4mi) loop*

Approx. time *30min return*

Trailhead *North from the Headwaters Trail*

This ironically named trail goes through a conifer plantation and then through a mixed beech and maple forest. You don't get a clear view of anything other than trees.

Lookout Side Trail

Level of difficulty 🚶

Distance *.5km (.3mi) extension*

Approx. time *30min return*

Trailhead *South from the Headwaters Trail*

This trail leads straight up the escarpment for the best lookout in the park.

Hilltop Side Trail

Level of difficulty 🚶

Distance *1km (.6mi) loop*

Approx. time *30min return*

Trailhead *South from the Headwaters Trail, Lions outdoor pool*

This trail leads up to a hill next to Ancaster Community Centre for a panoramic view of Dundas Valley. This is another good spot to see migrating turkey vultures.

North of the Visitor Centre

Spring Creek Trail

Level of difficulty *🚶*

Distance *3.3km (2mi) linear*

Approx. time *1.5hrs each way*

Trailhead *Outdoor bird exhibit beside the trail centre*

This trail follows the south shore of Spring Creek up the Niagara Escarpment. The trail crosses the creek several times until it reaches Sanctuary Park. It then follows the north shore of the creek until it reaches the top of the escarpment at Tallyho Road.

Exercise Side Trail

Level of difficulty *🚶*

Distance *.5km (.3mi) loop*

Approx. time *1hr return*

Trailhead *Spring Creek Trail, east from the bird exhibit*

This mini-loop is perfect for trail users who want to take advantage of equipment that encourages stretching, sit-ups, chin-ups and other warm-up exercises before or after hiking.

John White Side Trail

Level of difficulty *🚶*

Distance *5km (3mi) linear*

Approx. time *2hrs each way*

Trailhead *Spring Creek Trail*

This trail, which is named after a treasurer of the province of Ontario, leads north around the parking lots, beside a pond, then across Governor's Road to the McCormack Trail.

Sawmill Side Trail

Level of difficulty *🚶*

Distance *3km (.2mi) loop*

Approx. time *1hr return*

Trailhead *McCormack Trail, Spring Creek Trail*

This trail leads north of the trail centre, past the parking lots and around a pond.

Durham Regional Forest

Location *County Rd. 21 (Goodwood Rd.) and Concession 7, south of Uxbridge*

Number of trails *4*

Total distance *11km (6.8mi)*

Interesting features *Wildflowers, rolling hills of grass*

Other *Dogs on leashes permitted; links to the Trans Canada Trail*

Facilities/services *Parking, toilets, telephones, visitor information centre, convenience store, canoe and kayak rental and launch, playgrounds, fishing, swimming beach, cycling, camping, laundry area, showers*

The Durham Regional Forest is located on the Oak Ridges Moraine in an area that was once farmed. In the 1920s and 30's, it was replanted with pine and white spruce that give the area its current beauty. Red-breasted nuthatches, purple finches and northern goshawk all live within its confines.

The area is very popular with mountain bikes, but hikers are also welcome. Two main hiking trails are available from the main parking lot, and two others extend beyond them from Coyote Junction. The hiking trails include the 2.9km (1.7mi) White Pine Loop, the 2.4km (1.4mi) Maple Loop, the 3.6km (2mi) Red Oak Loop and the 2.5km (1.5mi) Spruce Loop.

› Getting There

Take Lakeridge Road (Durham Regional Road 23) south from Uxbridge or north from Highway 401 east of Whitby. Turn left (east) on Durham Regional Road #21 and continue to Uxbridge Township Concession #7. Turn left (south). The main entrance is on the west side of the road.

› Further Information

Lake Simcoe Region Conservation Authority
PO Box 282, 120 Bayview Parkway
Newmarket, ON L3Y 4X1
905-895-1281 or 800-465-0437
www.lsrca.on.ca

Ganaraska Forest

Location *Northeast of Newcastle*

Number of trails *50*

Total distance *300km (180mi)*

Interesting features *Oak Ridges Moraine,pine and hardwood forests*

Other *Dogs on leashes permitted; horseback riding permitted*

Facilities/services *Parking, toilets, telephones, visitor information centre, 42-bed accommodation,indoor gym*

Encompassing 4,228ha (10,443 acres), the Ganaraska Forest is the largest such tract in southern Ontario. It includes more than 300km (180mi) of hiking trails, including single–and double–track trails, plus roads. Twenty percent of the trails are reserved for hiking. Detailed maps are available on site.

As an example of what's available, there are six trails in one small non-motorized area. They are the 9.9km (5mi) Orange Trail; the 6.3km (4mi) Blue Trail; the 4.2km (2.5mi) Yellow Trail; the 3km (1.8mi) Orange A loop; the 5.6km (3.4mi) Orange B loop and the 3.7km (2.2mi) Orange C loop.

Also be sure to visit the new Ganaraska Forest Centre, a multi-use building with meeting and sleeping facilities that includes a new Oak Ridges Moraine Information Centre. Built with green roofs, recycled water systems and heat recovery shower drains, the building will eventually be self-sustaining in terms of energy output.

› Getting There

From Highway 401, take the Port Hope exit from the east or the Highway 115 exit from the west. Travel north on either County Road 28 or Highway 115 to County Road 9. Turn left (west). Drive for 16km (9.6mi) to Cold Springs Camp Road. Turn right (north) and continue for 4km (2.4mi) to the main entrance.

› Further Information

Ganaraska Forest Centre
10585 Cold Springs Camp Rd.
Campbellcroft, ON L0A 1B0
905-797-2721

Ganaraska Region Conservation Authority
PO Box 328, 2216 County Rd. 28
Port Hope, ON L1A 2W5
905-885-8173
www.grca.on.ca

Glen Haffy Conservation Area

Location *19305 Airport Rd., between Hwy. 9 and Caledon East*

Number of trails *3*

Total distance *5.6km (3.6mi)*

Interesting features *Niagara Escarpment, Oak Ridges Moraine*

Facilities/services *Parking, toilets, telephones, fishing, group camping*

Other *Dogs on leashes permitted*

A Pumpkinfest, with a 4ha (10-acre) corn maze, a Falconry Centre with birds of prey, hay bale playgrounds, and a petting zoo make Glen Haffy Conservation Area a very popular destination for families every weekend from late September to late October. **Bruce Trail Conservancy** (see p. 58) members are also quite familiar with the 325ha (803-acre) park, because their trail winds along portions of the Red and Blue trails.

Located at the juncture of the Oak Ridges Moraine and the Niagara Escarpment, this wonderful park is popular with hikers in general. The trails provide ample opportunities for bird-watching at dawn, before they get crowded. Species that live in the park include black-throated green warblers, eastern bluebirds, wild turkeys and yellow-billed cuckoos. The area is also known for the several species of grape ferns that grow throughout the forests.

› Getting There

Take Airport Road south from Highway 9 or north from Caledon East to the entrance of Glen Haffy, on the east side of the highway.

› Further Information

Toronto and Region Conservation Authority
5 Shoreham Dr.
Downsview, ON M3N 1S4
905-584-2922 or 416-667-6299
www.trca.on.ca

Red Trail

Level of difficulty

Distance *2.7km (1.7mi) loop*

Approx. time *45min return*

Trailhead *Northwest side of the Lookout Point parking lot*

The Red Trail is a narrow path leading through a mixed forest into a valley, over a small stream, through a cattail marsh, and then through a maple and beech forest up towards the top of the Niagara Escarpment. It ends at the Hilltop North picnic area where you'll get a great view of the Humber River Valley. The trail then follows along the edge of the picnic area to return to the parking lot.

Green Trail

Level of difficulty

Distance *.85km (.5mi) loop*

Approx. time *30min return*

Trailhead *Northwest side of the Lookout Point parking lot*

After leading down an old stone staircase, this trail crosses and loops around a spring-fed cold-water stream that eventually flows into the Humber River.

Blue Trail

Level of difficulty

Distance *2.3km (1.4mi) double loop*

Approx. time *1hr return*

Trailhead *Green Trail*

This trail begins from the Green Trail at the north side of the spring-fed creek. It leads past the group camping area to a maple and beech forest and then through meadows that used to be cleared farm fields. It leads to two ponds stocked with rainbow trout and then back to the Green Trail. A short extension cuts the loop in half.

Humber Valley Trail

Location *Between Lake Ontario and Steeles and between Bolton and Palgrave*

Number of trails *2*

Total distance *55km (33mi)*

Interesting features *Niagara Escarpment, Oak Ridges Moraine, Humber marshes, old mill, Harbour Arboretum, Wilson-Stewart ruins*

Other *Dogs on leashes permitted*

Facilities/services *Parking*

Eventually, trail users hope to have a single main trail that runs for the full 126km (76mi) of the Humber River from the Niagara Escarpment to Lake Ontario. For now, two main trails exist: one in the north and the other in the south.

In the northern section, 26km (16mi) of trails lead from **Albion Hills Conservation Area** (see p. 118) through the town of Bolton, with a soon-to-be side loop through Cold Creek Valley.

At the southern end, there are 29km (17mi) of trails from Lake Ontario to Thackeray Park on Steeles Avenue, with a side trail to the Humber Arboretum on Finch Avenue West.

➤ Getting There

Access the northern section from Palgrave or Bolton. In Bolton, begin at the junction of Columbia Way and Regional Road 50. There's a parking lot at the sports fields on the east side of Regional Road 50, while the trail begins in the road maintenance yard on the west side. In Palgrave, the trail begins on Humber Station Road about 2km (1.2mi) north of Old Church Road. Or take the easy way, and just begin in the Albion Hills Conservation Area.

Access the southern section from Rowntree Mills Park on Steeles Avenue or Humber Bay Park on the Toronto waterfront. Humber Bay Park is on Lake Shore Boulevard just south of Park Lawn. You'll have to walk east to get to the junction of the Humber River and the southern terminus of the trail. There's a parking lot in Rowntree Mills Park, but it's not visible from Steeles Avenue. Get there by taking Islington Avenue south from Steeles Avenue West and turning right (west) at Rowntree Mill Road. You can also get to the Humber Valley Trail from the Humber Arboretum.

> Further Information

Toronto and Region Conservation Authority
5 Shoreham Dr.
Downsview, ON M3N 1S4
905-584-2922 or 416-667-6299
www.trca.on.ca

The Humber Valley Heritage Trail Association
PO Box 273
Bolton, ON L7E 5T2
www.humbertrail.org

McLaughlin Bay Wildlife Reserve and Second Marsh Wildlife Area

Location *Oshawa*

Number of trails *3*

Total distance *11.3km (7mi)*

Interesting features *Second Marsh, McLaughlin Bay, Lake Ontario*

Facilities/services *Parking*

The McLaughlin Bay Wildlife Reserve surrounds the General Motors headquarters, which is right next to Second Marsh.

One main pathway made up of several trails link Second Marsh and **Darlington Provincial Park** (see p. 125) and forms part of the **Waterfront Trail** (see p. 71). A second pathway loops between the main trail and headquarters and offers a view of the shoreline of McLaughlin Bay. A third trail, the Dogwood Loop, is a multisensory pathway that has won awards for its ability to offer accessibility to people with visual and mobility impairments.

> Getting There

From Highway 401, take the Harmony Road exit. Turn south on Farewell Street and continue to Colonel Sam Drive. Turn left (east) and continue either to the parking lot just south of Farewell Drive or to three larger lots next to the General Motors headquarters. Trails lead from all four lots.

> Further Information

General Motors of Canada Limited
1908 Colonel Sam Dr.
Oshawa, ON L1H 8P7
905-644-1689
www.mclaughlinbay.org

Friends of Second Marsh
PO Box 26066, 206 E. King St., RPO King St.
Oshawa, ON L1H 8R4
905-723-5047
www.secondmarsh.com

The McLaughlin Bay Second Marsh Shoreline Trail

Level of difficulty

Distance *7.29km (4.4mi) linear*

Approx. time *2hrs each way*

Trailheads *Farewell Road,* ***Darlington Provincial Park*** *(see p. 125); links to parking lot on Colonel Sam Drive and parking lot at GM headquarters*

A series of trails (Marshland, Cool Hollow, Shoreline, Ghost Road Bush, Bob Mills Boardwalk and the Ed Kroll Memorial Walkway) leads along the promontory between McLaughlin Bay and Lake Ontario and along the shoreline of Second Marsh. Highlights include two boardwalks over the marsh and a bridge.

McLaughlin Bay Loop

Level of difficulty 🚶

Distance 2km (1.2mi) loop

Approx. time 1hr return

Trailhead The information post next to the General Motors headquarters

Several trails (the Beaten Path, the Woodland Trail, the Oshawa Trail, the Bayside Trail and the Darlington Trail) provide a scenic loop between the General Motors headquarters, Lake Ontario and McLaughlin Bay.

Dogwood Trail

Level of difficulty 🚶

Distance 490m (.3mi) loop

Approx. time 30min return

Trailhead The information post next to the General Motors headquarters

The Dogwood Trail is a multi-sensory loop around a stormwater pond of the same name. The trail is hard-packed for wheelchairs and includes a guide rope. Information panels are in Braille to allow visually impaired people to read about the natural and cultural history of the region.

Mountsberg Conservation Area

Location Campbellville Rd., west of Campbellville

Number of trails 5

Total distance 16km (9.9mi)

Interesting features Raptor centre, elk, bison, sugar bush

Facilities/services Parking, toilets, telephones, visitor information centre, canoe and kayak launch, fishing, wagon and sleigh rides

Mountsberg Conservation area is named after a 202ha (499-acre) water reservoir created in 1966 when conservation officials dammed Bronte Creek to block some of its flow to Lake Ontario. The expanded wetlands prevent flooding, filter sediments and are important feeding areas for migrating waterfowl, bald eagles, tundra swans, osprey and blue herons. The hike along the edge of the giant lake-like body is pleasant.

This 472ha (1,166-acre) park is more than just a water reservoir, however. It's also a sugar bush, a mixed forest where hooded mergansers, pileated woodpeckers and ring-necked pheasants nest, as well as the home of the Cameron Playbarn for children and the Douglas G. Cockburn Raptor Centre. Staff at the Douglas G. Cockburn Raptor Centre treats injured birds of prey, including hawks, kestrels, eagles, owls and turkey vultures. They also house and train birds that can't be released back into the wild because of human imprinting or permanent damage. This makes a fascinating outing for hikers.

› Getting There

Take Campbellville Road west of Campbellville to Milburough Line. Turn north on Milburough Line to the park entrance and visitor centre.

> Further Information

Conservation Halton
RR2, 2596 W. Britannia Rd.
Milton, ON L9T 2X6
905-854-2276 or 905-336-1158
www.hrca.on.ca

Wildlife Walkway

Level of difficulty

Distance *1.6km (1mi) loop*

Approx. time *30min return*

Trailhead *South of the raptor centre*

Other *Wheelchair accessible*

This hard-packed trail passes enclosures for bison, elk and permanently injured eagles, falcons, hawks, owls and turkey vultures. It leads to a boardwalk with a lookout blind over the reservoir.

Nature Trivia Trail

Level of difficulty

Distance *1.5km (.9mi) loop*

Approx. time *15min return*

Markers *Yellow*

Trailhead *Road north of the visitor centre and over the Millborough Line train track, Pioneer Creek Trail*

Young children will appreciate the nature trivia questions along this hike.

Sugar Bush Trail

Level of difficulty

Distance *1.5km (.9mi) linear*

Approx. time *20min each way*

Trailhead *Road north of the visitor centre and over the Milburough Line train track, Pioneer Creek Trail*

This trail passes a stone house built by Duncan Cameron in 1880 and through a sugar maple stand to a picnic pavilion. The sugar and candy houses are busy during March and April, when staff uses traditional methods to collect and boil maple tree sap to turn it into sweet confections.

Lakeshore Lookout Trail

Level of difficulty

Distance *5.6km (3.5mi) linear*

Approx. time *4.5hrs return*

Markers *Blue*

Trailhead *Road north of the visitor centre and over the Millborough Line train track, Sugar Bush Trail, Pioneer Creek Trail*

This trail leads past a viewing tower over the centre of the Mountsberg Reservoir. It then shadows the shoreline of the reservoir before passing a sawmill, workshop and nursery. It ends at an observation tower over a cattail marsh that attracts numerous blue herons.

Pioneer Creek Trail

Level of difficulty

Distance *6.5km (4mi) linear*

Approx. time *5hrs return*

Markers *Orange*

Trailhead *Road north of the visitor centre and over the Milburough Line train track, Sugar Bush Trail, Pioneer Creek Trail*

This trail leads east over boardwalks through a marsh that harbours many types of turtles. One portion leads through a small deciduous forest to a pioneer lime kiln. The trail then heads through old farmers' fields and across several creeks. Notice the stone walls, cedar rail fences and hedgerows typical of farms in the 1800s and early 1900s.

Niagara Glen

Location *On the Niagara Pkwy. between the Niagara Spanish Aero Car and the Lewiston-Queenston Bridge*

Number of trails *7*

Total distance *3.6km (2.13mi)*

Interesting features *The Niagara Gorge, Carolinian forest, fall gull migrations, Cripps Eddy, Devil's Hole Rapids*

Facilities/services *Parking, toilets, telephones, gift and birding shop*

The Niagara Glen was created about 8,000 years ago, when Lake Erie dumped water into Lake Ontario via a waterfall called Wintergreen Falls, which was located at the site of the present-day Niagara Glen.

The park consists of a section of dry riverbed called Wintergreen Terrace (also known as the Wintergreen Flats) at the level of the Niagara Parkway, and a jut of land 36m (118ft) below called the Wilson Terrace. The Wilson Terrace lies at the edge of the Niagara River, and provides a good view of the river's narrowest point, known as Devil's Hole, and the Cripps Eddy, a small bay with .6m (2ft) tidal surges caused by cross currents from the whirlpool to the southwest. The hiking trails are all located on the Wilson Terrace. You begin with a walk down a spiral steel staircase that was built in 1908. The staircase was refitted in 2008 with a turnstile so that visitors to the Wilson Terrace can be tracked. The turnstile is locked at night.

Bird-watchers spend a lot of time in the glen looking for American kestrels, black-capped chickadees, Bonaparte's gulls, canvasback ducks, common goldeneyes, eastern phoebes, glaucous gulls, great black-backed gulls, greater scaups, herring gulls, house finches (probably the descendants of those released in New York City in the 1940s), lesser black-backed gulls, lesser scaups, little gulls, northern orioles, oldsquaw ducks, purple finches, red-tailed hawks, ring-billed gulls, savannah sparrows, yellow-bellied sapsuckers and yellow warblers.

› Getting There

Take the Niagara Parkway south from Highway 405 or north from Horseshoe Falls.

› Further Information

The Niagara Parks Commission
PO Box 150
Niagara Falls, ON L2E 6T2
☎ 905-371-0254 or 877-642-7275
www.niagaraparks.com

Cliffside Path

Level of difficulty 🚶

Distance *.36km (.2mi) linear*

Approx. time *10min each way*

Markers *White blazes*

Trailhead *Steel staircase*

This path is a narrow walkway next to the Wintergreen cliff and a large overhang where Wintergreen Falls once fell, until erosion moved it further towards its present location and exposed the Wintergreen Flats portion of the riverbed.

Eddy Path

Level of difficulty 🚶

Distance *.24km (.14mi) linear*

Approx. time *10min each way*

Markers *Green blazes*

Trailhead *Cliffside and Woodland paths*

This path is a short extension past fallen cliff boulders towards a well-known fishing spot on the Cripps Eddy. You'll walk down a cast iron staircase and through a hole in the rock.

Woodland Path

Level of difficulty 🚶

Distance *.25km (.15mi) linear*

Approx. time *10min each way*

Markers *Yellow blazes*

Trailhead *Eddy or River paths*

The Woodland path enables hikers to avoid the portion of the **River Path** (see p. 143) that passes the sometimes dangerous, fast-moving waters at Cripps Eddy and Devil's Hole.

Terrace Path

Level of difficulty 🚶

Distance *.97km (.58mi) linear*

Approx. time *40mins each way*

Markers *Red blazes*

Trailhead *Cliffside, River, Cobblestone and Trillium paths*

This path contains many interesting formations, including potholes, a leaning rock, Scaz Cave—which was formed by ground water dissolving limestone—and two massive boulders with a narrow path between them called the "devil's arch."

Trillium Path

Level of difficulty 🚶

Distance *.11km (.07mi) linear*

Approx. time *5min each way*

Markers *Light blue blazes*

Trailhead *Terrace or River path*

This path cuts between the River Path and the Terrace Path to make smaller loops back to the steel staircase.

Cobblestone Path

Level of difficulty 🚶

Distance *.22km (.13mi) linear*

Approx. time *5min*

Markers *Purple blazes*

Trailhead *Terrace or River path*

This is a second path that cuts between the River Path and the Terrace Path to make smaller loops back to the steel staircase.

River Path

Level of difficulty 🚶🚶

Distance *1.4km (2mi) linear*

Approx. time *1hr each way*

Markers *Blue blazes*

Trailhead *Eddy, Woodland, Terrace, Cobblestone and Trillium paths*

This path leads along the rocky cliff edge of the Niagara River, past two dangerous spots next to the Cripps Eddy and past a seep (natural spring) that flows from the sandstone cliff.

Niagara River Recreation Trail

Location *Fort Mississauga in Niagara-on-the-Lake to Historic Fort Erie*

Number of trails *1*

Total distance *56km (35mi)*

Approx. time *28hrs*

Interesting features *Niagara Falls, Whirlpool Rapids, Fort Mississauga, Fort George, Paradise Grove, McFarland House, Floral Clock, Butterfly Conservatory,* ***Niagara Glen*** *(see p. 141), White Water Walk, Floral Showhouse,* ***Dufferin Islands*** *(see p. 128), Fort Erie Riverwalk, Peace Bridge, Mather Arch, Historic Fort Erie*

Other *Dogs on leashes permitted; part of the* ***Trans Canada Trail*** *(see p. 55) and the* ***Waterfront Trail*** *(see p. 71)*

Facilities/services *Parking, toilets, telephones, visitor information centre, retail outlets, indoor attractions, hotels, motels*

Most of the Niagara River Recreation Trail is maintained by the Niagara Parks Commission and consists of a smooth paved pathway linking various attractions in Niagara Falls, Ontario. Portions at either end, however, follow local roads along the Niagara River in Niagara-on-the-Lake and Fort Erie.

Natural highlights include Lake Ontario, the Chinquapin Oak Savannah in Paradise Grove, the garden in McFarland House, Inniskillin grape vines, the Lilac Garden, the Floral Clock, the Botanical Gardens and Butterfly Conservatory, the **Niagara Glen** (see p. 141), the Whirlpool Rapids, the American (Rainbow) Falls, the Luna (Bridal Veil) Falls, the Horseshoe Falls, Queen Victoria Park, Table Rock, the **Dufferin Islands** (see p. 128), Ussher's Creek, Black Creek, Miller Creek, Frenchman's Creek, Riverwalk, Lake Erie and of course, the Niagara River.

Those who only have one day in Niagara Falls should park in the **Dufferin Islands** (see p. 128) and walk along the trail to the **Niagara Glen** (see p. 141). Such a tour provides insights into the natural beauty of the city that might otherwise go unnoticed.

› Getting There

A pedestrian walkway to Fort Mississauga is located in the Niagara-on-the-Lake Golf Club. To get there from the Queen Elizabeth Way (QEW) at St. Catharines, continue east to Highway 55. Turn northwest on Highway 55 into the town of Niagara-on-the-Lake, where it turns into Mississauga Street. Continue north to Queen Street. Turn right and continue one block to Simcoe Street. Turn left and continue to Front Street. At the northwest junction of Simcoe and Front, you'll see the pedestrian walkway.

To get to Historic Fort Erie, take Lakeshore Road south from Mather's Arch or north from Waverly Beach to the parking lot.

Access to the trail is also available from Fort George, McFarland House, Queenston, the Niagara Glen, Whirlpool Rapids, the Rainbow Bridge, Table Rock, the Dufferin Islands, King's Bridge, the Willoughby Museum, or the Niagara Parks Marina.

› Further Information

The Niagara Parks Commission
PO Box 150
Niagara Falls, ON L2E 6T2
✆ 905-371-0254 or 877-642-7275
www.niagaraparks.com

Niagara-on-the-Lake Chamber of Commerce and Visitor & Convention Bureau
26 Queen St.
Niagara-on-the-Lake, ON L0S 1J0
✆ 905-468-1950
www.niagara-on-the-lake.com

Rouge Trail

Location *Along Rouge River between Lake Ontario and Meadowvale Road and north and south of Steeles Avenue*

Number of trails *1*

Total distance *17km (10.2mi)*

Interesting features *Rouge River, Glen Eagle Vista, Carolinian forests, Pearse House*

Other *Dogs on leashes permitted*

Facilities/services *Parking, toilets, telephones, visitor information centre, campground*

The Rouge Trail will eventually follow the Rouge River from Lake Ontario up into the Oak Ridges Moraine for a total of 250km (150mi). Already, the area is a park, with 4,657ha (11,500 acres) in the Rouge River, Petticoat Creek and Duffins Creek watersheds protected.

So far, only the southernmost portion in Toronto has been completed, but even this section is fabulous. It's hard to tell that you're in a major city from these trails, which go through Carolinian forests. Highlights in this section include Glen Rouge Campground, Celebration Forest and an overview of the entire river valley. It then goes to the Rouge Valley Conservation Centre, which is housed in a former farmhouse, which once operated in the valley.

There is an additional 2.5km (1.5mi) Woodland Trail, south of Steeles and north of the train tracks as well.

› Getting There

Access the southern trails from the Glen Rouge Trailhead, 7450 Kingston Road or from Pearse House, on Meadowvale Road, just to the right of the Toronto Zoo entrance. The Woodland Trail begins on Steeles Avenue between the south–and north–bound sections of Reesor Road.

› Further Information

Rouge Valley Conservation Centre
(owned by the Rouge Valley Foundation)
1749 Meadowvale Rd.
Toronto, ON M1B 5W8
✆ 416-282-8265
www.rvcc.ca

Rouge Park Office (not in the park)
50 W. Bloomington Rd.
Aurora, ON L4G 3G8
905-713-6038
www.rougepark.com

Rouge National Park Proposal
www.rougenationalpark.ca

St. Catharines Trail System

Location *West side of St. Catharines*

Number of trails *4*

Total distance *31.5km (18.9mi)*

Interesting features *Port Dalhousie, Lakefront Park, Green Ribbon Trail, Twelve Mile Creek, Montebello Park, Rodman Hall*

Facilities/services *Parking, toilets*

Other *Dogs on leashes permitted; cycling and in-line skating permitted; links to* ***Bruce Trail*** *(see p. 57) through Short Hills Provincial Park on the Niagara Escarpment; links to* ***Waterfront Trail*** *(see p. 71)*

A public trail system leads from the shores of Lake Ontario at the north end of St. Catharines to Short Hills Provincial Park, a 688ha (1,700-acre) protected area on the Niagara Escarpment at the southwest end of the city. This hike makes a very pleasant urban walk beside the waterfront, along tree-lined streets and through city parks.

For a good 5hr or 15km (9.3mi) walk, begin on the Waterfront Trail at the beach in Port Dalhousie's Lakeside Park, where the restored 1898 Looff Carousel still offers merry-go-round rides for $0.05 each. Then, either follow the Waterfront Trail to the Merritt Trail or link through Malcolmson Park to the Welland Canals Parkway Trail.

The Merritt Trail leads south along Lakeshore Road to Lakefront Park. From there, it continues down Martindale Road to the Green Ribbon Trail, a trail dedicated to missing children that was inspired by the killings of Kristen French and Leslie Mahaffy. From there, the Merritt Trail continues down Martindale Road until the park narrows between Second and Third avenues. Then it moves eastward to follow Twelve Mile Creek.

A footpath leads across the creek just north of Welland Avenue, and the Merritt Trail then leads into Montebello Park, the former estate of Welland Canal founder William Hamilton Merritt and the site of the largest rose garden in St. Catharines. After purchasing the property in 1887, the City of St. Catharines hired Frederick Law Olmsted to design the city's first public park. Along with a commemorative rose garden and ornamental fountain, he built a pavilion on the foundation of the original Merritt estate in 1888. Edwin Nicholson, a local builder who also built the Henley Grandstand in Port Dalhousie, added a covered circular bandstand in 1904. Both structures are listed as important Ontario heritage sites.

After Montebello Park, the Merritt Trail follows the east shore of Twelve Mile Creek past St. Paul Street. It then leads under Highway 406 and then back north along the west shore of Twelve Mile Creek to a pedestrian crossing south of St. Paul Street.

The Merritt Trail then passes through the Walker Arboretum behind Rodman Hall. The arboretum includes an original Samuel Richardson garden that was designed for Thomas Rodman Merritt in 1862. Exotic trees from Europe, China and the Carolinas have been included in an arboretum of more than 200 plants and shrubs, 15 magnolias, a North African cedar and one of Canada's largest empress trees.

Your path then continues south to St. Paul Street and the Participark Trail, which leads to Glendale Avenue. At this point, hikers can stop or carry on by crossing Twelve Mile Creek to join a 20km (12.4mi) section of the **Bruce Trail** (see p. 57). The Bruce Trail continues south through Brock University, past Lake Moodie and into Short Hills Provincial Park.

› Getting There

Take the Queen Elizabeth Way to St. Catharines and take the Ontario Street exit. Take Ontario Street north to Lakeport Road. Turn left on Lakeport Road and follow it north to a parking lot on the west side of the harbour at Port Dalhousie.

› Further Information

City of St. Catharines Recreation and Community Service Department
PO Box 3012, 50 Church St.
St. Catharines, ON L2R 7C2
905-937-7210 or 905-688-5600
www.stcatharines.com

Port Dalhousie Harbour Walkway Waterfront Trail

Level of difficulty

Distance *9km (5.6mi) linear*

Approx. time *4hrs each way*

Markers *Posts with three-colour trail logo*

Trailheads *East Port Weller, West Dalhousie*

The section of the **Waterfront Trail** (see p. 71) within St. Catharines runs along the shore of Lake Ontario from Trenton to Niagara Falls. Attractions along the way include the Welland Ship Canal, Happy Rolph's Bird Sanctuary, the St. Catharines Municipal Beach, Lakeside Park, the Port Dalhousie Harbour Walkway and the Royal Canadian Henley Regatta Course.

Merritt Trail

Level of difficulty

Distance *11km (6.8mi) linear*

Approx. time *4hrs each way*

Trailheads *Martindale Rd., Bradley St.*

Named after a leader in the construction of the Welland canal in the 1850s, this wide stone-dust path leads along Twelve Mile Creek and past remnants of the structure William Hamilton Merritt engineered. (The current eight-lock canal is the fourth such structure.)

Green Ribbon Trail

Level of difficulty 🚶

Distance *.529km (.3mi) linear*

Approx. time *10min each way*

Markers *Dedicated benches*

Trailhead *Old Martindale Rd. between Martindale Rd. and Third St. in Louth*

The Green Ribbon Trail opened on September 29, 1996 as a symbol of hope for all missing children. Donated benches line both sides of the trail and a ribbon-shaped garden at the trail entrance. The trail leads past and over a class-one wetland beside Martindale Pond. Expect Canada geese and mallards to follow you for food. You'll also see blue herons and wood ducks on the marsh.

Participark Trail

Level of difficulty 🚶

Distance *2km (6.8mi) linear*

Approx. time *45min each way*

Trailheads *Glendale Ave., St. Paul Cr.*

This wide crushed-stone path leads along the east bank of Twelve Mile Creek, past sections of the old Welland Canal.

Welland Canals Parkway Trail

Level of difficulty 🚶

Distance *9km (5.4mi) linear*

Approx. time *3.5hrs each way*

Trailheads *Flight Locks, Lock 1*

This paved trail traces the routes of the various Welland Canals. Highlights include the current functioning locks, the St. Catharines Museum and the Welland Canals Centre at Lock 3.

Seaton Hiking Trail

Location *Along West Duffins Creek between Pickering and Highway 7*

Number of trails *1*

Total distance *9.7km (6mi) linear*

Approx. time *4hrs each way*

Markers *White metal blazes*

Trailheads *Hwy 7; Forestream Trail, Pickering*

Interesting features *West Duffins Creek, Green River*

Other *Dogs on leashes permitted*

Facilities/services *Parking*

The Seaton Hiking Trail follows West Duffins Creek between Pickering and Highway 7 in three distinct sections that make up the hiking experience. They are the Heritage Trail, the Wilderness Trail, and the Walking Trail. A group of residents have gathered together under the "Friends" banner to clean up the trail and reconstruct several sections. In the future, they will decide how to link to other trails in the region.

➤ Getting There

There are parking lots at both the north and south entrances. The north entrance is on Hwy. 7 east of Green River. The south entrance is on the Pine Heights Trail at the south end of the Forestream Trail south of Whites Road.

➤ Further Information

Friends of the Seaton Hiking Trail
76 Sylvan Ave.
Scarborough, ON M1M 1K1
www.seatonhikingtrail.org

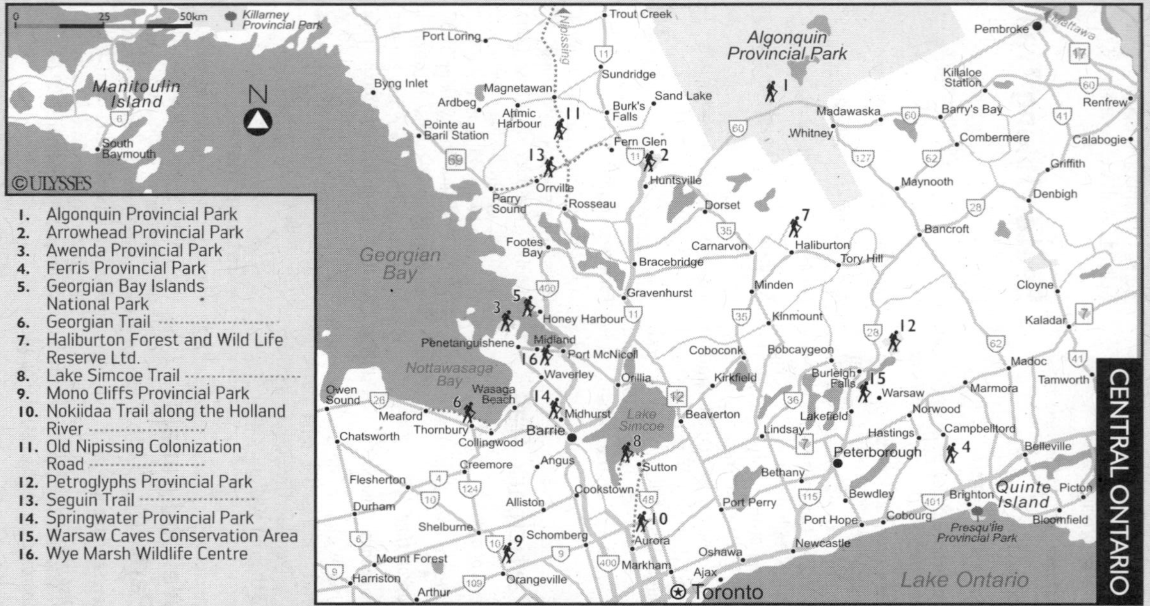
CENTRAL ONTARIO
0 25 50km
Killarney Provincial Park
N
©ULYSSES
Manitoulin Island
South Baymouth
Georgian Bay
Nottawasaga Bay
Lake Simcoe
Lake Ontario
Algonquin Provincial Park
Presqu'ile Provincial Park
Quinte Island
Nipissing
Mattawa
Port Loring
Byng Inlet
Pointe au Baril Station
Ardbeg
Magnetawan
Ahmic Harbour
Trout Creek
Sundridge
Burk's Falls
Sand Lake
Fern Glen
Huntsville
Parry Sound
Orrville
Rosseau
Footes Bay
Dorset
Carnarvon
Bracebridge
Gravenhurst
Honey Harbour
Penetanguishene
Midland
Port McNicoll
Waverley
Orillia
Owen Sound
Meaford
Thornbury
Collingwood
Wasaga Beach
Midhurst
Barrie
Chatsworth
Creemore
Angus
Flesherton
Durham
Shelburne
Alliston
Cookstown
Sutton
Beaverton
Schomberg
Aurora
Markham
Ajax
Oshawa
Toronto
Mount Forest
Harriston
Arthur
Orangeville
Haliburton
Tory Hill
Minden
Kinmount
Coboconk
Kirkfield
Bobcaygeon
Lindsay
Bethany
Port Perry
Burleigh Falls
Warsaw
Lakefield
Peterborough
Hastings
Norwood
Campbellford
Bewdley
Port Hope
Newcastle
Cobourg
Brighton
Belleville
Picton
Bloomfield
Marmora
Madoc
Tamworth
Kaladar
Cloyne
Bancroft
Maynooth
Whitney
Madawaska
Barry's Bay
Combermere
Killaloe Station
Pembroke
Renfrew
Calabogie
Griffith
Denbigh
1. Algonquin Provincial Park
2. Arrowhead Provincial Park
3. Awenda Provincial Park
4. Ferris Provincial Park
5. Georgian Bay Islands National Park
6. Georgian Trail
7. Haliburton Forest and Wild Life Reserve Ltd.
8. Lake Simcoe Trail
9. Mono Cliffs Provincial Park
10. Nokiidaa Trail along the Holland River
11. Old Nipissing Colonization Road
12. Petroglyphs Provincial Park
13. Seguin Trail
14. Springwater Provincial Park
15. Warsaw Caves Conservation Area
16. Wye Marsh Wildlife Centre

Central Ontario

People familiar with Central Ontario often call the region "cottage country." So many generations of cottage-goers have been attracted to the lakeshores in this area that the names of many of its lakes have taken on mystical meanings associated with relaxation, warmth and sun.

Just mention Lake Simcoe, Lake Couchiching, the Kawartha Lakes, Lake Joseph, Lake Muskoka, Lake Rosseau, Sparrow Lake or Rice Lake to anyone in the know, and watch their eyes sparkle with memories of restful summer vacations.

Part of this mystique began with nomadic Aboriginal people who began visiting the area thousands of years ago. Hikers will be particularly interested in exploring the areas around a deeply spiritual site: **Petroglyphs Provincial Park** (see p. 173). Petroglyphs refer to 900 rock carvings of birds, animals and other symbols that were made by Algonquian-speaking peoples between 600 and 1,100 years ago.

Central Ontario begins about an hour's drive or roughly 200km (124mi) north, east and northeast of Toronto and follows the shore of Georgian Bay to the French River. Much of the region was initially settled along a few principal thoroughfares. Some sense of the welcome these early pioneers faced can be seen by hiking the **Old Nipissing Colonization Road** (see p. 172), between Nipissing Village and Seguin Falls. Later, the railways came through, and many of these have recently been turned into rail trails, such as the **Seguin Trail** (see p. 176).

Today, there are only four major towns—Barrie, Huntsville, Peterborough and Orillia—in central Ontario. Small towns and hamlets dot the rest of the region. Many of these towns feature trails along their waterways, such as the ones on Ferry Lake in Huntsville and Jackson Creek in Peterborough (see **Trans Canada Trail**, p. 55).

Anyone who likes beach walking as a form of hiking will be attracted to the shores of Nottawasaga Bay, Severn Sound, Lake Simcoe and Georgian Bay. Wasaga Beach, the world's longest freshwater beach and home to the largest and least disturbed parabolic dunes in Ontario, is located along Georgian Bay, while the **Georgian Bay Islands National Park** (see p. 164) sits within it.

Inland trails, such as the **Georgian Trail** (see p. 166), which leads from Meaford to Collingwood, and the **Seguin Trail** (see p. 176), which leads from Parry Sound to Fern Glen Road, are also good places to explore the region's marshes and lakes.

Prefer bird-watching? Parts of Katchewanooka Lake and the Otonabee River north of Peterbourough don't freeze and so attract waterfowl all winter and early in the spring migration. Other good bird-watching locations include major wetlands, such as **Wye Marsh** (see p. 179) on the east side of Midland, the Minesing Swamp, west of Barrie, and Lake Scugog Marsh, east of Port Perry. A few hours at **Springwater Provincial Park** (see p. 177) is also time well spent. The park serves as a refuge for injured and human-imprinted birds and other wildlife that can't be re-released into the wild.

If scenic heights are more attractive to you, the Nipissing and Algonquin scenic bluffs rise 60m (197ft) above Georgian Bay at **Awenda Provincial Park** (see p. 161), as does the rounded Algonquin Dome on which **Algonquin Provincial Park** (see p. 152) and neighbouring Haliburton are located. At **Haliburton Forest** (see p. 167), a privately owned reserve on the southern portion of the Algonquin Dome, owner Peter Schleifenbaum has turned a spectacular part of his pine forest into a new kind of experience for North American hikers by building a suspended path through the canopy. The 0.5km-long (0.3mi) suspension bridge brings hikers 18m (60ft) up into the pines to see the forest from a bird's-eye view.

The area is also full of features created by glaciers. The Niagara Escarpment passes right along the edge of this region, although it's well hidden below 100m (328ft) of glacial till, except in the little-known **Mono Cliffs Provincial Park** (see p. 169), near Mono Centre. Hiking trails at **Arrowhead Provincial Park** (see p. 160) explore the glacial meltwater hills known as kames, while those at **Ferris Provincial Park** (see p. 163) traverse a particularly good example of a drumlin. The rounded holes in rock known as potholes or kettles and underground caves formed by glacial rivers can be seen at **Warsaw Caves Conservation Area** (see p. 178).

All of these features can be found in the newly created **Kawartha Highlands**, a 37,587ha (92,953-acre) protected area that includes the current Kawartha Highlands Provincial Park. The area falls between highways 507 and 28 and encompasses Anstruther Lake, Bottle Lake, Catchacoma Lake, Gold Lake, Sucker Lake and Wolf Lake. It's north of Big Cedar Lake and south of Eels Lake. Canoeing remains the most popular activity in the area now, but a strong network of hiking trails and camping sites has already been established, particularly on the Apsley side. For a map of the area, refer to the "Park Management Planning" section of the park's Web site at *www.ontarioparks.com/english/kawa.html*.

› Tourist Information

Georgian Triangle Tourist Association
30 Mountain Rd.
Collingwood, ON L9Y 5H7
705-445-7722 or 888-227-8667
www.georgiantriangle.com
www.georgianbay.com
www.visitsouthgeorgianbay.ca

Haliburton Highlands Trail and Tours Network
15500 Hwy. 35
Carnarvon, ON K0M 1J0
705-489-4049
www.trailsandtours.com

Kawartha Lakes Chamber of Commerce
PO Box 537, 12 Queen St.
Lakefield, ON K0L 2H0
705-652-6963 or 888-565-8888
www.kawarthachamber.ca

Muskoka Tourism
RR2, 1342 N. Hwy. 11
Kilworthy, ON P0E 1G0
705-689-0660 or 800-267-9700
www.discovermuskoka.ca

Peterborough and the Kawarthas Tourism
RR5, 1400 Crawford Dr.
Peterborough, ON K9J 6X6
705-742-2201 or 800-461-6424
www.thekawarthas.net

Algonquin Provincial Park

Location *North of Haliburton, east of Huntsville, west of Pembroke*

Number of trails *21*

Total distance *272.7km (169mi)*

Interesting features *Lakes, forests, cliffs, rock faces, waterfalls, rapids, bogs, 250 bird species, homestead ruins*

Other *Pets permitted on all trails, except Mizzy Lake*

Facilities/Services *Parking, toilets, telephones, visitor information centre, convenience store, maps, camping, canoe rentals*

When the government of Ontario passed the Algonquin Park Act, which set aside 18 townships as a "health resort and pleasure ground" and logging forest reserve in 1893, they didn't know that their park would eventually attract about a million visitors a year to see 45 species of mammals, 138 breeding birds and a variety of plants, trees and fungi. Nor did they know that future ministers would increase the amount of land protected within their province's oldest park another 12 times so that it now includes a territory of 772,500ha (1,908,000 acres).

The area is so large that a number of trails run from four distinct areas, each of which is a 1 to 4hr drive away from the others. They are: the Frank McDougall Parkway, a Highway 60 corridor that goes through a southern portion of the park; the Brent crater at the northern edge of the park; the eastern Achray campground area, and the southern Kingscote Lake region.

Most of the hiking trails run from the Frank McDougall Parkway,

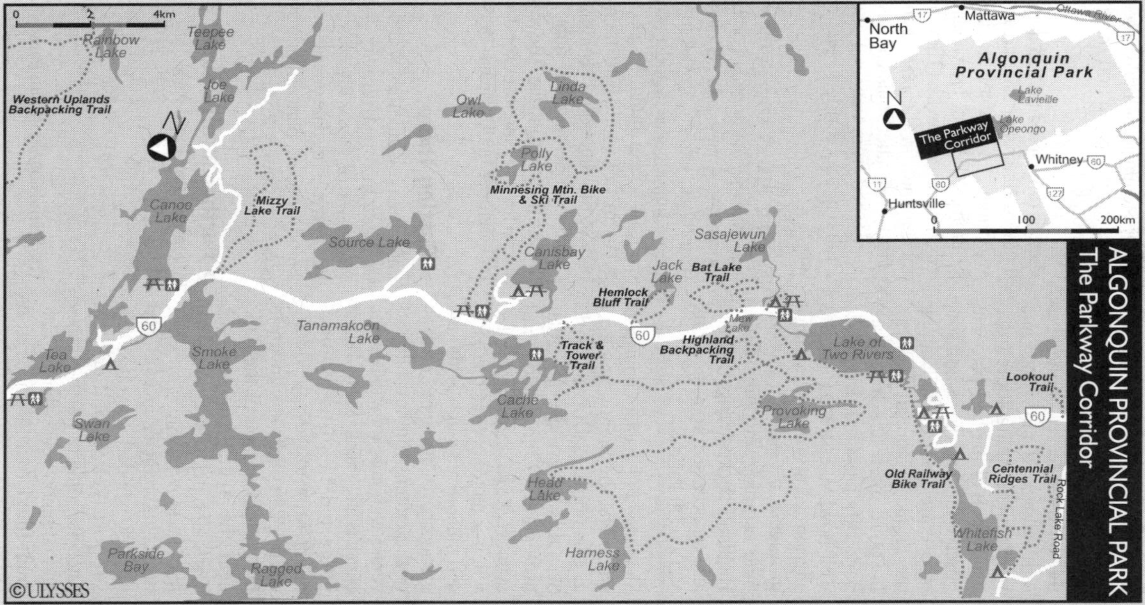
ALGONQUIN PROVINCIAL PARK
The Parkway Corridor
North Bay
Mattawa
Ottawa River
Algonquin Provincial Park
Lake Lavieille
Lake Opeongo
The Parkway Corridor
Whitney
Huntsville
N
0
100
200km
17
11
60
127
0
2
4km
Rainbow Lake
Teepee Lake
Joe Lake
Western Uplands Backpacking Trail
N
Canoe Lake
Mizzy Lake Trail
Source Lake
Owl Lake
Linda Lake
Polly Lake
Minnesing Mtn. Bike & Ski Trail
Canisbay Lake
Sasajewun Lake
Jack Lake
Bat Lake Trail
Hemlock Bluff Trail
Mew Lake
Tanamakoon Lake
Track & Tower Trail
Highland Backpacking Trail
Lake of Two Rivers
Lookout Trail
Tea Lake
Smoke Lake
Cache Lake
Provoking Lake
Swan Lake
Head Lake
Old Railway Bike Trail
Centennial Ridges Trail
Rock Lake Road
Whitefish Lake
Harness Lake
Parkside Bay
Ragged Lake
©ULYSSES

and they can be busy. Expect company on long weekends and on every weekend during the fall when leaves on the trees turn yellow, red and orange in a spectacular, multicoloured display. Some of the best places to observe the fall colours and spot moose are from the hills along the Frank McDougall Parkway. If you're interested in wolves, park officials conduct public wolf howl hikes throughout this area on warm summer evenings in August. If you want to combine camping and hiking, the Highland Backpacking Trail can also be accessed from the Frank McDougall Parkway.

Meteorite and glacier enthusiasts will prefer the Brent Crater Trail at the north end of the park. Scientists believe that a circular hole 4km (2.5mi) wide and 600m (1,969ft) deep was created when a meteorite hit the earth 450 million years ago. Although glaciers have since removed most of the crater's rim and filled its centre with limestone debris, the crater is still visible today. Hikers interested in plate tectonics might want to view the 100m-deep (328ft) Barron Canyon in the eastern portion of the park, near the Achray campground. The cliffs are nesting areas for barn swallows, eastern phoebes, ravens and red-tailed hawks, and the dry, wooded canyon slopes support yellow-bellied flycatchers, northern water thrushes and common yellowthroats. Calcium-filled rock crevices also support rare plants such as maidenhair spleenwort and bulblet fern. Other rare plants in the area include encrusted saxifrage, purple-stemmed cliffbrake, rock-cress, slender naiad and mountain woodsia.

There is only one short trail in the southern Kingscote Lake area of Algonquin Park, but it is the best location in the park for viewing red-shouldered hawks. (They are not common in the rest of the park.) Two other trails can also be reached from this area after a full-day canoe ride to Scorch Lake.

Autumn hikers who want to explore either the northeast or the southern regions should definitely wear hunter orange. A week-long moose-hunting season and a two-week-long deer hunting season occur in the south, and members of the Algonquin Nation of Ontario are permitted to hunt in the northeast from the Tuesday after Thanksgiving weekend in mid-October until January 15.

› Getting There

Enter the park at either Whitney or Dwight on Highway 60; Petawawa or Deux Rivieres on Highway 17; Emsdale on Highway 11; or Harcourt, Bancroft or Maynooth on County Road 10.

› Further Information

Algonquin Provincial Park
PO Box 219
Whitney, ON K0J 2M0
☎ 705-633-5572 or 800-667-1940
www.ontarioparks.com

The Friends of Algonquin Park
PO Box 248
Whitney, ON K0J 2M0
☎ 613-637-2828
www.algonquinpark.on.ca

Mini-Trails less than 3km (1.9mi) long

Beaver Pond

Level of difficulty 🚶

Distance *2km (1mi) loop*

Approx. time *1hr return*

Trailhead *Frank McDougall Pkwy., 45.2km (28mi) from the west entrance near Dwight or 10.8km (6.7mi) from the east entrance near Whitney*

This trail leads past two beaver dams and Amikeus Lake, which was created by a beaver dam. The trail runs along dirt paths and boardwalks past lodges and dams. Visitors along this trail have a good chance of seeing one or two members of the 4,500 beaver colonies in Algonquin Park or the frogs, great blue herons, moose, otters, ring-necked ducks and turtles that depend on beaver ponds and meadows for their food or habitat.

Hardwood Lookout

Level of difficulty 🚶

Distance *1km (.6mi) double loop*

Approx. time *30min return*

Trailhead *Frank McDougall Pkwy., 13.8km (8.6mi) from the west entrance near Dwight or 42.2km (26mi) from the east entrance near Whitney*

This trail leads through hardwood forests of sugar maple, yellow birch, American beech and hop hornbeam, with occasional stands of beech, hemlock and cherry that are typical of Algonquin Park. The path ends at a lookout over Smoke Lake and the surrounding hills. A short extension past the parking lot leads to a stand of red spruce, a tree species usually found only in New England and the Maritimes.

Peck Lake Trail

Level of difficulty 🚶

Distance *1.9km (1.2mi) loop*

Approx. time *1hr return*

Trailhead *Frank McDougall Pkwy., 19.2km (12mi) from the west entrance near Dwight or 36.8km (23mi) from the east entrance near Whitney*

The Peck Lake Trail follows dirt paths and boardwalks to circle the shoreline of Peck Lake, where loons, otters, mink, perch and splake make their homes. Loesel's twayblade and ragged fringed orchids grow to the west of the trail.

Spruce Bog Trail

Level of difficulty 🚶

Distance *1.5km (.9mi) loop*

Approx. time *1hr return*

Trailhead *Frank McDougall Pkwy., 42.5km (26mi) from the west entrance near Dwight or 13.5km (8.4mi) from the east entrance near Whitney*

A dirt track leads through black spruce and balsam fir. Boardwalks lead across the Sunday Creek bog and a second bog 9m (30ft) deep, in what once was a kettle or pothole formed by a glacier.

Whiskey Rapids Trail

Level of difficulty 🚶

Distance *2.1km (1.3mi) loop*

Approx. time *1hr return*

Trailhead *Frank McDougall Pkwy., 7.2km (4.5mi) from the west entrance near Dwight or 49km (30mi) from the east entrance near Whitney*

This trail gets its name from two loggers who once lost a keg of whiskey in the rapids of the Oxtongue River. This trail provides a stunning view of a river reshaping the land it traverses, taking soil from one side and placing it on the other as it flows around curves. You'll notice trees falling or on the verge of falling into the river on one side and new areas of sandy growth on the other. After the view of the rapids, the trail leads along an old corduroy road (made of tree trunks) that was originally built for hauling timber. The log paving looks like corduroy, which was also named after the French phrase for "King's road" or *corde de roi*. Bird-watchers should be on the lookout for winter finches, black-backed woodpeckers, boreal chickadees, brown creepers and northern parulas.

Barron Canyon

Level of difficulty 🚶🚶

Distance *1.5km (.9mi) loop*

Approx. time *1hr return*

Trailhead *A parking lot on Lake Travers Rd., 11km (6.8mi) past the Sand Lake Gate on the Park's east side*

This trail leads along the north rim of a 100m-deep (328ft) gorge with gneiss walls once known as "the Capes." The gap is constantly widening as annual frost shatters the cliffs leaving talus boulders at the gorge bottom to attract yellow-bellied flycatchers, northern water thrushes and common yellow-throats. The Barron River running along the centre of the gorge is all that remains of a huge torrent of glacial melt water that once ran from the Algonquin glacier to the Champlain Sea.

Brent Crater

Level of difficulty 🚶🚶

Distance *2km (1mi) loop*

Approx. time *1hr return*

Trailhead *Brent Rd., 32km (20mi) from Hwy. 17 near Deux-Rivieres*

The trail begins with a good overview of the 4km-wide (2.5mi) and 100m-deep (328ft) Brent Crater from an observation tower built for a field excursion of the 24th International Geological Congress, which met in Montréal in 1972. You'll see the eroded remains of a circular hole that was probably created when a meteor hit the Canadian Shield 450 million years ago. The trail then leads down the crater wall past shattered rock, where you'll see rare bulblet bladder ferns, liverworts, mosses and wildflowers growing. Once you reach the bottom, you'll see Tecumseh Lake, one of two lakes in the park resistant to acid rain.

Lookout Trail

Level of difficulty 🚶🚶

Distance *1.9km (1.2mi) loop*

Approx. time *1hr return*

Trailhead *Frank McDougall Pkwy., 40km (25mi) from the west entrance near Dwight or 16km (10mi) from the east entrance near Whitney*

This trail takes the hiker up a fairly steep climb to the top of a cliff where a fabulous view awaits, 125m (400ft) above the Lake of Two Rivers and Whitefish Lake.

Two Rivers Trail

Level of difficulty 🚶 🚶

Distance *2km (1mi) loop*

Approx. time *1hr return*

Trailhead *Frank McDougall Pkwy., 31km (19mi) from the west entrance near Dwight or 25km (15mi) from the east entrance near Whitney*

The Two Rivers Trail leads through a forest of white and red pine, spruce, balsam fir, aspen and birch. The trail then gently climbs to the top of a cliff for a view over the North Madawaska River.

Trails from 3km (1.9mi) to 10km (6.2mi) long

Bat Lake Trail

Level of difficulty 🚶

Distance *5.6km (3.5mi)*

Approx. time *2hrs return*

Trailhead *Frank McDougall Pkwy., 30km (19mi) from the west entrance near Dwight or 26km (16mi) from the east entrance near Whitney*

This trail passes through white pine, balsam fir and white spruce, then into a deciduous forest dominated by sugar maple. It then leads into Algonquin Park's largest mature stand of eastern hemlocks called "cathedral grove" and then into a black spruce and tamarack area at the northern part of Davies' Bog. The trail then continues on to Bat Lake, one of 15 lakes in the park known to be naturally acidic. Although no fish live in Bat Lake, it does support crustaceans, ghost midge larvae, two types of predatory beetles, yellow-spotted salamander tadpoles and an unusual migrating northern duck called the bufflehead. A boardwalk leads across a wide, moist creek called an "alder-swale" because speckled alders grow along the bottom.

Berm Lake Trail

Level of difficulty 🚶

Distance *4.5km (2.8mi) loop*

Approx. time *2hrs return*

Trailhead *Achray Campground on the Park's east side*

This path circles Berm Lake and leads through white pine, then red pine, blueberry patches, and finally red oak forests. You'll spot lots of red squirrels and see or hear many seed-eating birds, including red crossbills and pine warblers.

Booth's Rock Trail

Level of difficulty 🚶

Distance *5.1km (3mi) loop*

Approx. time *2hrs return*

Trailhead *8km (5mi) south of the Rock Lake Campground on Rock Lake Rd., off Frank McDougall Pkwy., 40km (25mi) from the west entrance near Dwight or 16km (10mi) from the east entrance near Whitney*

This trail allows hikers to relive the influence of J.R. Booth, one of Canada's first self-made millionaires. Booth made his fortune by logging Egan Estate, a pine forest in what is now the Rock Lake (or Booth's Rock) area of Algonquin Park. By 1894, his company ran the world's largest mill. Booth's Rock Trail leads up to a beautiful lookout over Rock

Lake and the old mill site, down several staircases to the foundations of Booth's cousin's estate, and then returns along part of his abandoned railway. Take the short extension leading along the railway bed away from the trail for a good shoreline view of Rock Lake.

Hemlock Bluff

Level of difficulty 🚶

Distance *3.5km (2mi) loop*

Approx. time *2hrs return*

Trailhead *Frank McDougall Pkwy., 27km (17mi) from the west entrance near Dwight or 29km (18mi) from the east entrance near Whitney*

This trail leads through a mixed forest of eastern hemlock, yellow birch, maple and beech, which is home to yellow-bellied sapsuckers, brown creepers, winter wrens, golden-crowned kinglets, Swainson's and hermit thrushes, northern parulas and black-throated, green and Blackburnian warblers. The trail leads up to the top of a cliff with an impressive view of Jack Lake.

Full-Day Trails, from 10km (6.2mi) to 16km (10mi)

Mizzy Lake

Level of difficulty 🚶🚶

Distance *11km (6.8mi) loop plus a 2km (1mi) extension*

Approx. time *5hrs return*

Trailhead *Frank McDougall Pkwy., 15km (9mi) from the west entrance near Dwight or 41km (25mi) from the east entrance near Whitney*

Other *Dogs not permitted on this trail*

The Mizzy Lake Trail leads past Mizzy, West Rose, March Hare and Dizzy lakes, Wolf Howl Pond, beaver dams, and a marsh, and along an old railway causeway.

Centennial Ridges

Level of difficulty 🚶🚶🚶

Distance *10km (6.2mi) loop*

Approx. time *6hrs return*

Trailhead *A parking lot 2km (1mi) south of Frank McDougall Pkwy., 38km (23mi) from the west entrance near Dwight or 18km (11mi) from the east entrance near Whitney*

This demanding trail was created in 1993 to celebrate Algonquin Park's 100th birthday. It consists of a total vertical climb of 360m (1,200ft) and offers fabulous views from five different cliffs along two high ridges.

Eastern Pines Backpacking Trail

Level of difficulty 🚶🚶🚶

Distance *6km (3.7mi) loop or 15km (9.3mi) loop*

Approx. time *2hrs return for the shorter loop or 6hrs return for the longer loop*

Trailhead *Achray Campground, off the Barron Canyon Rd., which is off County Rd. 26*

Other *Camping sites are available along the trail*

Both the Johnston Lake and Stratton/Bucholtz Lake loops of the Eastern Pines Trail are short enough to finish in a day, if you don't mind a few climbs; however, the area they cover is so stunningly beautiful that campsites have been set up along the shores of Stratton Lake to accommodate overnight stays. You'll see glacial boulder gardens, the cascading High Falls, an osprey nest and lots of blue herons. The Johnston Lake loop of this trail shares one side of the Berm Lake Trail as it passes through red and white pine forests.

Track and Tower

Level of difficulty 🚶 🚶 🚶

Distance *7.7km (4.8mi) loop, plus a 5.5km (3.4mi) extension*

Approx. time *4hrs for the loop; 7hrs for the loop and the extension one-way (with an arranged pick-up at the other end); or 12hrs for the loop and the extension, return*

Trailhead *Frank McDougall Pkwy., 25km (15.5mi) from the west entrance near Dwight or 31km (19.2mi) from the east entrance near Whitney*

This trail features a huge cattail marsh, an old airfield, three train trestles (two wooden and one steel), a 1967 dam at the outlet of Cache Lake, the foundation of the old Skymount fire tower and the site of a former hotel, train station and park headquarters.

Overnight Trails

Bruton Farm Trail

Level of difficulty 🚶

Distance *2.4km (1.5mi) each way*

Approx. time *2 hrs return, after a full-day canoe ride*

Trailhead *About 237m (778ft) along the Scorch Lake Lookout Trail, which begins at Scorch Lake, a one-day canoe ride from the Kingscote Lake Access Point Rd. parking lot in season, or a gate 5km (3mi) away near County Rd. 10 from the end of Oct until May*

This trail begins on an old carriage road and continues through a swamp, gradually climbing to the top of a hardwood ridge. You'll follow a stone fence to the old Bruton farm site, which was built in 1875 by the Bronson Co. to provide food for their loggers.

Highland Backpacking Trail

Level of difficulty 🚶 🚶 🚶

Distance *Provoking Lake 18.5km (11.7mi) loop and the Head and Harness Lakes 35.3km (22mi) loop*

Approx. time *8hrs return for the Provoking Lake loop or 15hrs return for both loops*

Markers *Blue (Provoking Lake loop) and yellow (Head and Harness Lake loop)*

Trailhead *Pewee Lake parking lot south of Frank McDougall Pkwy., 29.7km (18mi) from the west entrance near Dwight or 26.3km (16mi) from the east entrance near Whitney*

Other *Many 9-person campsites along the trail; reservations required*

This is a very wet, boggy trail, so wear lots of mosquito repellent. A scenic waterfall over the Madawaska River appears just before the Highland Trail crosses the Track and Tower Trail.

Scorch Lake Lookout Trail

Level of difficulty 🚶 🚶 🚶

Distance *.9km (.6mi) linear*

Approx. time *2hrs each way, after a full-day canoe ride*

Trailhead From Scorch Lake, a one-day canoe ride from the Kingscote Lake Access Point Rd. parking lot in season or a gate 5km (3mi) away near County Rd. 10; from the end of Oct until May

This very steep climb leads through a deciduous forest onto an oak barren where old twisted, gnarled trees bear witness to the strong wind and cold they face in this site. Look for the tracks of bears and deer, both of which appreciate the acorns.

Western Uplands Backpacking Trail

Level of difficulty 🚶 🚶 🚶

Distance Blue, 32.4km (20mi) loop; Yellow, 41km (25.4mi) loop; Red Pincher Tern Lakes, 26.8km (16.6mi) loop; Red East End Lake, 15.2km (9.4mi) loop; Rainy Lake extension, 8.4km (5mi) each way

Approx. time 14hrs return (Blue loop), 7 days return (all the loops)

Trailheads North of the Frank McDougall Pkwy. corridor 3km east of the west entrance near Dwight or 53km (33mi) from the east entrance near Whitney; or the Rain Lake Access Point, 35km (22mi) east of Hwy. 11 at Emsdale

Other Many 9-person campsites along the trail; reservations required

This multi-looped trail leads through deciduous forests, along lakes and across a particularly swampy area near the Oxtongue River. There are two lookouts: one over Susan Lake and the other over Stammer Lake.

Arrowhead Provincial Park

Location Huntsville

Number of trails 3

Total distance 13km (7.8mi)

Interesting features Stubbs Falls, Arrowhead Lake, East River, Mayflower Lake, former shore of glacial Lake Algonquin, kame hills

Other Dogs on leashes permitted

Facilities/Services Parking, toilets, telephones, convenience store, maps, camping, canoe rentals

Arrowhead Provincial Park lies just north of the town of Huntsville. Primarily known as a camping and canoeing destination, the park also offers three small trails for hikers to explore. There is also a pretty lookout over the bend in the Big East River in the Roe Campground.

› Getting There

From Huntsville, take Highway 11 north to the Arrowhead Provincial Park exit and follow the signs.

› Further Information

Arrowhead Provincial Park
451 Arrowhead Park Rd.
Huntsville, ON P1H 2J4
☎ 705-789-5105 or 800-667-1940
www.ontarioparks.com

Stubbs Falls Trail

Level of difficulty 🚶

Distance 2km (1.2mi) linear

Approx. time 45min each way

Trailheads The parking lot at the edge of Arrowhead Lake or the one at the east end of the East River Campground

This trail leads along the shore of Little East River past Stubbs Falls.

Beaver Meadow Trail

Level of difficulty 🚶

Distance *7km (4.2mi) linear*

Approx. time *2hrs return*

Trailhead *On the north side of Lumby Campground, near Arrowhead Lake*

This trail leads past the one-time shoreline of glacial Lake Algonquin, around a beaver pond, and past the remnants of the Oke Homestead site. In spring and summer, you'll be able to see Porcupine Bluffs, where the ancient lake once stood.

Homesteader and Mayflower Lake Trails

Level of difficulty 🚶

Distance *4km (2.4mi) double loop*

Approx. time *1.5hrs return*

Trailhead *On the east side of Lumby Campground at Mayflower Lake*

This trail leads along the shore of the spring-fed Mayflower Lake and past the former farm fields of pioneers.

Awenda Provincial Park

Location *15min from Penetanguishene*

Number of trails *7*

Total Distance *30km (18.6mi)*

Interesting features *Nipissing Bluff, Algonquin Bluff, Giant's Tomb Island, homestead ruins*

Facilities/Services *Parking, toilets, telephones, visitor information centre, convenience store, fishing, swimming beaches, camping, laundry area, showers*

Anyone interested in glacier-created landforms will want to visit Awenda Provincial Park on the edge of the Penetanguishene Peninsula, which juts into Georgian Bay to create Nottawasaga Bay and Severn Sound. The most impressive visual element of Awenda is Nipissing Bluff, a beach rising 60m (197ft) into the air. The park also includes most of Giants Tomb Island, which it shares with the Township of Tiny.

Awenda Provincial Park also contains the remains of abandoned Aboriginal villages that are now archaeological sites. Researchers are trying to find evidence of four different Aboriginal cultures—the Paleo, the Laurentian Archaics, the Middle Woodland and the Huron—who are assumed to have inhabited these sites.

› Getting There

Take Highway 93 to Penetanguishene. Turn left on Robert Street and right on Lafontaine (at the Shell gas station). Turn right at the first stop sign. Awenda Park Road is the first road on the left. The park is about 5min along, on the left.

› Further Information

Awenda Provincial Park
PO Box 5004
Penetanguishene, ON L9M 2G2
☎ 705-549-2231 or 800-667-1940
www.ontarioparks.com

Friends of Awenda
www.awendapark.ca

Beaver Pond Trail

Level of difficulty 🚶

Distance *1km (.6mi) loop*

Approx. time *30min return*

Trailhead *Trail centre*

Other *Wheelchair accessible*

The Beaver Pond Trail circles an active beaver pond. You'll also see historic remnants of logging in the area, including an old bridge and a logging building.

Brûlé Trail

Level of difficulty 🚶

Distance *4km (2.5mi) loop*

Approx. time *1.5hrs return*

Trailhead *Trail centre*

The Bluff Trail follows the Nipissing and Bluff trails across the summer road, and then turns off before the set of stairs to cross the main road and continue through a mature deciduous forest along an old logging road from 1880s.

Nipissing Trail

Level of difficulty 🚶🚶

Distance *.5km (.3mi) linear*

Approx. time *30min return*

Trailhead *Trail centre*

The Nipissing Trail leads up 155 steps onto the 8,000-year old Nipissing Bluff. It then leads through a lowland forest of cedar and white birch, ending in an upland forest of maple and oak.

Dunes Trail

Level of difficulty 🚶🚶

Distance *1.5km (.9mi) linear*

Approx. time *1.5hrs return*

Trailhead *Trail centre*

The Dunes Trail begins with a 90m (295ft) climb up the 12,000-year old Algonquin Bluff cliff. It levels off on a sand dune and passes the remnants of two homesteads along the way.

Beach Trail

Level of difficulty 🚶🚶

Distance *5km (3mi) linear*

Approx. time *4hrs return*

Trailhead *Trail centre*

The Beach Trail leads to an observation deck and then past it for 32m (105ft) straight down the face of the Nipissing Bluff to a birch, cedar and hemlock forest below. There are two steep points along the trail. Continue along the Georgian Bay shoreline to Methodist Point to get a good view of Giant's Tomb Island.

Bluff Trail

Level of difficulty 🚶🚶

Distance *13km (8mi) loop*

Approx. time *5hrs return*

Trailhead *Trail centre*

The Bluff Trail shares the Nipissing Trail stairs up onto the 8,000-

year old Nipissing Bluff. You'll get some good views of Georgian Bay and of several forested sand dunes.

Wendat Trail

Level of difficulty 🚶

Distance 5km (3mi) loop

Approx. time 2hrs return

Trailhead The Bluff Trail or a sign posted along the summer road

The Wendat Trail circles around the glacial Kettle Lake, passing the ruins of the Brabant family homestead, and through marshes and forest. You're very likely to see great blue herons, common loons, snapping turtles and beavers.

Ferris Provincial Park

Location Near Campbellford

Number of trails 4

Total distance 5.5km (3.4mi)

Interesting features Three drumlins, scenic bluffs, Ranney Gorge Suspension Bridge, Ranney Falls, Osprey Nest, Trent River, white trilliums in May, 4ha (10-acre) stand of old growth beech trees

Other Pets on 2m (7ft) leashes welcome

Facilities/Services Parking, toilets, telephones, camping, laundry area, showers, fishing, boat launch

Ferris Provincial Park, which was donated to the province by Kathleen Ferris, is highly recommended either for a relaxing, easy day-hike on an almond-shaped drumlin or for a longer hike on the Trans Canada Trail, which goes through the park. The suspension bridge over Ranney Falls is worth stopping for, and the day hike past the falls is worth the effort. Or you can take a longer journey along the Trans Canada Trail, on which you'll find Devil's Valley to the east and the Godolphin Esker Wetland Complex to the west.

› Getting There

Take Exit 509 from Highway 401 to County Road 30 north, or County Road 30 south from Havelock on Highway 7, to Campbellford. Turn right onto Centre Street at the top of the hill and continue past the town limits to the park.

› Further Information

Ferris Provincial Park
PO Box 1409
Campbellford, ON K0L 1L0
☎ 705-653-3575 (summer), 705-653-1566 (winter) or 800-667-1940
www.ontarioparks.com

Friends of Ferris Park
☎ 705-653-5548
www.friendsofferris.ca

Gorge Trail

Level of difficulty 🚶

Distance 2km (1.2mi) linear

Approx. time 2hrs return

Trailhead Day-use parking lot

The Gorge Trail begins on a limestone ridge that provides a beautiful view of Ranney Falls. It then continues through a deciduous forest along the Trent

River gorge past the boat launch area and ends with a view of an old osprey nest at the top of a telephone pole. You can also get onto the Ranney Gorge Bridge from this trail.

Drumlin Trail

Level of difficulty 🚶 🚶

Distance *2km (1.2mi) triple loop*

Approx. time *1hr return*

Trailhead *Day-use parking lot*

The Drumlin Trails weave up a cigar-shaped drumlin to a fork that leads either to a road leading back to the day-use parking lot or to the second loop. The second loop goes down the drumlin into a valley and then follows a creek bed to the Ranney Falls Trail. A third section leads back to a road towards the day-use parking lot.

Ranney Falls Trail

Level of difficulty 🚶

Distance *.5km (.3mi) loop*

Approx. time *10min each way*

Trailhead *The end of the Drumlin Trail, the end of the Gorge Trail or the day-use parking lot*

The trail is a loop next to Ranney Falls.

Milkweed Trail

Level of difficulty 🚶

Distance *1km (.6mi) linear*

Approx. time *1hr*

Trailhead *The end of the Gorge Trail*

The trail leads through fields to the south of the campgrounds for pleasant views of the butterflies and jewel weed in the area.

Georgian Bay Islands National Park

Location *Honey Harbour*

Number of trails *4*

Total distance *28km (17mi)*

Interesting features *Drumlins, old-growth hemlock stand, Brebeuf Lighthouse*

Facilities/Services *Parking, water-taxi, camping, toilets, telephones, ice, showers, firewood, swimming*

Other *Pets on leashes permitted; Massasauga rattlesnake and black bear country; full service camping with gear available on particular weekends in the autumn; alcohol Ban for ten days up to and including Victoria Day (May 24 weekend)*

Georgian Bay Islands National Park includes 63 islands in the world's largest freshwater island archipelago. Known as the 30,000 islands, the area actually contains at least 90,000 islands on the eastern shore of Georgian Bay, which is part of Lake Huron. Most visitors know the largest of these, Beausoleil Island, where the campgrounds and hiking trails are located. Visitors travel to the island by boat: their own, the park service's *DayTripper* or a private operator's. Camping services operate from mid-May to Canadian Thanksgiving. Day trips are also possible from Thursday to Monday in July and August and on Saturdays in the fall. The trip includes two 15-minute water taxis and a six-hour stay on Beausoleil Island.

Hikers will be fascinated by the many remnants of glaciers found on the trails, but Beausoleil Island also has a deep cultural history. In prehistoric times, it served as a summer settlement site for Aboriginals as far back as 7,000 years ago. Several permanent settlements have been recorded on the island too. For instance, an Algonquian village was mentioned in explorer field notes from 1634. In 1836, a permanent Anishinabe (Ojibway) settlement moved from Coldwater to Beausoleil Island, although sandy soil led most of these settlers to move to Christian Island by 1856. The few who remained were joined by European settlers from France, Scotland and the United States. The tough conditions led many of the families to leave, however, and only three families remained by the time the National Park was set up in 1929.

› Getting There

Georgian Bay Islands National Park can only be accessed by watercraft from one of four marinas in Honey Harbour. To get to Honey Harbour, follow Hwy 400 north to exit 156 and continue to Muskoka Road 5.

› Further Information

Georgian Bay Islands National Park
PO Box 9, 901 Wye Valley Rd.
Midland, ON L4R 4K6
705-526-9804 or 888-773-8888
www.pc.gc.ca

DayTripper Water Taxi
705-526-8907

Private Water Taxis:

Bayview Marina
705-756-2482

CnC Marina
705-756-3231

Georgian Bay Water Services
705-627-3062

Honey Harbour Boat Club
705-756-2411

Brebeuf Lighthouse Trail

Level of difficulty 🚶

Distance *6.2km (4mi) linear*

Approx. time *2.5hrs each way*

Trailhead *Day use area/dock*

This trail follows the north part of the Huron Trail and the Georgian Trail to get to the historic Brebeuf Lighthouse on the western shore of the island. This part of the Huron Trail follows a former fire tower road, so it's wide and flat, but the Georgian Trail goes along narrow forest portages and leads out to a rocky shoreline. At the top of the Huron Trail lies a renowned stand of 60 to 80 year-old hemlock trees.

The rocks next to the historic lighthouse are a great spot to see the sunset.

Northern Loop

Level of difficulty 🚶🚶

Distance *10.8km (6.5mi) quadruple loop*

Approx. time *From 1 to 6.5hrs return*

Trailhead *Top of the old Fireroad (north end of Huron Trail)*

Other *Campsites at Sandpiper, Oaks, Chimney Bay and Honeymoon Bay*

The northern loop encompasses six park trails and can be done as one of five loops. It goes through the Canadian Shield portion of the island, which means rocky, mossy trails.

The shortest possible loop includes part of the Massasauga and Rockview trails plus the Portage Trail. It takes about an hour to complete. Highlights include views of the most pristine wetland in the Great Lakes and an overlook over Long Bay. As this trail feels almost entirely inland, however, few hikers will want to limit themselves to it.

The longest loop includes most of the Massasauga and Rockview trails plus the Fairy, Cambrian and Dossyonshing trails. It follows the northeastern and northwestern shores of Beausoleil Island. There are beautiful scenic overlooks over various bays, many of which seem to be popular for boaters washing their dogs. The Cambrian Trail overlooks Main and Little Dog channels and is well worth the trip. The Fairy Trail is the easiest of the three add-on trails, while the mossy Dossyonshing is the most challenging and remote.

Southern Loop

Level of difficulty 🚶

Distance *7.5km (4.5mi) loop*

Approx. time *2.5hrs return*

Trailhead *Day use area/dock*

Other *Campsites at Beausoleil Point*

This trail follows the southern portions of the Huron and Georgian trails through the St. Lawrence Lowland region of Beausoleil Island. It then follows the entire Christian Trail or a portion of the Christian Trail and the Heritage Trail along the eastern and western shores of the island in a loop past Papoose Bay or Christian Beach south to Beausoleil Point.

Highlights include a cemetery, a large drumlin, black cherry trees and osprey nests.

Treasure Trail

Level of difficulty 🚶🚶

Distance *3.8km (2.3mi) linear*

Approx. time *2hrs each way*

Trailheads *Day use area/dock, Tonch East*

This trail follows the eastern coast of the island between the main dock and Tonch East. It's a much more rugged route than the old fire road and features a lookout over Thumb Point. The trail is named because of a myth that Jesuit priests buried treasure in this area.

Georgian Trail

Location *Meaford Waterfront to Collingwood*

Number of trails *1*

Total distance *34km (20.4mi)*

Interesting features *Meaford Harbour, Peasmarsh Beach, Christie Beach, Council Beach, Craiglaith Provincial Park, Collingwood Harbour*

Facilities/Services Parking, toilets

The Georgian Trail follows the path of the former Northern Railway Line, which operated from 1872 until 1984. It runs along the southern shore of Nottawasaga Bay, which is a smaller bay within Lake Huron's Georgian Bay.

Several beaches and parks provide lots of space for picnicking or swimming along the way. There are also bridges over Ash Creek, Silver Creek, Indian Brook and the Beaver River, all of which flow into the bay.

› Getting There

Reach the shoreline from Harbourview Park in Collingwood, or from Meaford Harbour. You can also join the trail along the way in Northwinds Beach, Craigleith Provincial Park (day-pass required), Council and Peasmarsh Beach, the village of Thornbury Harbour or Bayview Park and Meaford Harbour.

› Further Information

Georgian Cycle & Ski Trail Association
PO Box 151
Collingwood, ON L9Y 3Z5
☎ 705-445-4209
www.georgiantrail.ca

Haliburton Forest and Wild Life Reserve Ltd.

Location North of Haliburton

Number of trails 4

Total distance 10km (6.2mi)

Interesting features Canopy Trail, Wolf Centre, cabin observatory

Facilities/Services Parking, toilets, telephones, visitor information centre, restaurant, gift store, maps, lodge and room rental, camping, laundry area, showers, canoe and mountain bike rentals, fishing

The 24,300ha (60,000 acres) of land that Peter Schleifenbaum inherited from his father will draw any hiker who appreciates diversity. This is the forest's hallmark, whether in the activities available, the trees, the birds, the mammals, the stars or the trails. Diversity also describes the business operation itself and the philosophy behind timber management, which garnered a certification as Canada's first sustainable forest.

Most hikers will initially be attracted by the canopy tour, a guided opportunity to view a pine forest from a suspended bridge 18m (60ft) in the air. There are other trails too, and each provides an opportunity to explore a mixed forest that encompasses both deciduous and coniferous species, including maple, beech, birch, hemlock, spruce, cedar, white pine and red pine. Birds common to both boreal and southern forests are frequently seen here.

A captive pack of wolves lives in a 6ha (15-acre) enclosure, which is visible from a cabin with a one-sided viewing window. Research has been conducted on the wolves since the centre opened in 1996. The Wolf Centre also conducts public wolf howls on several evenings throughout the summer.

Astronomy enthusiasts will surely appreciate the country-style observatory, which opened in 2001. A map table outside helps visitors identify stars, with closer observations possible from a telescope placed within a log cabin with a retractable roof. Other activities include mountain biking, canoeing and camping.

› Getting There

From West Guilford on Highway 118, take County Road 7 (also known as Kennisis Lake Road) north for 20km (12mi) to the base camp entrance.

› Further Information

Haliburton Forest & Wild Life Reserve Ltd.
RR1, 1095 Redken Rd.
Haliburton, ON K0M 1S0
☎ 705-754-2198
www.haliburtonforest.com

Canopy Trail

Level of difficulty 🚶🚶🚶

Distance *4km (2.5mi) linear*

Approx. time *4hrs total, including short van ride, canoeing and walking*

Trailhead *Guided tour only, van leaves from visitor centre*

You'll join 11 other hikers on a guided tour that begins with a short van ride on which you'll hear about the Schleifenbaum family and their efforts to create a sustainable forest. You'll then walk a short distance to a lake, where you'll be provided with a life jacket and paddle so that you can join your fellow hikers in two eight-person canoes for a short ride across the lake. A short lesson in how to wear a harness and how to work with a partner for safety adds a bit of drama as the group walks up a short hill to the beginning of a 600m-long (0.3mi) suspended bridge that's raised 18m (60ft) up into the pines. If you can relax as you walk along the 3m-wide (10ft) and 3.6m-wide (12ft) boards, you'll see chipmunks, squirrels and a variety of birds and birds' nests at very close range. A platform part way along gives you a break.

Wolf Centre Trail Extension

Level of difficulty 🚶

Distance *.5km (.3mi) linear*

Approx. time *15min each way*

Trailhead *North end of the base camp beyond the cabins*

This short trail leads through a deciduous forest and along a boardwalk over a short boggy section leading from the base camp to the Wolf Centre.

Wolf Centre Trail

Level of difficulty 🚶

Distance *1.5km (.9mi) loop*

Approx. time *30min return*

Trailhead *Next to the Wolf Centre*

This hike begins at the Wolf Centre and leads through a mixed forest up to a natural platform overlooking MacDonald Lake.

Wild Woods Walk

Level of difficulty *🚶*

Distance *4km (2.5mi) loop*

Approx. time *1.5hrs return*

Trailhead *North end of the base camp beyond the cabins*

Other *Mountain bikes also permitted*

This wide dirt and boardwalk path leads through mixed forests and over wetlands and marsh.

Lake Simcoe Trail

Location *South shore of Lake Simcoe*

Number of trails *1*

Total distance *50km (30mi)*

Interesting features *Eildon Hall Memorial Museum, Sibbald Point Provincial Park, St. Georges Church, Stephen Leacock burial plot, Jackson's Point Harbour, Red Barn Theatre, Roches Point, 1863 stone church*

Facilities/Services *Parking*

The Lake Simcoe Trail traces the southern shore of Cooks Bay and Lake Simcoe between Lake Drive South in East Gwillimbury and Virginia Boulevard in the town of Virginia. The route follows local roads and the bed of the former Lake Simcoe Junction Railway through Georgina, across the Black River and through Sibbald Point Provincial Park.

› Getting There

The trail can be accessed from parking lots on Ravenshoe Road, Young's Harbour, Glenwoods Drive, Church Street, Maple Leaf Park, Civic Centre, Willow Beach Wharf on Kennedy Road, De La Salle Park, Jackson's Point, Sibbald Point Provincial Park or Virginia Hall.

› Further Information

Town of Georgina
RR2 , 26557 Civic Centre Rd.
Keswick, ON L4P 3G1
705-437-2210 or 888-436-7446
www.town.georgina.on.ca

Mono Cliffs Provincial Park

Location *East of Mono Centre, Off Hwy. 10 between Shelburne and Orangeville*

Number of trails *7*

Total distance *21.5km (13.3mi)*

Interesting features *Niagara Escarpment, cliffs, dolostone outliers, glacial spillway, a kettle lake, white trilliums, ferns*

Other *Pets on leashes permitted*

Facilities/Services *Parking, toilets*

Mono Cliffs Provincial Park protects 750ha (1,853 acres) of scenic land along the Niagara Escarpment. To the glacier enthusiast, Mono Cliffs is a Mecca. Besides walking along, past and up the main escarpment face, you can also walk past two dolostone outliers, through the Violet Hill glacial spillway, on top of the Orangeville moraine, and past a glacial kettle lake called McCarston's Lake, also known locally as Mono Lake.

The area's more recent rural past is also in evidence, with cedar rail fences, foundations of abandoned farm buildings, a stone fountain, stone fences, lilacs and apple orchards.

Getting There

Take Highway 10 north from Orangeville or south from Shelburne to County Road 8 at Camilla. Turn east and continue for 8km (5mi) past Mono Centre to Third Line. Turn left. The park entrance is on the left.

Further Information

c/o Earl Rowe Provincial Park
PO Box 872
Alliston, ON L9R 1W1
705-435-2498 or 800-667-1940
www.ontarioparks.com

Carriage Trail

Level of difficulty 🚶

Distance *1km (.6mi) linear*

Approx. time *30min each way*

Markers *Red*

Trailhead *Entrance parking lot*

Other *Mountain biking and horseback riding permitted*

This trail follows a glacial spillway and leads to the South Outlier Trail, the Spillway Trail and the Bruce Trail, past butternut trees and up wooden stairs to the Cliff Top Trail. Notice the talus boulder slopes along the walls of the escarpment. There is no other way to or from the park entrance, unless you want to take one of the side roads.

Spillway Trail

Level of difficulty 🚶

Distance *1.5km (.9mi) linear*

Approx. time *45min each way*

Markers *Blue*

Trailhead *Carriage Trail*

Other *Mountain biking and horseback riding permitted through portions*

This trail leads along the base of the south outlier with the main escarpment to the other side so that it feels as though you're walking through a canyon. It runs parallel to, and leads to and from, the Bruce Trail.

South Outlier Trail

Level of difficulty 🚶🚶

Distance *3km (1.9mi) loop*

Approx. time *2hrs return*

Markers *Yellow*

Trailhead *Carriage (steep climb) or Bruce trails*

This trail begins (or ends) with a climb up the south outlier, a rock island created by glacial ice eroding the weakened bedrock surrounding it. The trail then loops along the top of the outlier.

Bruce Trail

Level of difficulty 🚶🚶

Distance *6km (3.7mi) linear*

Approx. time *2.5hrs each way*

Markers *White blazes*

Trailhead *The Carriage Trail, County Rd. 8 or 25th side road*

Other *Mountain biking and horseback riding permitted through portions*

This trail leads straight through the park from County Road 8 in the south to the 25th side road in the north. The main escarpment runs parallel to one side of the trail, while the south outlier runs parallel to the other side for about 2km (1.2mi), making you feel as though you are walking through a canyon.

Cliff Top Trail

Level of difficulty 🚶 🚶

Distance *3km (1.9mi) linear*

Approx. time *1.5hrs each way*

Markers *Green*

Trailhead *Carriage Trail, Bruce Trail, Lookout Trail or McCarston's Lake Trail*

This trail leads up a metal staircase and boardwalk called Jacob's Ladder, along the top of the Niagara Escarpment, past two ponds and a stone fountain, across two boardwalks, through an open meadow, and past the foundations of an old farm homestead.

McCarston's Lake Trail

Level of difficulty 🚶 🚶

Distance *4km (2.5mi) semi-circle extension*

Approx. time *2hrs each way*

Markers *Orange*

Trailhead *Two access points from the Cliff Top Trail, one west of the cliff with the metal staircase and another .5km (.3mi) south of the viewing platform*

This loop circles past a glacial kettle lake called McCarston's Lake. It begins on the Cliff Top Trail at the metal staircase and boardwalk, which has been nicknamed Jacob's Ladder, past stunted white cedars and unusual ferns. It then leads along the stony glacial till of the Orangeville moraine, before climbing a glacial bank surrounding the lake into a sugar maple and beech forest, and then onto an old farm lane back to the Cliff Top Trail.

Lookout Trail

Level of difficulty 🚶 🚶

Distance *1km (.6mi) linear*

Approx. time *30min each way*

Markers *Grey*

Trailhead *From the McCarston's Lake, Bruce or Cliff Top trails*

Perhaps not surprisingly, this trail leads up a moraine hill on top of the escarpment to the highest point in Mono Cliffs park. It then returns along the Orangeville moraine.

Nokiidaa Trail along the Holland River

Location *Between Holland Landing and Fairy Lake, Aurora*

Number of trails *1*

Total distance *35km (21mi)*

Approx. time *14hrs*

Interesting features *Holland River*

Trailheads *McKenzie Marsh, Taylor Park, Aurora Leisure Complex, Aurora Town Hall, Lambert Wilson Park, Sheppards Bush Conservation Area, Aurora Community Arboretum, Paul Semple Park, Fairy Lake Park, Roger's Reservoir, Mabel Davis Conservation Area*

Other *Dogs on leashes permitted*

Facilities/services *Parking, toilets, telephones*

The Nokiidaa Trail follows along the shores of the Holland River, which runs from the Oak Ridge Moraine to drain into Cook's Bay on Lake Simcoe. Construction on it began in the year 2000 in three different municipalities—Aurora, Newmarket and East Gwillimbury. By 2006, it had reached 20km (12mi), but didn't yet link together. Today, with the last bridge and underpass completed, it reaches the full 35km (21mi) originally planned. In the future, it may link to the **Lake Simcoe Trail** (see p. 169).

In East Gwillimbury, the Nokiidaa Trail includes five different trails: the Sutton-Zephyr, Simcoe, Anchor Park, Holland River and Roger's Reservoir trails. In Aurora, it includes the Holland River Valley Trail. In Newmarket, it includes the Tom Taylor Trail.

› Getting There

In East Gwillimbury, the trail can be accessed from Ravenshoe Road, Holborn Road, Achor Park, Holland River Boulevard and Roger's Reservoir.

There are several access points in Aurora, including the junction of St. John's Sideroad and Industrial Parkway North, Taylor Park, the Soccer Dome, the Town Hall and Vandorf Sideroad at the Vandorf Woodlot, just west of Bayview Avenue.

In Newmarket, access points are on Mulock Drive, at the junction of Lorne Avenue and Cane Parkway, on Water Street and on Davis Drive.

› Further Information

East Gwillimbury
19000 Leslie St.
Sharon, ON L0G 1V0
☎ 905-478-4282
www.eastgwillimbury.ca

Town of Aurora
PO Box 1000, 1 Municipal Dr.
Aurora, ON L4G 6J1
☎ 905-727-1375 or (905) 727-3123
www.town.aurora.on.ca

Newmarket
PO Box 328, 395 Mulock Dr., STN Main
Newmarket, ON L3Y 4X7
☎ 905-895-5193 or 877-550-5575
www.newmarket.ca

Old Nipissing Colonization Road

Location *Nipissing to Rosseau*

Number of trails *1*

Total distance *112km (67mi)*

Interesting features *Orange Hall, Commanda General Store Museum, homestead ruins*

Facilities/Services *Parking, toilets, telephones, convenience store inns, resorts*

The Old Nipissing Colonization Road Trail follows the steps of early immigrants to Ontario between 1870 and the construction of a railway along a different route in 1886.

The trail wanders through the **French/Severn Forest**, a crown forest that extends for 880,000ha (2.1 million acres), which is now managed by Westwind Forest Stewardship Inc. You'll cross the new Commanda Bridge just past the Commanda General Store Museum, the Rye Crest Hunt Club and the former town of Mecunoma. The Rye Cemetery offers insight into former tragedies in the area, including deaths during childbirth and a big typhoid epidemic.

A white frame house built on the foundations of Alfred Russell's hotel is now labelled "Bummers Roost." Another highlight along the way is an old stone lime kiln that farmers once used to melt down limestone for lime.

South of the village of Magnetawan, the trail follows the road past the Spence cemetery and the Cornball General Store. The trail joins the Seguin Falls Rail Trail (which is part of the **Trans Canada Trail**, see p. 55) in the former village of Seguin Falls. There's also some old ruins of the village, including some stone fireplace and chimneys at this junction.

The trail then leaves the road again to get to Rosseau, on Highway 141.

› Getting There

Join the trail anywhere between Nipissing on Highway 534 and Rosseau, on Highway 141. It also links with the Seguin Trail. For services, it's definitely easiest to explore from a base in Magnetawan.

› Further Information

Woodland Echoes Cottage Resort
PO Box 59
Magnetawan, ON P0A 1P0
☎ 705-387-3866
www.nipissingroad.ca

Discovery Routes Association
1375 Seymour St.
North Bay, ON P1B 9V6
PO Box 248
Whitney, ON K0J 2M0
☎ 705-472-8480
www.discoveryroutes.ca

Petroglyphs Provincial Park

Location *Stoney Lake, 55km (34mi) north of Peterborough*

Number of trails *6*

Total distance *27km (16.7mi)*

Interesting features *Canada's largest concentration of prehistoric Aboriginal rock carvings, glacial lake, waterfalls, white-tailed deer, wolves, coyotes, wild turkeys, ruffed grouse, spring wildflowers*

Facilities/Services *Parking, toilets, telephones, cultural interpretive visitor centre*

Other *Dogs on 2m (7ft) leashes permitted on the trails, but not in the protective building; wheelchairs available at the gatehouse; no camping permitted*

A special outcrop of white crystalline marble (metamorphosed limestone) north of Stoney Lake made a perfect canvas for Algonquian-speaking shamans passing through the area 600 to 1,100 years ago. Over the years, these visitors carved 900 different symbols into the rock, although the reasons for their selection of this site and the precise meaning of the symbols died with the carvers. Still, locals somehow knew to protect the sacred site, and it wasn't until mining prospectors publicized their find in the *Peterborough Examiner* in May 1954 that the world became aware of the petroglyphs. The site became a provincial park in 1976. Today, a giant glass building protects 300 distinct and another roughly 600 faded carvings from wind, frost, algae growth and people.

Known as "Kinomagewapkong" or the "teaching rocks" by the United Anishnaabeg Council, these symbols include turtles, cranes or herons, spiritual boats, snakes, thunderbirds and rabbits. The Curve Lake First Nation has been designated spiritual custodians of the site and often conduct praying, meditation and fasting ceremonies at the site. Visitors might see offerings of sage, tobacco, sweet grass, cedar, feathers, shells and stones left beside particular symbols on the rock. Members of the Curve Lake First Nation also operate the front gate and have been involved in setting up the new visitor centre.

Another important site at this park is McGinnis Lake, a 15 to 16m-deep (45ft) glacial lake. The water in McGinnis is meromictic, which means that the waters at the top and bottom of the lake do not exchange biannually as most lakes do. Instead, this lake has three distinct water layers, each with its own chemical composition. No oxygen exists below 12m (39ft). In July and August, the lake appears a brilliant jade colour, thanks to increased algae at that time. The algae also causes the lake to produce an excess of calcium carbonate so that a whitish-gray clay-like substance, called marl, gets deposited along the basin and shorelines of the lake. In some areas this marl is more than 10m (33ft) deep.

Note: This is a day use only park, so anyone wanting to hike all the trails should begin as soon as it opens at 10am or perhaps park outside the park and walk in. Also, pets are not permitted inside the protected petroglyph building.

› Getting There

Take Northey's Bay Road from Lakefield on Highway 28 or take County Roads 46, 44 and 6 north from Havelock or Norwood on Highway 7.

› Further Information

Petroglyphs Provincial Park
General Delivery
Woodview, ON K0L 3E0
✆ 705-877-2552 or 800-667-1940
www.ontarioparks.com

McGinnis Lake Trail

Level of difficulty 🚶

Distance *2.5km (1.6mi) loop*

Approx. time *1hr return*

Trailhead *East day-use parking lot*

This 2.5km (1.6mi) loop leads to and from glacial McGinnis Lake. You'll notice the jade colour of the water and the white marl deposits. Well worth stopping at, not because it's a long walk, but because it's a pleasant view and easy to get to on the way to the petroglyphs.

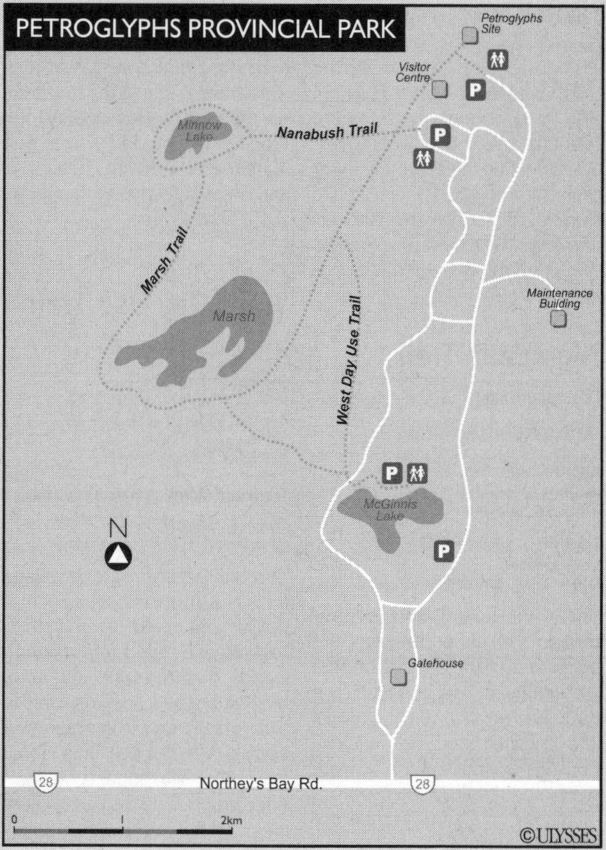

Petroglyphs Trail

Level of difficulty *🚶*

Distance *1km (.6mi) linear*

Approx. time *1hr each way*

Markers *Signs*

Trailhead *Main parking lot*

Other *Wheelchair accessible*

This paved path leads past the washrooms and past the visitor interpretation building to the protective building that has sheltered the petroglyphs since 1984. Please stay on the trail, as there is a lot of poison ivy in the area.

Nanabush Trail

Level of difficulty *🚶*

Distance *5.5km (3.4mi) loop*

Approx. time *2hrs return*

Markers *Red blazes*

Trailhead *Main parking lot*

This trail leads along two long boardwalks, across a bridge, up a steep hill and then along the north shore of Minnow Lake. The granite outcrops here are beautiful and you're likely to see a white-tailed deer running away as you approach. An interpretive booklet describes the Aboriginal legends behind the symbols drawn on the petroglyphs.

High Falls Trail

Level of difficulty 🚶🚶🚶

Distance *8km (5mi) linear*

Approx. time *3hrs each way*

Markers *Blue blazes*

Trailhead *Nanabush Trail*

Other *Camping not permitted*

This is the longest and prettiest trail in the park. It shares the beginning of the Nanabush Trail across a boardwalk and then continues through open meadows and along exposed rock outcroppings. You must climb several steep, rocky hills. Outcroppings of marble and pink granite are visible in places.

The trail ends at the impressive and namesake set of vertical rapids on Eels Creek.

Marsh Trail

Level of difficulty 🚶🚶

Distance *7km (4mi) loop*

Approx. time *3hrs return*

Markers *Yellow blazes*

Trailhead *Main parking lot, close to the washroom*

This is a very hilly trail that leads along a rocky path through a dense red pine forest. You may see beavers, ducks or muskrats on the marshy portion, and the forest is full of chickadees. The Marsh Trail joins the Nanabush and High Falls trails to continue past Minnow Lake.

West Day Use Trail

Level of difficulty 🚶🚶

Distance *5km (3mi) loop*

Approx. time *2hrs return*

Markers *Orange blazes*

Trailhead *Across the road from the west day-use parking lot, in the opposite direction from McGinnis Lake*

This trail begins in a low wetland marsh with occasional stands of poplar and cedar up to a drier, rockier, root-filled trail through stands of pine, oak, and then birch. A bridge leads over a valley created millions of years ago by a glacial meltwater river. In autumn, the path is surrounded by stunning green followed by yellow and orange.

Seguin Trail

Location *Fern Glen Road, just west of Hwy. 11 to Hwy. 69/400 at Parry Sound*

Number of trails *1*

Total distance *75km (45mi)*

Interesting features *Canadian Shield; significant marshes between Bartlett, Doe and Compass lakes*

Other *Pets on leash permitted*

Facilities/Services *Parking*

The Seguin Trail follows the path of the former Ottawa, Arnprior and Parry Sound Railway, which was built in the late 1800's by J.R. Booth. Today, the trail is maintained by the Ontario Ministry of Natural Resources and managed by the Park to Park Association, which promotes the trail between Algonquin and Killbear parks.

› Getting There

Trailheads can be found just across from the Visitor Centre in Parry Sound or on Fern Glen Road, but the trail can be accessed via Highway 518, where it intersects with the highway.

› Further Information

Park to Park Trail Association
70 Church St.
Parry Sound, ON P2A 1Y9
☎ 705-746-7663 x 26 or 888-213-8134
www.parktoparktrail.com

Springwater Provincial Park

Location *Midhurst*

Number of trails *5*

Total distance *15km (9mi)*

Interesting features *Birds of prey, bears, beavers, coyotes, owls, porcupine, raccoons, turkeys and wolves*

Facilities/Services *Parking, toilets, telephones, visitor information centre*

If you have kids, Springwater Provincial Park is an absolute must. The Ontario Ministry of Natural Resources houses injured, orphaned and human-imprinted birds and wildlife that can't be released into nature in specially designed enclosures that provide the animals with an appropriate level of space. Your kids will spend hours watching snowy owls, hawks, porcupines, beavers, raccoons, wild turkeys, wolves, coyotes, bears and other wild animals up close.

For a longer walk through the park, take advantage of three cross-country ski trails that lead through forests and meadows.

› Getting There

Take Highway 26 north from Barrie.

› Further Information

Springwater Provincial Park
1331 Hwy. 26
Midhurst, ON L0L 1X0
☎ 705-728-7393 or 800-667-1940
www.ontarioparks.com

Animal Display Path

Level of difficulty 🚶

Distance *1km (.6mi) multi-loop*

Approx. time *1hr return*

Trailhead *Park office*

Other *Wheelchair accessible; maintained for walking year-round*

This paved path meanders alongside enclosures with glass windows and fences housing a variety of birds and animals that can't be released back into the wild because of permanent injuries or human imprinting that has prevented them from learning to hunt. They might include snowy owls, hawks, porcupines, beavers, raccoons, wild turkeys, wolves, coyotes, white-tailed deer and bears.

William R. Wilson Trail

Level of difficulty 🚶

Distance *1.5km (.9mi) loop*

Approx. time *1hr return*

Trailhead *Parking lot 2*

Other *Maintained for walking in the summer, snowshoeing in the winter*

This nature trail for children describes animals that live in two types of forest and a marsh.

Red Trail

Level of difficulty 🚶 🚶

Distance *5.5km (3.4mi) loop*

Approx. time *3hrs return*

Trailhead *Main parking lot*

This trail leads through a cedar ash forest and a mature red and white pine forest and up and down hills to loop around the periphery of the park.

Green Trail

Level of difficulty 🚶 🚶

Distance *4km (2.5mi) loop*

Approx. time *2hrs return*

Trailhead *Main parking lot*

This trail leads past the waterfowl and wildlife display area through pine, maple and oak forests, into meadows, and along old logging roads to loop around the south end of the park.

Blue Trail

Level of difficulty 🚶

Distance *2.5km (1.6mi) loop*

Approx. time *1hr return*

Trailhead *Main parking lot*

This trail makes a small loop to join some of the best parts of the woodland and nursery trails.

Warsaw Caves Conservation Area

Location *Warsaw*

Number of trails *3*

Total distance *15km (9mi)*

Interesting features *Caves, potholes*

Facilities/Services *Parking, toilets, telephones, showers, swimming*

Other *Dogs on leashes permitted*

Warsaw Caves Conservation Area was closed for eight years before local hero Ian Guest took on the job of running the campground and park in 1999. Lucky for hikers that he did too, because the 224ha (553-acre) site includes some of Ontario's best caves, including one with ice that doesn't melt, plus a lot of potholes, an underground stream, several alvars and a good view of the Drummer moraine. The caves were created when meltwater from the Indian River spillway that drained glacial Lake Algonquin into glacial Lake Iroquois weakened the limestone bedrock.

Bring a flashlight, a helmet and solid boots to explore the caves.

› Getting There

Take County Road 4 north from Warsaw.

› Further Information

White Pine Land Stewardship Services and Otonabee Conservation
250 Milroy Dr.
Peterborough, ON K9H 7M6
☎ 705-652-3161 (summer), 705-745-5791 (winter) or 877-816-7604
www.warsawcaves.com

Scenic Lookout Trail

Level of difficulty 🚶

Distance *4km (2.5mi) linear plus loop*

Approx. time *2hrs return*

Markers *Orange blazed L's*

Trailhead *Cave parking lot*

This hike begins on flat bedrock and leads to an extension that lets you view a variety of potholes (also known as kettles). From here, you either follow a small portion of the trail back to the lookout route or keep following the extension down the edge of the cliff to the Limestone Plain Trail. The Scenic Lookout Trail leads up along a granite ridge, past cedar fences, into a meadow to a lookout. The trail then loops back to the linear section that leads to the parking lot and the kettles.

Limestone Plain Trail

Level of difficulty 🚶🚶

Distance *4km (2.5mi) loop*

Approx. time *2hrs return*

Markers *Orange blazed P's*

Trailhead *Campground*

This relatively flat but rocky trail loops through a rocky forest and along the Indian River. It provides good views of the Drummer moraine, along which the Lookout Trail passes. An extension leads up the side of the moraine to the potholes area.

Limestone Plain Trail

Level of difficulty 🚶🚶🚶

Distance *7km (4mi) loop*

Approx. time *4hrs return*

Trailhead *Cave parking lot*

This trail connects the kettles, the easy Limestone Plain Trail and the Lookout Trail into one long hike. It involves at least four very steep climbs and lots of diverse habitats, including rock plain, forest and meadow.

Wye Marsh Wildlife Centre

Location *Across from the Martyrs' Shrine in Midland*

Number of trails *6*

Total distance *5km (3mi)*

Interesting features *Cattail marsh, trumpeter swans, wildflower garden, bee keeping*

Facilities/Services Parking, toilets, telephones, visitor information centre, gift store

The Wye Marsh Wildlife Centre isn't known for its extensive hiking trails, but what they lack in length, they make up for in content. This 1,000ha (150-acre) nature discovery centre features rare trumpeter swans, a floating boardwalk through the cattail marsh, canoe rentals, an observation tower, a sugar shack and lots of great bird-watching.

Your experience begins at the indigenous wildflower garden right at the entrance of the park. From there, you'll wander back towards the swan pond, where the giant white beauties gather. Then you'll walk across the bridge to the floating boardwalk above the cattail marsh.

Hikers can also take advantage of guided hikes and presentations about snakes, birds of prey, edible plants and astronomy conducted by naturalists throughout the summer.

› Getting There

Take Highway 12 east from Midland.

› Further Information

Wye Marsh Wildlife Centre
16160 E. Hwy. 12, PO Box 100
Midland, ON L4R 4K6
705-526-7809
www.wyemarsh.com

Berm Loop to Tower, via the Floating Boardwalk

Level of difficulty

Distance *.75km (.5mi) loop*

Approx. time *30min return*

Trailhead *Adult swan pond corner fence*

Wye Marsh's fame is due, at least in part, to this floating boardwalk. The boardwalk meanders directly into the marsh to allow hikers a good up-close view of cattails and other wetland plants.

Hardwood Trail

Level of difficulty

Distance *.25km (.2mi) linear*

Approx. time *10min each way*

Trailhead *Visitor centre, adult swan pond*

The Hardwood Trail leads between the visitor centre and the adult swan pond, where you can see the results of Wye Marsh's successful breeding of trumpeter swans.

Return Trail

Level of difficulty

Distance *.25km (.2mi) linear*

Approx. time *10min each way*

Trailhead *Visitor centre, adult swan pond*

The Return Trail also leads between the visitor centre and the adult swan pond.

ID Trail

Level of difficulty *🚶*

Distance *.5km (.3mi) linear*

Approx. time *20min each way*

Trailhead *Visitor centre, adult swan pond corner fence*

The Identification Trail leads from the visitor centre to the adult swan pond. Along the way, placards explain the types of plants that grow in a marsh and the many interesting uses for them, including cattail flour and a fern scrub brush.

Woodland and Muskrat Trails

Level of difficulty *🚶*

Distance *3km (1.9mi) loop*

Approx. time *1hr return*

Trailhead *Adult swan pond corner fence*

The Woodland and Muskrat trails lead in loops through a pine forest at the edge of the marsh.

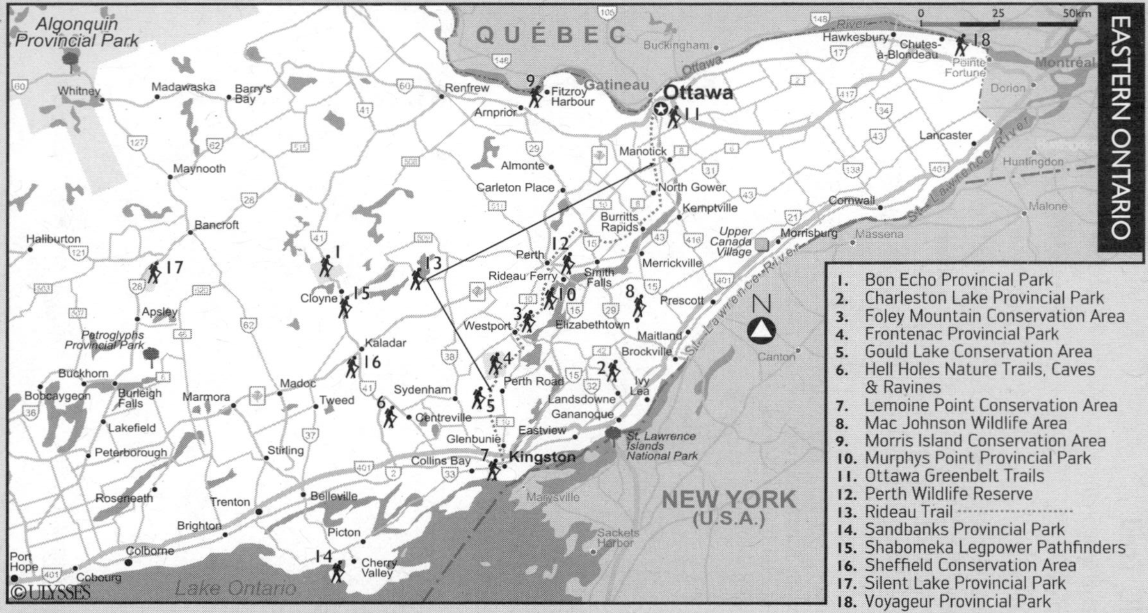
EASTERN ONTARIO
QUÉBEC
NEW YORK
(U.S.A.)
Lake Ontario
Ottawa
Kingston
Algonquin Provincial Park
Petroglyphs Provincial Park
St. Lawrence Islands National Park
Upper Canada Village
St. Lawrence River
Ottawa River
1. Bon Echo Provincial Park
2. Charleston Lake Provincial Park
3. Foley Mountain Conservation Area
4. Frontenac Provincial Park
5. Gould Lake Conservation Area
6. Hell Holes Nature Trails, Caves & Ravines
7. Lemoine Point Conservation Area
8. Mac Johnson Wildlife Area
9. Morris Island Conservation Area
10. Murphys Point Provincial Park
11. Ottawa Greenbelt Trails
12. Perth Wildlife Reserve
13. Rideau Trail
14. Sandbanks Provincial Park
15. Shabomeka Legpower Pathfinders
16. Sheffield Conservation Area
17. Silent Lake Provincial Park
18. Voyageur Provincial Park
0 25 50km
©ULYSSES

Eastern Ontario

Hiking trails in eastern Ontario showcase both natural wonders and marvels of human ingenuity. On the natural side, there are vast plains of gneiss, pink granite mountains and ridges, mixed forests of maple and pine, fields of orchids, vast marshes, beaver dams, smooth lakes and flowing rivers.

Three such natural wonders, **Bon Echo** (see p. 185), **Silent Lake** (see p. 214) and **Foley Mountain** (see p. 189), are so spectacular that they've become destinations in themselves. On the human side, there are rock paintings (such as those found at Bon Echo), stone houses, farm fields, the Rideau Canal, abandoned mines, vast orchards, mills and log cabins. Hikers interested in traces of historical human settlement will enjoy a visit to **Murphys Point Provincial Park** (see p. 203) or the Stony Swamp portion of the **Ottawa Greenbelt Trails** (see p. 205).

Although the Champlain Sea disappeared thousands of years ago, water still defines eastern Ontario's topography, thanks to two great rivers–the St. Lawrence and the Ottawa–that border the region, the Rideau River and canal that cut through the middle, and the many other rivers, lakes and marshes throughout the area. For a good short hike through marsh, woodlands and fields, walk the Coureur des Bois Trail at **Voyageur Provincial Park** (see p. 218) or along Collins Bay at the **Lemoine Point Conservation Area** (see p. 198). A similar but longer hike is possible at the **Morris Island Conservation Area** (see p. 200), which includes a view of a modern Ontario Hydro dam.

All the bodies of water in this region make it a good habitat for a variety of plant and animal species. Wild rice, little bluestem, Indian grass and tall cord grass grow in swamps, while tall wormwood, Russian thistle and sand cherry grow on the sand dunes bordering large lakes, such as those at **Sandbanks** (see p. 212) and **Charleston Lake** (see p. 187) provincial parks. Beavers, muskrats, turtles and river otters inhabit all the lakes and streams, which also attract migrating hawks, geese, herons and blackbirds in great numbers. Many of these creatures can be seen from the **Shabomeka Legpower Pathfinders** (see p. 215) trails. The **Perth Wildlife Reserve** (see p. 210) a refuge for Canada geese, celebrates the season with a migration festival over the best viewing weekend in late October, while the breeding trumpeter swans are almost always visible at the **Mac Johnson Wildlife Area** (see p. 199).

An extension of the Canadian Shield known as the Frontenac Axis (or Frontenac Arch) cuts through this region. For particularly good views of the landscape created by this landform, hike along the bedrock plains of the **Sheffield Conservation Area** (see p. 213), **Frontenac Provincial Park** (see p. 191), or the **Shabomeka Legpower Pathfinders** (see p. 215) area.

After European settlers came, soldiers set up forts while others began logging the forests and mining the rock. To experience a miniature version of the caves they explored, visit **Hell Holes Nature Trails, Caves and Ravines** (see p. 198).

More human ingenuity can be experienced along the **Rideau Trail** (see p. 211), a hiking path along the inland canal between Kingston and Ottawa.

› Tourist Information

Ontario East Economic Development Commission
18980 Beaverbrook Rd.
Martintown Ontario K0C 1S0
866-641-3278
www.onteast.com

Bon Echo Provincial Park

Location *Cloyne*

Number of trails *6*

Total distance *28km (17.5mi)*

Interesting features *Algonquian pictographs, Bon Echo Rock, Kettle Lake*

Facilities/services *Parking, toilets, telephones, visitor information centre, convenience store, canoe rental, playground, swimming beaches, camping, laundry area, showers, fishing, boat launch, Mugwump ferry*

Other *Dogs on leashes permitted, unleashed on* ***Pet Exercise Trail*** *(see p. 187)*

Bon Echo Rock on Mazinaw Lake has been an important spiritual site for at least the past 300 to 1,000 years during which it's estimated the more than 260 Algonquian pictographs on it were completed. The collection, which can only be seen from canoe or boat, is the largest example of Aboriginal rock paintings in Canada. It is so important that the federal government has designated the entire park a National Historic Site.

As impressive as the pictographs are, they aren't the only reason to visit Bon Echo. Another good reason is the rock itself. Known locally as both Bon Echo Rock and Mazinaw Rock, the sheer cliff of hardened pink granite and gneiss rises 100m (328ft) into the air, while it continues another 90m (295ft) below the waterline. The park's most popular hike leads hikers to the top of Bon Echo rock while another popular trail provides a good overall view of the rock from a lookout.

› Getting There

Take Highway 41 north from Kaladar or south from Denbigh.

› Further Information

Bon Echo Provincial Park
RR1
Cloyne, ON K0H 1K0
613-336-2228 or 800-667-1940
www.ontarioparks.com

The Friends of Bon Echo Park
16151 Hwy. 41, RR1
Cloyne, ON K0H 1K0
613-336-0830 or 613-336-9863
www.mazinaw.on.ca/fobecho

Cliff Top Trail

Level of difficulty 🚶

Distance *1km (.6mi) linear*

Approx. time *1hr return plus another 15min for the Mugwump ferry or canoe ride each way*

Trailhead *Mugwump Ferry Wharf past the South Beach parking lot.*

The initial trip across Mazinaw Lake provides a sense of mystery that makes this hike the most enjoyable one in the park. The hike itself leads up stairs to the top of the rock. You're now walking on the Canadian Shield itself!

The whole island has been set aside as a nature reserve zone. You'll often be walking on solid rock, although a couple of boardwalks protect the fragile red oak rock barrens that are capable of growing in the minuscule amount of soil that collects on top of bedrock. You'll see stunted oaks that don't show their 60 to 90 years, stunted white cedars, ground junipers, bush honeysuckles, bearberries and blueberries.

The Abes and Essens Trail

Level of difficulty 🚶 🚶 🚶

Distance *17km (10.5mi) triple loop*

Approx. time *8hrs return*

Markers *Red, yellow and orange disks*

Trailhead *North side of Joeperry Lake Rd., opposite the parking lot on the south side*

Other *Three outhouses and five interior campsites*

This scenic trail is by far the most versatile and interesting in the park. Three loops enable hikers to walk for about 1.5hrs (follow the red disks), 4hrs (follow the red and yellow disks) or the full trip (follow the red, yellow and orange disks).

Bon Echo Creek Trail

Level of difficulty 🚶

Distance *1km (.6mi) linear*

Approx. time *1hr return*

Trailhead *Either from the footbridge south of the Lower Mazinaw Lake parking lot or from the day-use area road, near the bridge*

This trail runs along the south side of Bon Echo Creek to a footbridge near the lake. You have a good chance of seeing beavers and kingfishers along this route.

High Pines Trail

Level of difficulty 🚶

Distance *1.4km (.9mi) loop*

Approx. time *45min return*

Trailhead *Visitors parking lot*

This trail leads along a ridge, through a stand of aspen, a wooded wetland of ferns, a hemlock grove and a stand of red pine to a Bon Echo Rock lookout .

The Shield Trail

Level of difficulty 🚶🚶

Distance *4.8km (3mi) loop*

Approx. time *2.5hrs return*

Trailhead *Parking lot on Joeperry Lake Rd., west of Hwy. 41*

This hike explores the landscape of the Bon Echo area as used by loggers, farmers, miners and resort owners. The trail starts along the Old Addington Road, which served as the entrance to Bon Echo until the construction of Highway 41 in 1935. Along with glacial erratics, fallen trees, an old beaver dam and the marsh, you'll see prospectors' test pits and a hill that used to be a log slide.

Pet Exercise Trail

Level of difficulty 🚶

Distance *2.4km (1.5mi) linear*

Approx. time *1hr each way*

Trailhead *Day-use area parking lot*

This trail, near Bon Echo Creek, is the only area where pets are permitted to roam off their leashes.

Charleston Lake Provincial Park

Location *Landsdowne*

Number of trails *7*

Total distance *35km (21mi)*

Interesting features *Aboriginal rock shelters, Frontenac Axis, pioneer settlement ruins, pitch pine, black rat snakes, pileated woodpeckers*

Facilities/services *Parking, toilets, telephones, visitor information centre, canoe and kayak rental, playground, swimming beaches, camping, laundry area, showers, fishing, boat launch*

Other *Dogs on leashes permitted*

Charleston Lake Provincial Park forms part of the UNESCO-designated Frontenac Arch Biosphere. With a surface area of 26.2km^2 (16 sq mi), its namesake lake is the largest body of water within the biosphere. The park itself covers 23.3km^2 (14 sq mi) or 2,400ha (5,928 acres) of land on the eastern and western shores of the Lake and includes 46 islands.

Currently, hiking trails pass by stands of hemlock, hickory, birch, maple, beech and red cedar which grow on a base of granite, sandstone and igneous rocks. Two additional trails may be built soon: one through Mud Lake and another through the Haskins property that the park purchased a few years ago.

› Getting There

From Highway 401, west of Brockville and east of Gananoque, take County Road 3 north towards Landsdowne. Continue north as the road turns into Outlet Road. Turn right at Charleston Lake Road.

› Further Information

Charleston Lake Provincial Park
148 Woodvale Rd.
Lansdowne, ON K0E 1L0
☎ 613-659-2065 or 800-667-1940
www.ontarioparks.com

Friends of Charleston Lake
www.friendsofcharlestonlake.ca

Charleston Lake Association
www2.ucdsb.on.ca/athens/CharlestonLakeAssoc/index.html

Tallow Rock Bay (Westside Trail)

Level of difficulty 🚶 🚶

Distance *10km (6mi) loop*

Approx. time *4hrs return*

Trailhead *The wheelchair accessible boardwalk west of the Visitor Centre*

This rocky loop leads to Tallow Rock Bay and then along the Charleston Lake shoreline past Beaver Pond and between Slim and Runnings bays.

Sandstone Island Trail

Level of difficulty 🚶

Distance *3.3km (2mi) loop*

Approx. time *2hrs return*

Trailhead *North of the Shady Ridge Campground at Boathouse Cove*

The Gordon Rock Shelter, pioneer home foundations and good views overlooking Charleston Lake are the highlights along this rocky path.

Blue Mountain Trail

Level of difficulty 🚶 🚶

Distance *4km (2.4mi) linear*

Approx. time *2hrs each way*

Trailheads *By water, from Huckleberry Hollow Lake or through private land from Mountain Street, Mallorytown*

This trail runs between Huckleberry Hollow Bay and Mountain Street. An midpoint extension leads to the top of Blue Mountain, the highest point in Leeds and Grenville County.

Quiddity Trail

Level of difficulty 🚶

Distance *2km (1.2mi) linear*

Approx. time *30 min each way*

Trailhead *To the west of the Visitor Centre, across the wheelchair accessible boardwalk*

This trail begins on wetland boardwalks and ends at rocky ledges overlooking Whitefish Island in Runnings Bay.

Hemlock Ridge Trail

Level of difficulty 🚶

Distance *2km (1.2mi) loop*

Approx. time *1.5hrs return*

Trailhead *Parking lot east of the Visitor Centre*

This trail features the most common trees of the Great Lakes–St. Lawrence Forest Region, including hemlock, hickory, hop hornbeam, red cedar, silver maple, American elm, black ash and yellow birch.

Beech Woods Trail

Level of difficulty 🚶

Distance *1.5km (.9mi) loop*

Approx. time *30min return*

Trailhead *East of the Visitor Centre*

This short loop passes through forest and old pioneer pasture. A guidebook highlights deer, the black rat snake and other park fauna.

Shoreline Centennial Trail

Level of difficulty 🚶

Distance *2km (1.2mi) loop*

Approx. time *1hr return*

Trailhead *Boathouse Cove*

The Shoreline Centennial Trail loops around the tip of Charleston Lake to some canoe-in/hike-in campsites on Buckhorn Bay.

Foley Mountain Conservation Area

Location *County Rd. 10 near Westport*

Number of trails *6*

Total distance *9km (5mi)*

Interesting features *Spy Rock, view over Westport, beavers*

Facilities/services *Parking, toilets, telephones, interpretive centre; cost of admission $5/vehicle, $2 to walk or bicycle in, $40 for an annual pass*

Foley Mountain sits on a granite ridge, 65m (200ft) above the village of Westport. Squirrels, white-tailed deer, rabbits, fishers, pine martens, bobcats and porcupines also live in the park. Sightings have been made of more than 100 species of birds, including warblers, which breed in the area. The conservation area's 325ha (800 acres) of land are owned and operated by the Rideau Valley Conservation Authority.

› Getting There

Take Highway 42 until it ends at Westport, and continue across the bridge to County Road 10 or take County Road 10 from Perth. The entrance is to the east on the hill.

› Further Information

Area supervisor
Rebecca Whitman

Friends of Foley Mountain
105 N. Perth Rd., PO Box 244
Westport, ON K0G 1X0
☎ 613-273-3255

Rideau Valley Conservation Authority
PO Box 599, 3889 Rideau Valley Dr.
Manotick, ON K4M 1A5
☎ 613-692-3571 or 800-267-3504
http://rvca.ca/careas/foley/index.htm

Blue Circle Trail

Level of difficulty 🚶🚶🚶

Distance *3km (1.8mi) loop*

Approx. time *2hrs return*

Trailheads *Spy Rock parking lot*

This loop trail leads from Spy Rock, past a lookout over Westport Pond and then through the forest. Rideau Trail hikers use almost half of it via both the main and side trails.

Beaver Trail

Level of difficulty 🚶

Distance *1.2km (.7mi) loop*

Approx. time *45min return*

Trailhead *The north side of the Foley Mountain Conservation Rd. (parking lot on south side)*

FOLEY MOUNTAIN CONSERVATION AREA

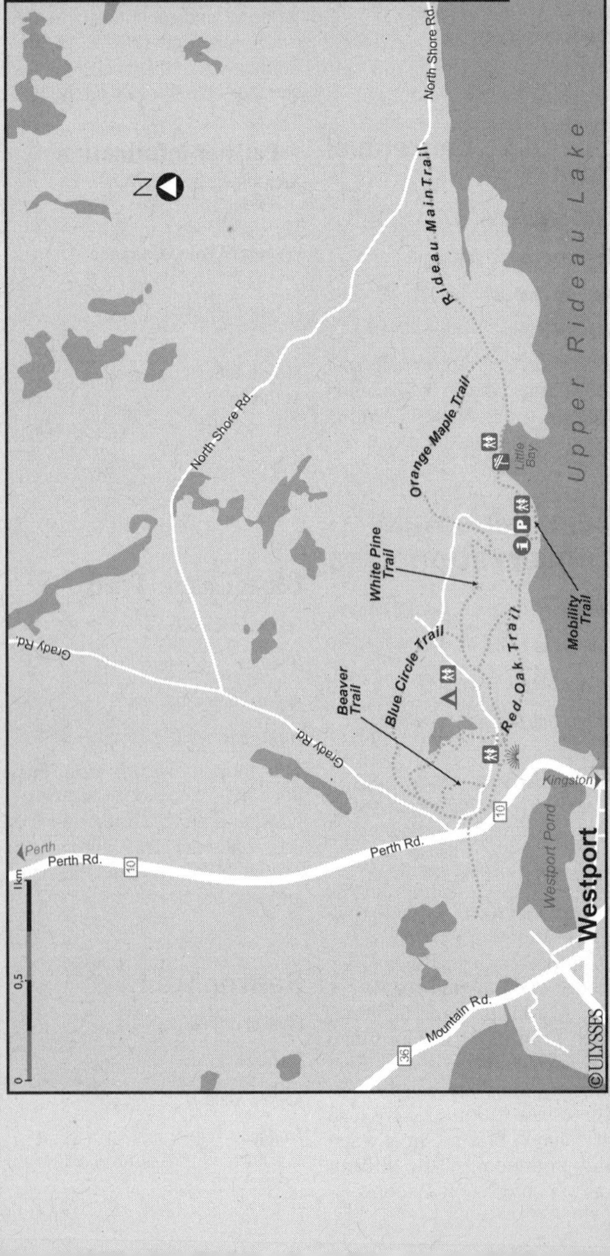

The Beaver Trail loops around an old beaver pond that is now transforming into marsh, providing ideal feeding grounds for herons. Most of the trail leads through pine forests, stands of trembling aspen and alongside the marsh. A large rock lookout offers a good view of the pond.

Orange Maple Trail

Level of difficulty 🚶 🚶

Distance *2.5km (1.5mi) loop*

Approx. time *1hr return*

Trailhead *Interpretive centre*

A rocky trail leads from the Interpretive Centre past a sandy beach and through the forest for a good view of the Frontenac Arch Biosphere.

Mobility Trail

Level of difficulty 🚶

Distance *291m (955ft) loop*

Approx. time *30min return*

Trailhead *Parking lot*

This short stone-dust trail offers a brief respite for wheelchair users or those with young children in strollers.

Red Oak Trail

Level of difficulty 🚶 🚶

Distance *1.8km (1mi) loop*

Approx. time *30min return*

Trailhead *Spy Rock parking lot*

A trail leads from the Spy Rock Lookout east along the ridge for a good look at Upper Rideau Lake and then loops back to join part of the Blue Circle trail

White Pine Trail

Level of difficulty 🚶

Distance *200m (650ft) linear*

Approx. time *10min each way*

Trailhead *Orange Maple, Blue Circle and Red Oak trails*

This short trail offers the easiest walk between the Interpretive Centre and the Spy Rock Lookout and is used as part of a Rideau side trail.

Frontenac Provincial Park

Location *Sydenham, 40km north of Kingston*

Number of trails *12*

Total distance *132km (82mi)*

Interesting features *beaver ponds, 20th century homestead remains, Moulton Gorge, abandoned mines, black rat snakes, waterfalls, rugged Canadian Shield hiking, numerous rock ridges and lookouts*

Facilities/services *Parking, toilets, telephones, visitor information centre and gift shop, interior camping, canoe launch, wilderness courses*

Other *Open year round; 48 interior campsites available year yound*
Reservations recommended and permits required for day use and interior camping
Dogs on leashes permitted

Frontenac park offers hikers a peaceful experience, living up to the creed of its first superintendent, R. Bruce Page, who believed that wilderness should be as untouched by humans as possible. Although once heavily settled by farmers, miners, loggers, and then cottagers, the park now feels relatively empty. The last seasonal resident left in 1991, and now only hikers, campers, anglers, cross-country skiers, snowshoers, backpackers and canoeing enthusiasts frequent the area. Unless you happen to visit on one of the weekends when volunteers offer a variety of wilderness survival courses, you're not likely to meet anyone other than the park employee who looks after your day permit or back country camping reservation and perhaps a park ranger, warden or interior volunteer in the backcountry.

What you *will* see, however, is a wide variety of plants and animals. The 5,214ha (12,878 acres) park lies directly on the southern tip of the Frontenac Axis and is a transition zone between southern and northern types of forest. It's a great location for identifying over 750 species of vascular plants. Thirty-nine different mammals live here, including bears, beavers, coyotes, deer, fox, minks, moose, otters, fishers, porcupines and wolves. There are 30 species of reptiles and amphibians, including the rare five-lined skink. About 197 bird species nest in or migrate through the park, including barred owls, great blue herons, hawks, eagles, kingbirds, kingfishers, ospreys, turkey vultures, wood ducks, and various woodpeckers.

› Getting There

Take County Road 38 south from Sharbot Lake or north from Kingston. Turn east on Desert Lake Road (County Road 19) at Verona. After 22km (14mi), turn north onto Salmon Lake Road and continue to the park entrance. If coming from Kingston up County Road 38, you can also turn right at Harrowsmith on Rutledge Road to Sydenham. Turn north on Bedford Road (County Road 19) and continue past the village for 12km (7mi) to the park entrance.

› Further Information

Frontenac Provincial Park
1090 Salmon Lake Rd., PO Box 11
Sydenham, ON K0H 2T0
☎ 613-376-3489, 888-668-7275 or 800-667-1940
www.ontarioparks.com

The Friends of Frontenac Park
PO Box 2237
Kingston, ON K7L 5J9
www.frontenacpark.ca

Arab Lake Gorge Trail

Level of difficulty 🚶

Distance *1.5km (.9mi) loop*

Approx. time *45min return*

Trailhead *Park Office*

This trail leads along the Arab Lake Gorge, a valley created either by a fault or crack in the earth's crust, or by an intrusion of softer rock that eroded faster than the hard diorite around it. Boardwalks and woodland trails lead through the valley, forest, and an abandoned field.

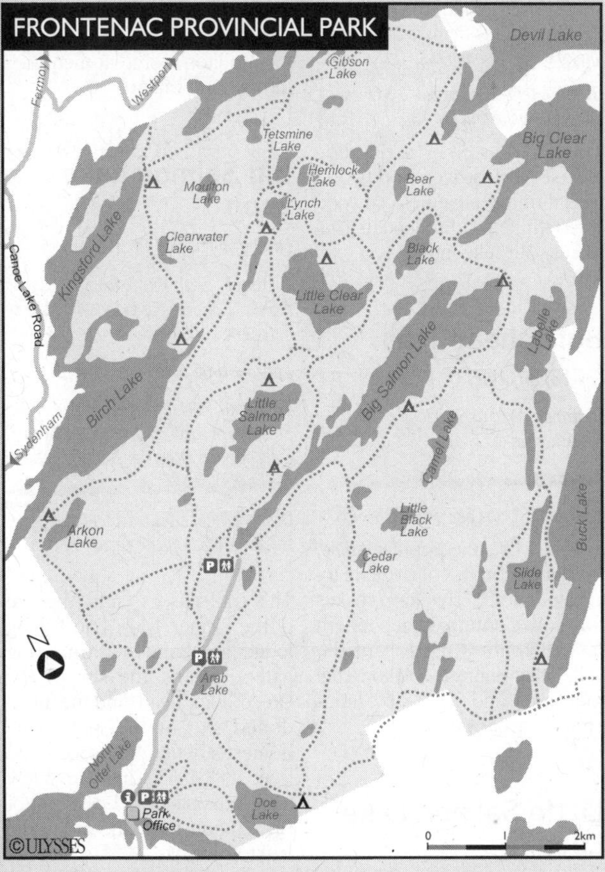

Doe Lake Trail

Level of difficulty

Distance *3km (1.9mi) loop*

Approx. time *1 to 2hrs return*

Trailhead *Park Office*

The Doe Lake Trail leads around the shores of two lakes past a few beaver ponds and the old Kemp mine dating from 1900. Two interesting lookouts–one a rock overlooking South Otter Lake and the other over Doe Lake–as well as many animals and a very easy walk make this a great trail to do with children.

Arkon Lake Loop

Level of difficulty

Distance *13km (8mi) loop plus 1.9km (1.2mi) linear extension*

Approx. time *4 to 5hrs return*

Trailhead Either of two parking lots at the Park Office or the Arab Lake parking lot on Big Salmon Lake Rd.

Other 4 tent sites available on Birch Lake, campsite cluster #7

This trail passes by a ring bog and several beaver ponds and then through a mature hardwood forest. Take the Bufflehead Trail to cut your hike in half.

Bufflehead Trail

Level of difficulty 🚶🚶

Distance 8km (4.8mi) loop (half of the Arkon Lake Loop)

Approx. time 2 to 2.5hrs

Trailhead Arab Lake parking lot

This trail cuts the popular Arkon loop in half to a comfortable 2–2.5 hour walk. This loop makes for a nice intermediate length trail. It follows the top of the valley that drains the Arkon Trail loop area and passes by numerous beaver ponds.

Little Salmon Lake Loop

Level of difficulty 🚶🚶

Distance 15km (9.3mi) loop plus 4km (2.4mi) linear extension if starting at the Park Office

Approx. time 4 to 5hrs return

Trailhead The parking lot at the end of Big Salmon Lake Rd., or the Big Salmon Lake or Arkon Lake Trail

Other 8 tent sites available along this loop: 4 on Big Salmon Lake at campsite cluster #3 and 4 on Little Salmon Lake at campsite cluster #6

This trail leads through mature hardwood bush to a view over the Moulton Gorge. It then goes through the valley.

Big Salmon Lake Loop

Level of difficulty 🚶🚶🚶

Distance 19km (12mi) loop plus 4.5km (2.8mi) linear extension if starting at the Park Office

Approx. time 4 to 6hrs return

Trailhead Parking lot at the end of Big Salmon Lake Rd., or park at the Arab Lake parking lot or the parking lots at the Park Office

Other 17 tent sites available along this loop, at campsite clusters #3, 4, 5, 6 and 13

This trail passes cliffs, the site of the former Trails End fishing lodge, an abandoned truck, the gateposts and the site of the Green homestead, and the abandoned site of the McComish homestead that was occupied from 1881-1953. There are a few high lookouts at the east end of Big Salmon Lake and along the trail to campsite 13.

Little Clear Lake Loop

Level of difficulty 🚶

Distance 9km (5.6mi) loop plus 7.5km (4.7mi) linear extension

Approx. time 5hrs return if starting at Big Salmon Lake parking lot

Trailhead Big Salmon Lake parking lot

Other Four tent sites available at cluster #9 on Little Clear Lake, also *available are 4 campsites at cluster #12 on Lynch Lake*

This trail leads around the shores of Little Clear Lake. The site of the Green homestead with its old gateposts, the abandoned truck "Old Thor" and the clearing and foundations of the Hardwood Bay Farm are all on or near this loop.

Tetsmine Lake Loop

Level of difficulty 🚶 🚶

Distance *12km (7mi) loop plus 9.6km (6mi) linear extension if starting at the Big Salmon Lake parking lot*

Approx. time *4 hours if starting at Kingsford Dam at the north end of the park, or 8 to 10 hrs return if starting from the Big Salmon Lake parking lot or the Park Office*

Trailhead *Kingsford Dam (at the north end of the park) or Big Salmon Lake / Park Office parking lots*

Other *12 tent sites available, 4 on Kingsford Lake at campsite cluster #11 and 4 on Birch Lake at cluster #8 and 4 at campsite cluster #12 on Lynch Lake*

Hemlock Lake Loop

Level of difficulty 🚶

Distance *5km (3mi) loop, plus 9.5km (6mi) linear extension if starting from the Big Salmon Lake parking lot or the Park Office parking lots*

Approx. time *6 to 9hrs return*

Trailhead *Big Salmon Lake parking lot*

This trail features mature hardwood trees, abandoned homestead fields, marshes, beaver ponds and Hemlock Lake.

Gibson Lake Loop

Level of difficulty 🚶 🚶 🚶

Distance *11km (6.8mi) loop, plus 11.5km (7mi) linear extension if starting from the Big Salmon Lake parking lot or the Park Office*

Approx. time *5 to 14hrs return (5 hrs from Kingsford Dam at the north end or 10 to 14hrs from the BIg Salmon Lake or Park Office parking lots)*

Trailhead *Kingsford Dam (at the north end of the Park) or Big Salmon Lake / Park Office parking lots*

Other *4 tent sites available at Hardwood Bay on Devil Lake at campsite cluster #10*

This trail crosses and follows rock ridges past the remains of the Crab Lake mining shanty, through mature hardwood forests and past the Rathkopf Fen.

Cedar Lake Loop

Level of difficulty 🚶 🚶

Distance *15km (9.3mi) loop, plus 1.8km (1mi) linear extension if starting at the Park Office*

Approx. time *5 to 6hrs return*

Trailhead *Park Office parking lot or Arab Lake parking lot down Big Salmon Lake Rd.*

Other *3 tent sites available at campsite cluster #2 on Doe Lake*

The Cedar Lake Trail leads through and over several wetlands. The trail also includes a lookout over Doe Lake. Part of the trail is shared with the **Rideau Trail** (see p. 211). Hikers on the Rideau Trail must report to the Park Office when hiking through the park.

Slide Lake Loop

Level of difficulty 🚶🚶🚶

Distance *21km (13mi) loop, plus 4.6km (2.9mi) linear extension if starting at the Arab Lake parking lot*

Approx. time *8 to 12hrs return*

Trailhead *Park Office or Arab Lake parking lots*

Other *7 tent sites available, 3 at Doe Lake at campsite cluster #2 and 4 at North Bay (Buck Lake) at cluster #1*

This remote trail leads through mixed forests as well as the rockiest, most rugged portion of the park. It can be arduous in the summer heat as it passes over bare exposed granite bedrock. Carry plenty of fluids and hike with a partner. Help is far away. The **Rideau Trail** (see p. 211) also passes through here and hikers must report to the Park Office before venturing into this area.

The trail name comes from an old log slideway at Slide Lake and a small waterfall leads from Slide to Buck Lake. Several good lookouts offer views over both lakes.

Gould Lake Conservation Area

Location *Glenburnie*

Number of trails *10*

Total distance *20km (12mi)*

Interesting features *Gould Lake, barn foundation, Millhaven Creek headwaters, former mica mines, beach, ospreys, turtles*

Facilities/services *Parking, toilets, barn, admission fee $4.50 per adult, $2 per child, $11 maximum per vehicle, $65 annual pass, canoe and kayak or paddle boat rentals*

Gould Lake Conservation Area protects 489ha (1,455 acres) of Frontenac Axis wilderness surrounding half of the 590ha (1,457 acres) lake shoreline. Gould Lake is cold and deep, roughly 21m (70ft) deep on average, although some spots go down to 60m (197ft).

Hikers will enjoy seeing the many species of birds in this region, including a great many sorts of ducks plus ospreys and blue herons.

› Getting There

From Highway 401 at Kingston, take Sydenham Road north to County Road 5. Turn left and continue to Wheatley Street. Continue north as Wheatly turns into George and Bedford streets and then becomes County Road 19. Turn left at Alton Road and turn right immediately onto Rosedale Road. Turn left onto Freeman Road and then right onto Gould Lake Road.

› Further Information

Cataraqui Region Conservation Authority
1641 Perth Rd., PO Box 160
Glenburnie, ON K0H 1S0
☎ 613-546-4228
www.cataraquiregion.on.ca/lands/gould.htm

Tom Dixon, East, Famous, Bedford Road and Wagon Loop

Level of difficulty 🚶🚶🚶

Distance *7.5km (4.5mi) loop*

Approx. time *3hrs return*

Trailhead *Parking lot next to the barn*

This loop combines four trails and a road to make a pleasant loop along the east shore of Gould Lake and the barn. It's best to begin on the Tom Dixon Trail, named after a student employee who drowned in 1971. This is the more difficult part of the loop.

Walking eases slightly past East Bay and on the East Trail, which swerves around the wetlands to Famous Trail. Famous Trail leads to a boardwalk to Bedford Road.

Turn right (south) on Bedford and look for the entrance to the Wagon Trail on the right. Wagon Trail follows an old road used to service the mica mines in 1890 and makes for a nice easy walk back to the barn.

Mica Loop

Level of difficulty ✦ ✦ ✦

Distance *2km (1.2mi) loop*

Approx. time *2hrs return*

Trailhead *Tom Dixon Trail*

This rocky winding loop follows the shore of Gould Lake past several mica pits and is a worthwhile extension to the Tom Dixon, East, Famous, Bedford Road and Wagon Loop.

Rideau Trail

Level of difficulty ✦ ✦ ✦

Distance *8.5km (5mi) linear*

Approx. time *3hrs each way*

Trailheads *Park entrance, Bedford Road north of Salmon Lake Road*

The Rideau Trail Association follows a trail along the western shore of Gould Lake, past several mica mine pits and along the Marion Webb Boardwalk bridge, which is named after a local social worker and was rebuilt in 2008.

Mine Loop with Crossover Trail

Level of difficulty ✦ ✦ ✦

Distance *2.2km (1.3mi) loop, divided by a .3km (.2mi) Crossover Trail in the middle*

Approx. time *2hrs return*

Trailhead *Rideau Trail, between Frog and Hill junctions*

This loop circles a section of land that juts into Gould Lake. Several mine pits are visible and part of the trail follows an old mining road.

Point Spur

Level of difficulty ✦ ✦ ✦

Distance *.3km (.2mi) linear*

Approx. time *20min each way*

Trailhead *Mine Loop*

This rocky trail leads to a point of land offering great overviews of Gould Lake all along its length.

Ridgewalk

Level of difficulty ✦ ✦

Distance *1.8km (1mi) linear*

Approx. time *1hr each way*

Trailheads *Rideau Trail in the middle and at the south end of Gould Lake*

This side trail lies to the west of the main trail and offers hikers a good loop alternative with the main trail.

Hell Holes Nature Trails, Caves & Ravines

Location *Centreville*

Number of trails *1*

Total distance *3.2km (1.9mi) loop*

Time *1hr return*

Interesting features *Stone bridge, caves*

Facilities/services *Parking, toilets, visitor information centre, convenience store, flashlight rental, mini-golf, admission fee $6.50, youth aged 5 to 15 $4.50*

› Getting There

From Highway 401 at Napanee, take Highway 41 north to Centreville Road. Turn right to get to the entrance of Hell Holes.

› Further Information

Hell Holes Nature Trails, Caves & Ravines
RR1
Centreville, ON K0K 1N0
☎ 613-388-2284
www.ruralroutes.com/hellholes

Rob and Evelyn Storring started up Hell Holes after receiving lots of requests to see the caves on their land. A short trail leads past a dynamited cave, a stone bridge and a marsh to the Hell Hole Cave. Climb a steel ladder down 7.5m (24 ft) and use your flashlight to explore a three-cavern cave.

Lemoine Point Conservation Area

Location *Kingston*

Number of trails *4*

Total distance *11km (6.6mi)*

Interesting features *Collins Bay, Lake Ontario, native plant nursery, spring wildflowers, red oak plantation*

Facilities/services *Parking, toilets, beach*

Lemoine Point offers a pleasant outdoor walk through the forest and along the shore of Lake Ontario for anyone in the Kingston area. Formerly settled by French immigrants, United Empire Loyalists, retired British Army officer William Lemoine (after whom it is named) and a prominent industrialist who used the farm nearby as a summer retreat from his business in the United States.

Local volunteers have planted a native plant garden and many trees. They also hold a native plant sale every spring.

› Getting There

Take Highway 33 west from Kingston to Baybridge Drive. Take Baybridge Drive south one block to Coverdale Drive. Turn right (west) on Coverdale Drive to get to the north entrance. To get to the south entrance, continue south on Baybridge Drive to Front Road. Turn right (west) to get to the conservation area.

> Further Information

Cataraqui Region Conservation Authority
1641 Perth Rd., PO Box 160
Glenburnie, ON K0H 1S0
☎ 613-546-4228
www.cataraquiregion.on.ca/lands/lemoine.htm

Shore Trail and Meadowlark Lane

Level of difficulty 🚶

Distance *9km (5.4mi) loop*

Approx. time *2hrs return*

Trailheads *North or south parking lots*

The main trail at Lemoine Point Conservation area loops around the edge of the conservation land. Highlights include views along the shore of Lake Ontario and the beach. A spur inland leads to the main road, where a wildflower garden is located.

Hickory Lane and Trillium Trail

Level of difficulty 🚶

Distance *2km (1.2mi) loop*

Approx. time *30min return*

Trailheads *Shore Trail at Lake Ontario in the south or at its link with the Meadowlark Lane in the north or from the middle of the service road that crosses through the centre of the Conservation area.*

An interior loop through the forest is known as the Trillium Trail. It can be reached from its own spur in the north or Hickory Lane in the south.

Mac Johnson Wildlife Area

Location *Elizabethtown (north of Brockville)*

Number of trails *5*

Total distance *11km (6.6mi) loop*

Time *2 hrs return*

Interesting features *Buells Creek Reservoir, trumpeter swans, Broome-Runciman Dam, osprey nest, cat tail swamps, boardwalk, farm ruins from 1860, glacial sea sand dunes*

Facilities/services *Parking, toilets, picnic shelter, barbecues, firepit*

Other *Canoeing on the Reservoir*

Although it was named after a local volunteer in 1987, locals still call the Mac Johnson Wildlife Area the "Back Pond" after the large body of water that helps prevent the Buells Creek System from overflowing. The reservoir has so many species of plant and animal life living in it that it has been classified as a class 1 provincially significant wetland. The Conservation Area contains 532 ha (1314 acres) of wetland, field and forest.

Although there are five separately named trails, they link together nicely into a single hike, starting and finishing next to the osprey nesting platform near the dock. The small loop around the picnic shelter, the osprey platform and the trumpeter swan compound is known as the Wildflower Loop. From there, you follow the shore of the reservoir along the Railway Trail, the Old Woods Trail, the Boardwalk Trail and the Jack Pine Trail, which loops along the shore of the reservoir to another parking lot.

The return walk goes through some fields, before crossing the boardwalk again. Highlights on the return section through a forest include some pioneer ruins, sand dunes that once bordered the glacial Champlain Sea and now serve as turtle habitat, and the Joyce Farmstead.

› Getting There

Take Highway 29 north from Brockville for 4km. Turn west at Tincap onto Debruge Road and continue for 3km to the main entrance of the conservation area.

› Further Information

Friends of Mac Johnson Wildlife Area
4671 Debruge Rd.
Elizabethtown, ON K6T 1A5
www.cybertap.com/~macjohnson/

Cataraqui Region Conservation Authority
1641 Perth Rd., PO Box 160
Glenburnie, ON K0H 1S0
☎ 613-546-4228
www.cataraquiregion.on.ca/lands/macj.htm

Morris Island Conservation Area

Location *On the Ottawa River between Arnprior and Fitzroy Harbour*

Number of trails *6*

Total distance *15km (9.3mi)*

Interesting features *Ottawa River Islands, view of Chats Falls Hydro Dam, marble outcrops, trilliums*

Facilities/services *Parking, toilets, canoe launch*

Other *Dogs on leashes permitted*

This 47ha (116-acre) conservation area is run by the Mississippi Valley Conservation Authority, but is used and maintained by local residents. The neighbours' caring attitude really shows: the conservation area is clean, litter free, and well cared for.

All the small islands and diverse habitats along the shores of the Ottawa River combine to make this conservation area special. You also get a good view of the Chats Falls Hydro Dam.

› Getting There

Take Highway 17 west from Kanata or east from Arnprior to County Road 22. Turn north towards Galetta. The next right after the town is Loggers' Way. Follow the road around until it reaches Morris Island Drive. Turn right. The conservation area is at the back of the first bend.

› Further Information

Mississippi Valley Conservation Authority
PO Box 268
Lanark, ON K0G 1K0
☎ 613-259-2421
www.mvc.on.ca

The Accessible Track

Level of difficulty 🚶

Distance *1km (.6mi) loop*

Approx. time *3hrs return*

Trailhead *Parking lot*

Other *Wheelchair-accessible*

This wheelchair-accessible path leads from the parking lot behind the washroom, along the shore

MORRIS ISLAND CONSERVATION AREA

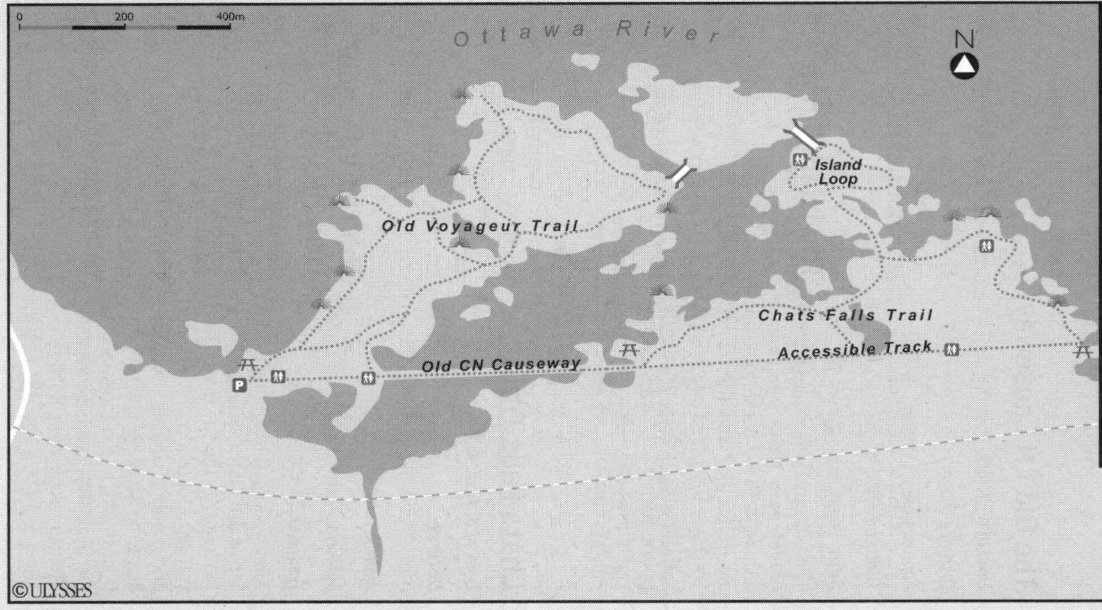

of the Ottawa River, to the canoe launch and the causeway.

The Old CN Causeway

Level of difficulty 🚶

Distance *2.5km (1.6mi) linear*

Approx. time *1hr return*

Trailhead *Parking lot*

Other *Wheelchair-accessible*

The old causeway makes a good gravel path that's wheelchair accessible. Two decks look out across the bay and the marsh. You'll see lots of old tree stumps, cattails and reeds, and many poison ivy bushes. There are several trails to the right towards the railway, but they're closed.

Chats Falls Trail

Level of difficulty 🚶 🚶

Distance *5km (3mi) semicircle to and from the causeway*

Approx. time *2hrs return*

Markers *Yellow triangles*

Trailhead *The CN Causeway*

After walking through the woods for about 2min, you get to a lookout over the bay from which you can spot resident blue herons and egrets. The path continues along the bay shore and over four boardwalks to the lookout over the Chats Falls hydroelectric dam. The dam dates from 1929.

Ambush Shortcut

Level of difficulty 🚶

Distance *100m (328ft) linear*

Approx. time *10min each way*

Trailhead *Chats Falls Trail*

This small extension shortens the Chats Falls Trail and leads to a good lookout.

The Island Loop

Level of difficulty 🚶 🚶

Distance *1km (.62mi) loop*

Approx. time *30min return*

Markers *Purple triangles*

Trailhead *Chats Falls Trail*

Lots of roots and rocks poke their way up along this trail and the path frequently loops around fallen trees. Three lookouts along the trail emphasize the Ottawa River's historical importance as a log transportation route.

The Old Voyageur Trail

Level of difficulty 🚶 🚶

Distance *5km (3mi) loop*

Approx. time *1.5hrs return*

Markers *Blue triangles*

Trailhead *Parking lot*

The trail system to the left of the parking lot includes a double loop with good views out onto the Ottawa River and the railway trestle.

Murphys Point Provincial Park

Location *South of Perth*

Number of trails *5*

Total distance *16.5km (10.2mi)*

Interesting features *McParlan House, Silver Queen Mine and Bunkhouse, Rocky Narrows Beach, black rat snakes (Ontario's only constrictor), waterfall*

Facilities/services *Parking, toilets, telephones, visitor information centre, convenience store, swimming beaches, camping, laundry area, showers*

Other *Dogs on leashes permitted*

Murphys Point's location directly on top of the Frontenac Axis gave European settlers many challenges. Shallow soil covers the bedrock in the area, and farming was next to impossible. Mining and logging was good, however, and a few farmers made a living supplying and housing the miners. Hiking trails at Murphys Point highlight the experiences of these successful early settlers.

One trail leads to McParlan House, a fully restored log cabin and shed originally built by Reuben Sherwood in 1812. The Sylvan Trail features a mature hardwood forest, similar to–although younger than–the forests Sherwood would have seen, and the Point Trail provides stunning views over Big Rideau Lake.

The Silver Queen Mine Trail, which begins at the Lally Homestead and leads to an abandoned mica mine, showcases both the mine and a farmer who sold food to miners. Lantern-lit guided hikes through the restored mine take place once or twice during the summer, or hikers can follow the Silver Queen Mine Trail past the site itself and a series of test pits.

› Getting There

Take County Road 1 south from Perth or north from the town of Rideau Ferry. (Stop at the General Store in Rideau Ferry for the best butter tarts in Ontario.) Turn west onto Lanark County 21, also known as Elm Grove Road. Drive for 12km (7.4mi). The provincial park is on the left.

› Further Information

Murphys Point Provincial Park
RR5
Perth, ON K7H 3C7
☎ 613-267-5060 or 800-667-1940
www.ontarioparks.com

Friends of Murphy's Point Park
www.friendsofmurphyspoint.ca

Silver Queen Mine and Beaver Pond Trails

Level of difficulty 🚶

Distance *2.5km (1.6mi) loop*

Approx. time *1.5hr return*

Trailhead *Parking lot at the Lally Homestead on Elm Grove Rd.*

This trail begins across from the Lally Homestead. It then follows a gravel roadbed through abandoned farm fields to a mica mine that opened in 1903. After passing several test pits and a bunkhouse, the path continues along a boardwalk, past an old beaver dam and back to the Lally Homestead.

McParlan House Trail and Loon Lake Loop

Level of difficulty 🚶

Distance *3km (1.9mi) loop plus extension*

Approx. time *1.5hrs return*

Trailhead *The road leading past campsites 40 to 46*

Instead of driving to the trail head, consider walking to this trail from the visitor centre/store parking lot. You'll probably see deer crossing the road near the lily-pad-covered pond between the store and the registration gate.

Although the Loon Lake Loop and the McParlan House Trail have separate trailheads from the road, they join together at a canoe portage. For a looped hike, begin at the Loon Lake trailhead and return via the better-marked McParlan House Trail. The Loon Lake Loop leads alongside a lake, while the McParlan House Trail follows an old carriage road through a maple and birch forest.

Both trails lead to an extension trail to the McParlan House and beyond to the **Rideau Trail** (see p. 211). You'll walk along Black Creek, past a bog to a small bridge with a waterfall. This trail is worth doing just for this view.

Walk over the bridge and up the hill to McParlan House, a one-and-a-half-storey log cabin and storehouse. The back door should be open, if you want to see inside.

Rideau Trail

Level of difficulty 🚶

Distance *6.5km (1.9mi) linear*

Approx. time *2.5hrs each way*

Trailhead *The McParlan House Trail*

The portion of the **Rideau Trail** (see p. 211) in this park follows Black Creek and Black Ance Road through open pastureland and some bush, past beaver floods and beyond the park to Big Rideau Lake.

Point Trail

Level of difficulty 🚶

Distance *5.5km (3.4mi) loop*

Approx. time *1.5hrs return*

Trailhead *Parking lot at the end of Rideau Rd.*

The Point Trail leads hikers around the very tip of Murphys Point, providing a good view of Big Rideau Lake and Noble Bay.

Sylvan Trail

Level of difficulty 🚶🚶

Distance *2.5km (1.6mi) loop*

Approx. time *1.5hrs return*

Trailhead *Day-use parking lot at Noble Bay*

Lots of rocks, a steep hill and big roots make this the most challenging trail at Murphys Point. The path leads through a mature coniferous forest to a lookout over Noble Bay.

Ottawa Greenbelt Trails

Location *A crescent-shaped area bordering the city of Ottawa to the south*

Number of trails *28 (two combined)*

Total distance *113km (70mi)*

Interesting features *Abandoned quarry that supplied the sandstone used in the Parliament Buildings, restored log farmhouse, orchards, sand dunes, marsh, sphagnum peat bog and boreal forest, mineral springs, migratory bird staging*

Facilities/services *None*

Other *Dogs on leashes permitted everywhere except Britannia Conservation Area*

The National Greenbelt encompasses 20,000ha (49,400 acres) of land that was set aside as a green space in 1950 to prevent the city of Ottawa from expanding in an urban sprawl. The important natural areas it encompasses include:

- Shirley's Bay, an 800ha (1,946-acre) backwater bay that forms an important staging area for migrating songbirds, shorebirds and waterfowl;
- Stony Swamp, 2,000ha (4,940 acres) of wetland and forest with more than 700 species of plants and the restored 1857 Bradley log farmhouse (access from Cedarvale Road) and the building foundations of at least two old farm buildings;
- Bruce Pit, a 300ha (741-acre) re-naturalized sand pit;
- Pinhey Forest, 300ha (741 acres) of mature coniferous trees;
- The Ministry of Natural Resources logging forest, 1,200ha (2,964 acres) of pine grove forest;
- Green's Creek, a 400ha (988-acre) valley where many post-glacial fossils of seals and other marine mammals have been found;
- Mer Bleue Bog, 2,300ha (5,681 acres) of boreal forest and sphagnum peat bog;
- Carlsbad Forest Reserve, a 1,100ha (2,717-acre) forest with mineral springs.

› Getting There

Trailhead access points are scattered along Anderson Road, Bearbrook Road, Cedarview Road, Dolman Ridge Road, Eagleson Road, Hunt Club Road, Moodie Drive, Range Road, Richmond Road, Ridge Road, Slack Road, Timm Road, and behind the Nepean Sportsplex.

› Further Information

The Greenbelt

National Capital Commission (NCC)
40 Elgin St.
Ottawa, ON K1P 1C7
☎ 613-239-5000 or 800-465-1867
www.canadascapital.gc.ca

Sarsaparilla Trail, Stony Swamp

Level of difficulty 🚶

Distance *.8km (.5mi) loop*

Approx. time *30min return*

Trailhead *Parking lot on Richmond Rd.*

Other *Wheelchair accessible*

This easy forest trail leads to a lovely lookout over Stony Swamp.

Watts Creek Pathway, Shirley's Bay

Level of difficulty *🚶*

Distance *8km (5mi) linear*

Approx. time *3hrs each way*

Trailhead *Moodie Dr. or Hertsberg Rd.*

Other *Wheelchair accessible*

This crushed gravel and asphalt pathway winds through mixed forests and open pastures between Moodie Drive and Hertzberg.

NCC Trail 30 and 31, Pinhey Forest

Level of difficulty *🚶*

Distance *3.5km (2mi) loop*

Approx. time *2hrs return*

Trailhead *Behind the Nepean Sportsplex, on Woodroffe south of Hunt Club*

Other *Wheelchair accessible*

This triple-looped trail leads through a mature coniferous forest that's planted on sand dunes. One of the loops offers suggestions for fitness activities.

Mer Bleue Trail, Mer Bleue Bog

Level of difficulty *🚶*

Distance *1.2km (.7mi) loop*

Approx. time *45min return*

Trailhead *Trail 53 or parking lot on Ridge Rd.*

This trails leads along a boardwalk which offers good views of the important sphagnum bog, considered an internationally significant area by the Ramsar Convention (an international agreement to protect wetlands signed in Ramsar, Iran in 1971).

NCC Trail 50, Mer Bleue Bog

Level of difficulty *🚶🚶*

Distance *4km (2.5mi) loop*

Approx. time *2hrs return*

Trailhead *Parking lot on Dolman Ridge Rd., Trail 51*

This trail leads through a boreal forest along a sandy escarpment called Dolman Ridge. A bird feeder attracts clay-coloured sparrows and palm warblers. Trail 51 passes through part of this trail, and a short extension of Trail 51 leads to another parking lot on Anderson Road.

NCC Trail 53, Mer Bleue Bog

Level of difficulty *🚶*

Distance *6.7km (4.2mi) loop*

Approx. time *3.5hrs return*

Trailhead *Parking lot on Ridge Rd.*

This trails leads through regenerated pastureland and connects with the Mer Bleue Trail.

NCC Trail 52, Mer Bleue Bog

Level of difficulty

Distance *3.5km (2.2mi) loop*

Approx. time *1.5hrs return*

Trailhead *Trail 51*

This trails leads through a boreal forest and along the edge of a major marsh. Look for red squirrels and chickadees. The eastern portion of the loop is shared with Trail 51.

NCC Trail 21, Stony Swamp

Level of difficulty

Distance *2.3km (1.4mi) loop*

Approx. time *45min return*

Trailhead *Trails 20 or 22*

An easy stroll through the forests and along boardwalks over Stony Swamp. An eastern extension leads to Trail 20, while a western extension leads across Hamel Road to the parking lot and Trail 22.

NCC Trail 22, Stony Swamp

Level of difficulty

Distance *2.4km (1.5mi) loop*

Approx. time *1hr return*

Trailhead *Parking lot on Timm Rd.*

This easy forest trail leads through a deciduous forest in Stony Swamp.

NCC Trail 23, Stony Swamp

Level of difficulty

Distance *2.3km (1.4mi) loop*

Approx. time *1hr return*

Trailhead *Old Quarry Trail*

This easy forest trail leads through Stony Swamp forest. The straight east end of the loop is the upper section of Trail 24.

Beaver and Chipmunk Trails, Stony Swamp

Level of difficulty

Distance *2.6km (1.6mi) linear*

Approx. time *1hr each way*

Trailhead *Parking lot on Moodie Dr.*

Two multi-looped trails meander through a pine plantation, along boardwalks over swamp, and across a bridge past a beaver pond. The parking lot, which also accesses the Wild Bird Care Centre, is on Moodie Drive. These trails also form part of the **Rideau Trail** (see p. 211), so you'll see orange triangles on them as well as the NCC signs.

Old Quarry Trail, Stony Swamp

Level of difficulty

Distance *2.7km (1.7mi) loop*

Approx. time *1.5hrs return*

Trailhead *Parking lot on Eagleson Rd., Trail 23*

Most of this trail leads through forests to an old stone quarry, although a boardwalk going over Stony Swamp divides the loop in two. A short extension leads to Trail 23.

NCC Trail 24, Stony Swamp

Level of difficulty

Distance *3km (1.9mi) semicircle*

Approx. time *1hr each way*

Trailhead *Trails 23 or 25*

This easy forest and boardwalk trail leads from Bells Corners through a deciduous forest in Stony Swamp and then loops along an old road that forms part of Trail 23.

NCC Trail 25, Stony Swamp

Level of difficulty

Distance *3.5km (2mi) loop*

Approx. time *1hr return*

Trailhead *Parking lot on Richmond Rd., Trail 24*

The eastern portion of this trail is an easy forest trail leading through Stony Swamp forests, while the western portion follows an old road. The northern portion of the loop is also part of Trail 24.

NCC Trail 27, Stony Swamp

Level of difficulty

Distance *2.7km (1.7mi) loop*

Approx. time *1.5hrs return*

Trailhead *North side of Hunt Club Rd., opposite the trailhead for Trail 26*

This trail leads through a forest. Look for the foundation of an old farmhouse; you'll also notice day-lilies and lilac trees in the area. Extensions connect to Trails 26 and 28.

NCC Trail 28, Stony Swamp

Level of difficulty

Distance *2km (1.2mi) loop*

Approx. time *1hr return*

Trailhead *Parking lots on Moodie Dr. and Hunt Club Rd.*

This trail leads through a meadow and then into a mature mixed forest with hemlocks, pine, maple and beech. Extensions connect to Trails 27 and 29.

NCC Trail 29, Stony Swamp

Level of difficulty

Distance *2.8km (1.7mi) loop*

Approx. time *1.5hrs return*

Trailhead *Parking lots on Moodie Dr. and Hunt Club Rd.*

This trail leads through a meadow and then into a mature mixed forest with hemlocks, pine, maple and beech. Extensions connect to Trails 27 and 29.

Jack Pine Trail, Stony Swamp

Level of difficulty

Distance *3.7km (2.3mi) loop*

Approx. time *2hrs return*

Trailhead *Parking lot on Moodie Dr.*

This triple-looped trail meanders through a jack pine forest where a huge birdfeeder attracts chickadees, nuthatches, woodpeckers, and evening grosbeaks. The parking lot on Moodie Drive also accesses Trail 26.

NCC Trail 45, MNR Logging Forest

Level of difficulty

Distance *3.7km (2.3mi) loop*

Approx. time *2hrs return*

Trailhead *Trails 44 and 46 and Hawthorne Rd.*

This trail leads through a mature pine grove managed by the Ministry of Natural Resources. The east side of the loop is shared with Trail 46 and an extension leads across Hawthorne Road to Trail 44.

NCC Trail 26, Stony Swamp

Level of difficulty

Distance *4km (2.5mi) loop*

Approx. time *2hrs return*

Trailhead *Parking lots on Moodie Dr. and Hunt Club Rd.*

This trail leads through a red pine plantation, past the limestone foundation of the Lenahan farmhouse and past a beaver pond. Extensions connect to the Jack Pine Trail and Trail 27.

NCC Trail 43, MNR Logging Forest

Level of difficulty

Distance *4km (2.5mi) loop*

Approx. time *2hrs return*

Trailhead *Trail 44 or parking lot on Davidson Rd.*

This trail leads through a mature pine grove managed by the Ministry of Natural Resources. A very active bird complex attracts a variety of songbirds. The east side of the square-shaped loop is shared with Trail 44.

NCC Trail 44, MNR Logging Forest

Level of difficulty

Distance *4km (2.5mi) loop*

Approx. time *2hrs return*

Trailhead *Trails 43 and 45*

This trail leads through a mature pine grove managed by the Ministry of Natural Resources. Parking is on Davidson Road. The west side of the loop is shared with Trail 43 and an extension leads across Hawthorne Road to Trail 45.

NCC Trail 46, MNR Logging Forest

Level of difficulty

Distance *4.3km (2.7mi) loop*

Approx. time *2hrs return*

Trailhead *Parking lot on Leitrim Rd.*

This trail leads through a mature pine grove managed by the Ministry of Natural Resources. The east side of the loop is shared with Trail 45.

NCC Trail 51, Mer Bleue Bog

Level of difficulty

Distance *2.8km (1.7mi) loop*

Approx. time *2hrs return*

Trailhead *Parking lot on Anderson Rd.*

This trails leads through a boreal forest and past a cattail marsh. Trail 50 passes through part of this trail and the eastern loop of it is shared with Trail 52.

Greenbelt Pathway

Level of difficulty

Distance *21.5km (13.6mi) linear*

Approx. time *9 hrs each way*

Trailhead *Watts Creek Pathway, Robertson Rd., St. Joseph Blvd., Woodroffe Ave., Merivale, Black Rapids Lock Station, Hunt Club Rd., Bruce Pit*

Other *Wheelchair accessible*

This compacted stone dust pathway leads south from the Watts Creek Pathway to Bruce Pitt and from Green's Creek to St. Joseph Boulevard. It is the first part of a 56km (35mi) recreational pathway that will eventually loop around the Green Belt between Shirley's Bay in the west to Green's Creek in the east.

Perth Wildlife Reserve

Location *Off County Rd. 1 between Perth and Rideau Ferry*

Number of trails *1*

Total distance *5km (3mi)*

Approx. time *1.5hrs*

Interesting features *Canada geese migration site, wood ducks, snakes, 2 marsh viewing towers and a duck viewing blind*

Trailhead *Parking lot*

Facilities/services *Parking, toilets, telephones, lookouts*

To really appreciate the size, sound and beauty of the Canada geese migration, visit the Perth Wildlife Reserve in October. More than 5,000 geese use a pond-field area at the wildlife area entrance, and you're likely to see several groups land and take-off in a very short period of time.

The area, which includes about half of the Tay Marsh along 2km (1.2mi) of the Tay River, opened in 1974 as a refuge for migrating Canada geese, snow geese and many ducks. Wildlife-friendly plants, such as the red elderberry, have been planted; ponds with geese nesting areas have been created; grazing areas have been planted; and nesting boxes have been set up to encourage wood ducks to nest along the creek. Other species have also been taken care of. A salt lick has been created for deer and apple trees have been pruned and weeded to produce more fruit for deer, squirrels, red foxes and birds. A marsh area attracts fish, muskrats, bullfrogs and marsh birds. It's also a very good place to see five different kinds of snakes, including the black rat snake, Ontario's only constrictor.

› Getting There

Take County Road 1 south from Perth or north from the town of Rideau Ferry. Turn east onto County Road 18.

› Further Information

Rideau Valley Conservation Authority
RR3, Armstrong Rd.
Maberly, ON K0H 2B0
☎ 613-692-5371 or 800-267-3504
www.rvca.ca

Rideau Trail

Location *Links Kingston and Ottawa*

Number of trails *1*

Total distance *387km (240mi)*

Markers *Orange isosceles triangles with yellow tips in the Kingston direction, tipped so that the point indicates trail direction. Side trails and loops marked with blue triangles*

Trailheads *Parking lot at the Cataraqui Marshlands Conservation Area, on the north side of King St. west of the Cataraqui Golf course in Kingston; or Richmond Landing, near the parking lot of The Mill Restaurant, on The Parkway in Ottawa*

Interesting features *View of Westport, graves of famous Canadians, limestone caves*

Facilities/services *None*

The Rideau Trail and the association that runs it began as a vision of Kingston-area resident Douglas Knapp. Knapp successfully communicated his dream to 27 students, who got a grant to build the entire path in the summer of 1971. In the meantime, Knapp recruited another 250 people who became members of the trail that first year. Today, the association has 1,200 members.

Hikers on the trail will appreciate many of the region's most important natural features, including rocky ridges, lakes, limestone caves ,the view from Spy Rock over Westport.

The trail passes a number of historical landmarks, including the graves of Canada's first prime minister, Sir John A. Macdonald, and Sir Alexander Campbell, a Father of Confederation; shallow and deep mica pits; Chaffey's Lock on the Rideau Canal; the Beverige Dam and Locks; the remains of a stone lime kiln; and houses built in a variety of architectural styles. The section along the Tay River in Perth features historical plaques about canal building, soldiers, prohibition and Canada's last fatal duel.

Many of the parks, conservation areas and locks offer camping, as do some of the private land owners along the way.

› Getting There

Access the trail from Ottawa, Richmond, Merrickville, Smith's Falls, Port Elmsley, Perth, Westport, Sydenham or Kingston or from the parks it goes through, including: Marlborough Forest, Mica Mine Conservation Area, Murphys Point Provincial Park, Foley Mountain Conservation Area, Frontenac Provincial Park, Gould Lake Conservation Area or Cataraqui Bay Conservation Area.

➤ Further Information

Rideau Trail Association
PO Box 15
Kingston, ON K7L 4V6
☎ 613-545-0823
www.rideautrail.org

Sandbanks Provincial Park

Location *South of Picton*

Number of trails *2*

Total distance *7km (4.2mi)*

Interesting features *World's largest fresh water baymouth barrier sand dune complex*

Facilities/services *Parking, toilets, telephones, visitor information centre, convenience store, swimming beaches, camping, laundry area, showers*

Other *Pets on leashes permitted. Please stay on trails–lots of poison ivy here, and the dunes house a very fragile ecosystem*

A long beach of soft, white sand, two major sand dune systems and a short nature hike that's good for children makes this 1,600ha (3,952-acre) park a good destination for walking.

Hikers can choose to walk along the sandy beach on Athol Bay; along the Woodland Trail, which leads past the West Lake freshwater sand dune system; or along the Cedar Sands Trail to explore four important habitats: the still-growing fore dunes, wet areas called pannes or dune slacks, stable back dunes and reforested sand ridges. Some of these dunes range from 15m to 25m (49ft to 82ft) in height. Plant enthusiasts will appreciate a wide variety of species that includes some rarities, such as the gray-stemmed goldenrod (*Solidago nemoralis ssp. Decemflora*), the ram's head lady's slipper (*Cypripedium arietinum*) and the internationally vulnerable swamp rose mallow (*Hibiscus moscheutos*). Sea rocket, marram grass, tall wormwood, Russian-thistle and sand cherry inhabit the fore dunes; sedges, rushes, orchids, Kalm's lobelia, silverweed and twayblades grow in the pannes; creeping juniper, white cedar, eastern hemlock, sugar maple, white spruce, balsam fir and white pines grow on the back dunes and ridges.

You may also want to look for signs of history in the sand. Two major Aboriginal groups visited this area beginning as early as AD 1000. Archaeologists named the first group the Princess Point Culture. The group seems to have lived by fishing in the spring, eating wild rice and growing some corn in the summer, and hunting in the fall. The second group, a band of Huron-affiliated Iroquois, appears to have used the site primarily for fishing between AD 1400 and 1550.

➤ Getting There

From Picton, follow County Road 10 to County Road 11. Turn right. Continue to County Road 18. Turn left. The park is on your left.

➤ Further Information

Sandbanks Provincial Park
RR1
Picton, ON K0K 2T0

613-393-3319 or 800-667-1940
www.ontarioparks.com

Friends of Sandbanks
PO Box 20007, 219 Main St.
Picton, ON K0K 3V0
www.friendsofsandbanks.org

Woodlands Trail

Level of difficulty *1*

Distance *5km (3mi) linear*

Approx. time *1hr return*

Trailhead *Parking lot on Dunes Beach or Outlet Beach*

This trail highlights historic changes in the area since settlers in the late 1800s allowed cows to use the dunes as pasture so they could plant their fields with barley. The cows trampled the vegetation, which eventually caused major sandstorms that destroyed their homes. This well-trodden path leads through the West Lake sand dunes, past stands of Scots pine planted in the 1950s, and the old site of the Lake Ontario Cement Ltd. Factory that operated on this site until 1973. Stop and look at the sand occasionally; you'll see the holes of giant sand spiders and the tracks of other sand creatures. The park offers guided tours throughout the summer.

Cedar Sands Trail

Level of difficulty *1*

Distance *2km (1.2mi) linear*

Approx. time *45min return*

Trailhead *Parking lot at the end of Outlet Beach*

This hike leads through a stabilized bay mouth sandbar. At one point, the trail leads onto a sandbar in the middle of Outlet River. There are two lookouts along the way.

Sheffield Conservation Area

Location *Hwy. 41, south of Kaladar*

Number of trails *1*

Level of difficulty *2*

Total distance *4km (2.5mi) linear*

Approx. time *1hr each way*

Trailhead *Parking lot beside Little Melon Lake*

Interesting features *Loons, granite rock plains, lookouts*

Facilities/services *Parking, toilets*

If you want to feel like an explorer, this conservation area is for you. Most of the trail goes right over open plains of bedrock around the shoreline of Little Melon Lake to eventually end up at a great lookout over Haley Lake. If you prefer to make your own trail, there's lots of space in this unexplored 466ha (1,150-acre) conservation area.

The well-travelled path begins beside the parking lot next to Little Melon Lake. You'll have to climb up a big boulder right away, but don't worry: this climb is the most difficult part of the tour. You'll continue along a huge expanse of rock and then onto a woodland path.

The trail follows the shores of Little Melon Lake for about

15min. Near the end of the lake, you'll notice the occasional yellow blazes that mark the path to Haley's Lake. You'll go through mixed forests and back onto rock. Lots of different creatures live here, including the five-lined skink, shining sumac, and Indiangrass and swallowtail butterflies.

› Getting There

Take Highway 41 south from Kaladar or north from Erinsville. The conservation area is on the east side.

› Further Information

Quinte Conservation
2061 Old Hwy. 2, RR2
Belleville, ON K8N 4Z2
☎ 613-968-3434
www.quinteconservation.ca

Silent Lake Provincial Park

Location *Hwy. 28 north of Apsley and south of Bancroft*

Number of trails *3*

Total distance *19.5km (12mi)*

Interesting features *Sunset over Silent Lake, Quiet Lake, bear nests*

Facilities/services *Parking, toilets, telephones, visitor information centre, convenience store, canoe rental, bicycle rental, playground, fishing, swimming beaches, pine lodge, camping, yurt (furnished year-round tent), laundry area, showers, canoe launch*

Other *Dogs on leashes permitted*

Other than the lake itself, this 1,450ha (3,582-acre) park doesn't have any particular feature that stands out, but it's still one of the top 10 places to go in Ontario. You'll love the astonishing diversity of habitats, the sunset over the beach, the changing leaf colours in fall, and just the relative emptiness of the place.

In addition to the three hiking trails offered by the park, there's another 38km (23.6mi) of mountain bike trails. Hikers who want to walk a bit longer will enjoy these trails, as long as they're careful to listen and watch for bike traffic.

› Getting There

Take Highway 28 north from Apsley or south from Bancroft.

› Further Information

Silent Lake Provincial Park
PO Box 219
Bancroft, ON K0L 1C0
☎ 613-339-2807 or 800-667-1940
www.ontarioparks.com

Lakehead Loop Trail

Level of difficulty *🚶*

Distance *1.5km (.9mi) loop*

Approx. time *30min return*

Trailhead *Either the day-use parking lot or the Granite Ridge Campground*

This short trail crosses a bridge over Silent Creek and follows the Lakeshore Hiking Trail along the shore of Silent Lake through cedar groves and black ash to a lookout. You can see the beach, Peaches Island and the narrows of Silent Lake from this point. Then the trail loops around through a deciduous forest of maple and red oak and then over an uneven rocky trail back to the bridge.

Bonnie's Pond Trail

Level of difficulty 🚶

Distance *3km (1.9mi) loop*

Approx. time *1hr return*

Trailhead *Pincer Bay Campground parking lot*

Although this trail takes its name from a logging horse that slid into the pond in the 19th century and drowned, it doesn't carry any negative vibes. You'll pass a beaver pond, a spectacular lookout and bear nests, which are created in the autumn by beechnut-craving black bears dropping leaves from the tops of beechnut trees as they eat.

Lakeshore Hiking Trail

Level of difficulty 🚶🚶🚶

Distance *15km (9mi) loop*

Approx. time *6hrs return*

Trailhead *Day use parking lot*

This trail follows the shoreline of Silent Lake and the smaller Quiet Lake. There's only one scenic lookout marked on the trail guide, but a number of large boulders at the edge of the lake perform just as admirably. Bonnie's Pond Trail and the Lakehead Loop both connect to this trail, so that you can cover all three in a day.

Shabomeka Legpower Pathfinders

Location *Cloyne*

Number of trails *11*

Total distance *66km (40mi)*

Interesting features *Shabomeka Lake, Dog Lake, Little Shabomeka Lake*

Facilities/services *Map*

Other *Avoid area in hunting season first two weeks of November*

Glen Pearce has spent more than two decades exploring and marking a series of paths through the crown land near his home, south of Bon Echo Provincial Park. The paths lead from either Shabomake Lake Road or Shawenegog Lake Lane and meander through a wide variety of habitats in the forest heartland surrounding Shabomeka Lake in the Madawaska Highlands. The narrow high pruned single-file paths are numbered sequentially. Hikers can return to the laneway (Path 1) by selecting the lower-numbered path in any intersection.

There are 49 individual paths in the network, so a map is almost essential. Maps are free at the pathhead or by sending a self-addressed stamped envelope to Shabomeka Legpower Pathfinders at the address provided below.

Walking on these paths means crossing beaver dams, weaving around marshes and spotting wildlife without seeing a single person anywhere nearby. As with all trails on crown land, you have the right to use the land, but no oversight or services are available. If you have a sense of adventure, this is the spot for you.

➤ Getting There

Take Highway 41 north from Kaladar or south from Denbigh to Head Road, 3.7km (2.2mi) north of Cloyne at the south end of Mazinaw Lake. Pass Cedar Lodge and cross the biridge. Just past Bon Echo Family Campsites, turn left onto Shabomeka Lake Road. Continue for 5.7km (3.4mi) to a short causeway where Shawenegog Lake Lane begins. After .4km (.2mi), turn left into driveway 1067B marked PEARCE 22/23/EKELI to pick up a map. Parking areas are shown on the map.

➤ Further Information

Shabomeka Legpower Pathfinders
PO Box 217
Cloyne, ON K0H 1K0
✆ 613-336-8036

Path 1

Level of difficulty 🚶

Distance *8.5km (5mi) linear*

Approx. time *2hrs each way*

Pathhead *1067 Shawenegog Lake Lane*

All the trails stem from Shabomeka Lake Road or Shawenagog Lake Lane which weaves through the region. Most of the trails lie to the south of this line, but Shabomeka Lake lies to the north.

Path 2

Level of difficulty 🚶🚶

Distance *6.2km (3.7mi) linear*

Approx. time *1hr return*

Pathhead *1067 Shawenegog Lake Lane, Paths 1, 3, 4 and 8*

This trail loops around Judyla Marsh and Box Canyon Falls. It crosses the marsh along a beaver dam.

Path 3

Level of difficulty 🚶

Distance *7.6km (4.6mi) quadruple loop*

Approx. time *2hrs return*

Pathhead *Paths 1, 2, 8 and 12*

This trail weaves around Levere's Marsh, Price Pond and Ferguson Swamp.

Path 4

Level of difficulty 🚶🚶

Distance *4.6km (2.8mi) quadruple loop*

Approx. time *2hrs return*

Pathhead *Paths 2, 5, 6 and 8*

This trail climbs up Forsey Rill and includes three crossover paths.

Path 5

Level of difficulty 🚶

Distance *8.2km (5mi) triple loop*

Approx. time *3hrs return*

Pathhead *Paths 1, 4, 6, 7 and 10*

The longest section of this path loops around the shore of Little Shabomeka Lake and links to two smaller interior loops with good lookouts.

Path 6

Level of difficulty 🚶🚶

Distance *8.4km (5mi) quadruple loop*

Approx. time *4hrs return*

Trailhead *Paths 4, 5, 6, 7 and 8*

The highlight of this path is a section that loopes around the south side of Little Shabomeka Lake. Other features include Greg Gulch, Lois Lane, Fortier Bluff and Pearce Creek.

Path 7

Level of difficulty 🚶🚶

Distance *8.7km (5.2mi) double loop*

Approx. time *4hrs return*

Trailhead *Paths 5, 6 and 8*

The larger of the two loops circumnavigates Tiny Shabomeka Lake, connecting to the Beech Bush, and a section of old logging road.

Path 8

Level of difficulty 🚶🚶

Distance *10.9km (6.5mi) triple loop and extensions*

Approx. time *4.5hrs return*

Pathhead *Paths 2, 3, 4, 6 and 7*

The largest loop circles around Meeka Creek and passes Cranberry and Head marshes. An extension leads around Gloria marsh. A second extension leads past Cranberry and Bingeman marshes to the shore of Missassagagon Lake. The small loop bypasses Lemke and Bev marshes with an extension to Perry's Hill.

Path 9

Level of difficulty 🚶🚶

Distance *3.5km (2mi) linear*

Approx. time *2hrs each way*

Pathhead *Path 1*

Path 9 leads north from Shawenegog Lake Lane past Green Lake and Horton Marsh to the southeastern shore of Horton Lake. Two loops are portages from Shabomeka Lake to Dog and Horton lakes.

Path 10

Level of difficulty 🚶

Distance *2.2km (1.3mi) loop*

Approx. time *1hr return*

Pathhead *Path 1*

Path 10 begins at the dam at the end of Higgins Lane and loops up next to Shabomeka Lake and along the shore of McDowall Lake.

Path 11

Level of difficulty 🚶

Distance *2.6km (1.6mi) linear*

Approx. time *1hr each way*

Pathhead *Paths 1 and 10*

Path 11 connects the two sections of Trail 10 together along Old Pines Path.

Voyageur Provincial Park

Location *On the Ottawa River between Chutes-à-Blondeau and Pointe Fortune*

Number of trails *2*

Total distance *7km (4.3mi)*

Interesting features *Diverse habitats and mammals, Carillon dam on former Long Sault rapids*

Facilities/services *Parking, toilets, telephones, visitor information centre, convenience store, playground, swimming beaches, camping, laundry area, showers, equestrian facilities*

› Getting There

From Hawkesbury, take Highway 417 east to Exit 5. Go north on County Road 4 to the park.

› Further Information

Voyageur Provincial Park
PO Box 130
Chutes-à-Blondeau, ON K0B 1B0
613-674-2825 or 800-667-1940
www.ontarioparks.com

Coureur des Bois Trail

Level of difficulty 🚶

Total distance *2.km (1.2mi) loop*

Approx. time *1hr*

Trailhead *Coureur des Bois parking lot, past the equestrian area*

The Coureur des Bois Trail leads through several diverse habitats including three different forests–a maple-beech deciduous forest, a grove of mature hemlock, and a mixed deciduous forest of pine and oak, as well as a swamp, an overgrown meadow and two ponds, one of which was created by a beaver dam.

Outaouais Trail

Level of difficulty 🚶

Total distance *2.5km (1.6mi) linear*

Approx. time *2hrs*

Trailheads *Campgrounds, day use area*

The Outaouais Trail simply links the three campgrounds with the beaches. You'll get a wonderful view of the Laurentian Mountains.

Northeastern Ontario

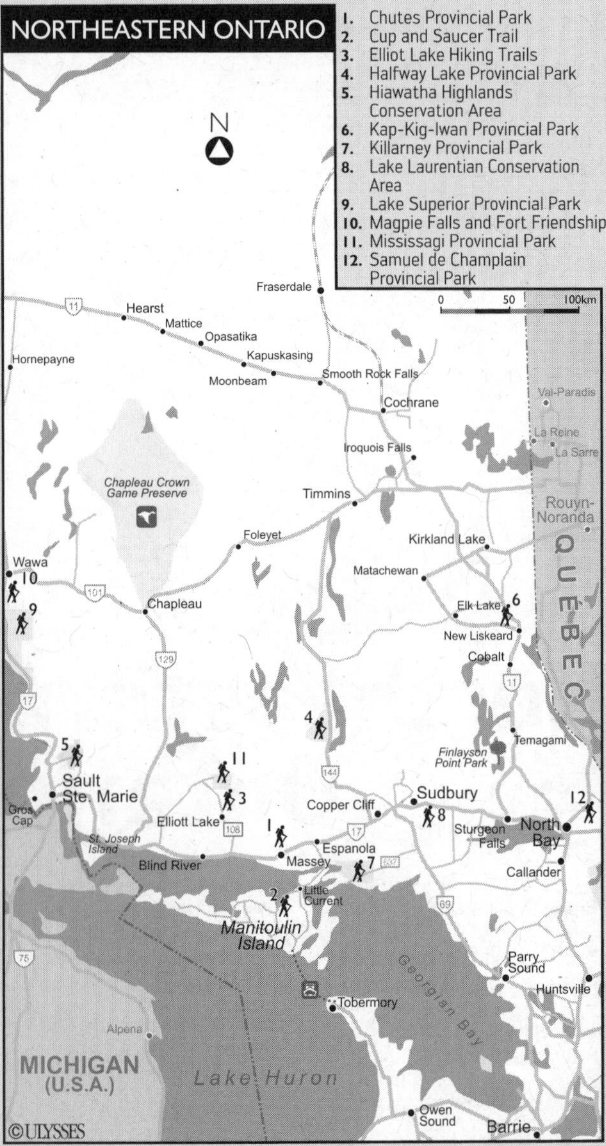
NORTHEASTERN ONTARIO
1. Chutes Provincial Park
2. Cup and Saucer Trail
3. Elliot Lake Hiking Trails
4. Halfway Lake Provincial Park
5. Hiawatha Highlands Conservation Area
6. Kap-Kig-Iwan Provincial Park
7. Killarney Provincial Park
8. Lake Laurentian Conservation Area
9. Lake Superior Provincial Park
10. Magpie Falls and Fort Friendship
11. Mississagi Provincial Park
12. Samuel de Champlain Provincial Park
N
0 50 100km
Fraserdale
Hearst
Mattice
Opasatika
Kapuskasing
Moonbeam
Smooth Rock Falls
Hornepayne
Cochrane
Val-Paradis
La Reine
La Sarre
Iroquois Falls
Chapleau Crown Game Preserve
Timmins
Rouyn-Noranda
Foleyet
Kirkland Lake
Wawa
Matachewan
Chapleau
Elk Lake
New Liskeard
Cobalt
QUÉBEC
Temagami
Finlayson Point Park
Sault Ste. Marie
Gros Cap
Sudbury
Copper Cliff
Elliott Lake
Sturgeon Falls
North Bay
St. Joseph Island
Espanola
Blind River
Massey
Callander
Little Current
Manitoulin Island
Parry Sound
Huntsville
Georgian Bay
Tobermory
Alpena
MICHIGAN (U.S.A.)
Lake Huron
Owen Sound
Barrie
©ULYSSES

More than two thirds of the vast region of northeastern Ontario, which begins at Lake Nipissing and ends at James Bay, lies north of the tree line in a sea of unending tundra.

The area south of the tree line, however, contains ancient rock formations, vast boreal forests, Aboriginal pictographs, historic engineering feats, and more recent ingenious creations that help turn hiking into a treasure hunt. You'll find yourself searching the landscape for clues to the past, present and future.

You don't need to go far from the cities to explore the northeastern Ontario landscapes. Ideal walking trails include the **Elliot Lake Hiking Trails** (see p. 223), the **Hiawatha Highlands Conservation Area** (see p. 225) in Sault Ste. Marie, **Lake Laurentian Conservation Area** (see p. 231) in Sudbury, and the **Kap-Kig-Iwan Provincial Park** (see p. 228) in Kirkland Lake.

As you explore the area, you'll understand why Northeastern Ontario has attracted so many prominent Canadian artists, including those from the Group of Seven.

Many famous Group of Seven paintings, including *Northern River*, *Canyon*, *Agawa*, *Algoma Waterfall* and *Agawa Canyon*, were inspired by two important provincial parks: **Lake Superior** (see p. 231) and **Killarney** (see p. 228). Frank Johnston, Lawren Harris, A.Y. Jackson and J.E.H. MacDonald each found inspiration in the views at Lake Superior, especially those in Agawa Canyon. Franklin Carmichael, A.J. Casson, Arthur Lismer and A.Y. Jackson all painted the Georgian Bay landscape from both the Killarney area and from the part of the Niagara Escarpment found on Manitoulin Island. Hikers today can explore these views on the **Cup and Saucer Trail** (see p. 222).

Other works feature major valleys such as those through which the Magpie, Spanish, Mattawa and Mississagi rivers flow. The best place to explore the Magpie River Valley is on the **Voyageur Trail** (see p. 70) as it passes through **Magpie Falls and Fort Friendship** (see p. 235). Perspectives on the extraordinarily large Spanish River valley can be seen from **Halfway Lake Provincial Park** (see p. 224). The Spanish connects to the fast-moving Aux Sables in the south and together they form what was once an ideal logging route to Lake Superior. Signs of this once-thriving business can be seen at **Chutes Provincial Park** (see p. 222). Look for the remains of a log chute on the Seven Sisters waterfall and bark chips in the beach sand. The ideal spot to see the Mississagi watershed is **Mississagi Provincial Park** (see p. 236). The Mattawa River valley can be explored on the trails or from the Canadian Ecology Centre at **Samuel de Champlain Provincial Park** (see p. 238).

› Tourist Information

Algoma Kinniwabi Travel Association
485 E. Queen St., suite 204
Sault Ste. Marie, ON P6A 1Z9
705-254-4293 or 800-263-2546
www.algomacountry.com

Rainbow Country Travel Association
2726 Whippoorwill Ave.
Sudbury, ON P3G 1E9
705-522-0104 or 800-465-6655
www.rainbowcountry.com

Almaguin Nipissing Travel Association
PO Box 351, 1375 Seymour St.
North Bay, ON P1B 8H5
705-474-6634 or 800-387-0516
www.ontariosnearnorth.on.ca

Conchrane-Timiskaming Travel Association
76 McIntyre Rd. (Timmins), PO Box 920
Schumacher, ON P0N 1G0
705-360-1989 or 800-461-3766
www.jamesbayfrontier.com

Chutes Provincial Park

Location *North of Hwy. 553, north of Massey*

Number of trails *1*

Level of difficulty

Total distance *6km (3.6mi)*

Interesting features *Seven Sisters waterfall on Aux Sables River*

Facilities/services *Parking, toilets, telephones, amusement park, swimming beach, camping, laundry area, showers, fishing*

Other *Dogs on leashes permitted*

The Ontario government decided to set aside 109ha (269 acres) of land to protect the rapids, waterfalls, wetlands, flood plain and terraces of the Aux Sables River in 1970. The river had been used as a logging waterway from the late 1800s until 1929. Remnants of the log chute can still be seen near the waterfalls.

Today, hikers can follow the Twin Bridges Trail around the waterfalls to the mouth of the river and then over a bridge and back up towards a sandy beach and day-use area. Look for the builder's mark: *J. Rivers, Stonecutter, 1883* on the bridge.

› Getting There

Take Highway 553 north from the Trans-Canada Highway at Massey. The park appears on the right.

› Further Information

Chutes Provincial Park
PO Box 37
Massey, ON P0P 1P0
705-865-2021 or 800-667-1940
www.ontarioparks.com

Cup and Saucer Trail

Location *Junction of Hwy. 540 and Bidwell Rd., Manitoulin Island*

Number of trails *3*

Level of difficulty

Total distance *16km (10mi)*

Interesting features *Niagara Escarpment*

Facilities/services *Parking, toilets*

The Cup and Saucer Trail runs along and below the centre of the highest part of the horseshoe-shaped Niagara Escarpment, following two small ridges. At 180m about sea level, the higher of the two ridges is also the highest point on Manitoulin Island. Both ridges are about 70m (230ft) high.

Although the escarpment itself is fascinating, the best views are those over the North Channel to the La Cloche Mountains along the upper trail.

Eventually, the Escarpment Biosphere Conservancy plans to build the 450km (279mi) Manitou Trail, which would link the Cup and Saucer to South Bay Mouth in the south and the Mississagi Lighthouse in the north.

› Getting There

Take Highway 69 south from Sudbury or north from Parry Sound to Highway 637. Turn west towards the town of Killarney. It's another 68km (42mi) to the campground.

› Further Information

Manitoulin Tourism Association
70 E. Meredith St., PO Box 119
Little Current, ON P0P 1K0
www.manitoulintourism.com

Escarpment Biosphere Conservancy
503 Davenport Rd.
Toronto, ON M4V 1B8
416-960-8121
www.escarpment.ca

Elliot Lake Hiking Trails

Location *Hwy. 108, Elliott Lake*

Number of trails *8*

Level of difficulty 🚶🚶

Total distance *25km (15.5mi)*

Interesting features *Matinenda Escarpment, Elliot Lake dam, neon-green mine tailings, lakes*

Facilities/services *Parking, toilets, telephones, playgrounds, beaches*

Other *The Lacnor and Nordic sites just north of the Westner Lake trail include more than 15 million tonnes of decommissioning radioactive uranium mine tailings*

The town of Elliot Lake offers hikers a multitude of linked trails, all located from various parking lots in the middle of town, including two on Highway 108 itself. If you want to do all the trails, begin at Spine Beach and follow the 3.5km (2.1mi) Westview Nature Trail with its many boardwalks and rocky areas.

You'll cross Highway 108 to the entrance of the Sheriff Creek Wildlife Sanctuary, which offers 11km (6.8mi) of trails past a cattail marsh and beaver meadow and into an upland forest and tamarack bog. The Tamarack Bog Trail ends along the Horne Lake Trail just past the entrance to the sanctuary.

Continue along the 6km (3.7mi) Horne Lake Trail and climb up some ridges and two steep hills. You'll pass many cliffs. You can either complete the loop around the lake or turn at the entrance to the Mount Dufour Skill Hill, which leads to the Fire Tower Lookout on the Matinenda Escarpment. The Fire Tower Lookout offers a 360-degree view of the entire area, including Manitoulin Island in the North Channel of Lake Huron to the south. Return to the Horne Lake Trail to get back to Highway 108. Look for Hillside Drive North, which turns into Spine Road and leads back to the beach where you started.

You can also join the **Voyageur Trail** (see p. 70) at Spine Beach or at the edge of Mount Dufour.

› Getting There

Take Highway 108 north from the Trans-Canada Highway between Blind River and Cutler.

› Further Information

Elliot Lake Economic Development Office
45 N. Hillside Dr.
Elliot Lake, ON P5A 1Z5
800-661-6192
www.cityofelliotlake.com

Halfway Lake Provincial Park

Location *Hwy. 144, north of Sudbury*

Number of trails *4*

Level of difficulty 🚶🚶

Total distance *29km (18mi)*

Interesting features *Boreal forest, 20 lakes, ground moraine, rolling bedrock, preglacial boulder fields, moose yard*

Facilities/services *Parking, toilets, telephones, playground, fishing, swimming beaches, camping, 9 back-country campsites, laundry area, showers, canoe launch*

Other *Dogs on leashes permitted*

Halfway Lake Provincial Park encompasses 4,735 ha (11,695 acres) on the Canadian Shield around and north of Halfway Lake. Most of the area is covered by boreal forest, although a tornado in 2002 did significant damage to many of the jack pine, trembling aspen and white birch stands.

A healthy moose population lives within the park, as do wolves, lynx, foxes, beavers, hares and more than 90 species of birds, including the great blue heron.

Although all the trails in this park feature rocky plains and many short climbs, hikers should expect major climbs to stunning vistas on three of the four. The Moose Trail, in particular, provides an excellent view over Halfway Lake itself. The Hawk Ridge Trail loops from Echo Pond trail past Lost Lake and around to Three Island, Crystal and Burnt Ridge lakes. Nine overnight campsites are available here. The Osprey Heights Trail leads from Highway 144 north of the main park entrance to a spectacular lookout over Antrim Lake. The Echo Pond Trail parallels Raven Lake and then climbs slightly until it crosses the stream leading from Echo Pond to Halfway Lake. If you're lucky, you'll see some of the moose that live near here.

› Getting There

Take Highway 144 north from Sudbury for 90km (55.8mi) until you see the park entrance on the left.

› Further Information

Halfway Lake Provincial Park
PO Box 560
Levack, ON P0M 2C0
705-965-2702, 705-966-2315 or 800-667-1940
www.ontarioparks.com

Hiawatha Highlands Conservation Area

Location *Fifth Line, 3km east of Hwy. 17 in Sault Ste. Marie*

Number of trails *6*

Total distance *35km (22mi)*

Interesting features *Waterfalls, red and white pines, sugar shack, 2 lookouts*

Facilities/services *Parking, toilets, telephones, playground, swimming*

Other *Dogs on leashes permitted*

The Hiawatha Highlands and Kinsmen Park include three main trail systems: the Crystal Creek System with five trails; the Lookout Trail System (locally known as the Pinder System after the family who donated the land), which includes three trails; and the Red Pine Trail System with three trails. All three systems branch out in different directions from the corner of Fifth Line East and Landslide Road.

The hiking trails go through forests, including 20ha (50 acres) of old-growth forest with trees that are at least 130yrs old. There are also several creeks, lakes and wetlands that are the ideal habitat for more than 70 species of birds, including bald eagles, redstarts, Blackburnian warblers, common yellowthroats, ovenbirds, parula warblers, red-eyed vireos, hermit thrushes and bluebirds. You'll have a good chance of seeing 18 species of mammals, including chipmunks, voles, and red foxes.

Each section covers a considerable territory: Kinsmen Park alone is 97ha (240 acres). The park includes Crystal Falls, a baseball diamond, a children's playground, picnic areas, change rooms and a stocked fishpond. Crystal Falls can be reached from the Crystal Creek Trail. Although the trail itself is not wheelchair-accessible, a wheelchair-accessible boardwalk has been constructed beside it to enable everyone to see the falls.

Wishart Park offers its own hiking trails that extend from the Wishart Extension south of Fourth Line East.

Backpackers will be interested in following either the Mabel Lake Backcountry or Beaver trails, both of which extend off of the Crystal Lake Trail. We recommend the Mabel Lake Trail, which runs for 15km (9.3m) to Mabel Lake.

The 40km (25mi) Saulteaux section of the Voyageur Trail also goes through the Hiawatha Highlands, with a side trail to Crystal Creek.

› Getting There

Take Highway 17 north of Sault Ste. Marie to Fifth Line East. Follow the road until it meets Landslide Road. Parking is available at the lodge or on a small lot on Landslide Road.

› Further Information

Sault Ste. Marie Region Conservation Authority
1100 E. Fifth Line
Sault Ste. Marie, ON P6A 5K7
705-946-8530
www.ssmrca.ca

Crystal Creek System

Kinsmen Lit

Level of difficulty 🚶

Distance *2km (1mi) loop*

Approx. time *45min return*

Trailhead *Behind the lodge, down the driveway, beside the children's playground*

Other *Wheelchair-accessible*

The Kinsmen Club has installed lights along this loop, which circles beside the children's playground. One side of the loop is shared with the Crystal Creek Trail. The path is very straight and much of it is paved.

Ecology Trail

Level of difficulty 🚶

Distance *2.5km (1.6mi) loop*

Approx. time *1hr return*

Trailhead *Off the Crystal Creek Trail or down a staircase behind the Hiawatha Lodge*

The Ecology Trail leads south to another view of Crystal Creek.

Crystal Creek Trail

Level of difficulty 🚶

Distance *5km (3mi) loop*

Approx. time *2hrs return*

Trailhead *Behind the lodge, down the driveway, beside the children's playground*

The Crystal Creek Trail circles around Crystal Falls, through the forest and past the swimming reservoir next to the W.C. Thayer Memorial Dam above Minnehaha Falls. The Kinsmen Club stocks the reservoir with rainbow trout and speckled trout so children can fish all summer.

Inner Loop

Level of difficulty 🚶

Distance *2km (1mi) loop*

Approx. time *45min return*

Trailhead *Crystal Creek Trail*

The Inner Loop winds through the woods between Crystal Creek and the Crystal Creek Trail so that hikers can increase the length of their walk.

Olympic Extension

Level of difficulty 🚶

Distance *2.5km (1.6mi) loop*

Approx. time *1hr return*

Trailhead *Crystal Creek Trail*

The Olympic Extension circles beyond the Crystal Creek path so that hikers can again easily lengthen the walk.

Lookout Trail System (Pinder System)

Lookout Trail

Level of difficulty 🚶

Distance *4km (2.5mi) loop*

Approx. time *2hrs return*

Markers *Red*

Trailhead *Fifth Line E. on the north side of the street just east of Landslide Rd.*

The Lookout Trail begins in a white pine forest, climbs up to a lookout towards Root River and then continues to a huge sundeck and another lookout over

Root River. Notice the pale grey granite base found throughout the Hiawatha Highlands.

White Pine Extension

Level of difficulty 🚶

Distance *2km (1mi) loop*

Approx. time *45min return*

Markers *White*

Trailhead *Lookout Trail*

This trail circles inside the Lookout Trail through a forest of huge white pine. White pine has always been an important source of lumber and was chosen as Ontario's tree emblem on May 1, 1984 to commemorate the province's bicentennial.

Sugar Bush Extension

Level of difficulty 🚶

Distance *1.5km (.9mi) loop*

Approx. time *45min return*

Markers *Yellow*

Trailhead *Lookout Trail*

This trail circles through a forest of sugar maples whose sap starts running in the spring. There's a sugar shack close to Fifth Line East.

Red Pine Trail System

Red Pine Trail

Level of difficulty 🚶 🚶

Distance *5km (3mi) loop*

Approx. time *2hrs return*

Markers *Red*

Trailhead *West side of Landslide Rd., just south of Fifth Line E.*

The Red Pine Trail begins in a forest of red pine that was planted in the 1930s.

Fish Hatchery Extension

Level of difficulty 🚶 🚶

Distance *5km (3mi) loop*

Approx. time *2hrs return*

Markers *Green*

Trailhead *Begins off the Red Pine Trail*

This trail leads throughout the Fish Hatchery forests, passing over Cold Water Creek and Root River and past the hatchery itself (although at too far a distance to see anything).

Cold Water Creek Extension

Level of difficulty 🚶 🚶

Distance *2.5km (3mi) loop*

Approx. time *1hr return*

Markers *Blue*

Trailhead *Begins off the Fish Hatchery Extension Trail*

This trail passes over Cold Water Creek twice.

Wishart Park Extension

Level of difficulty 🚶 🚶

Distance *2km (1mi) loop*

Approx. time *1hr return*

Markers *Purple*

Trailhead *Begins off the Fish Hatchery Extension, or from Fourth Line E. or from inside Wishart Park*

This trail leads to a lookout over Root River, where salmon spawn in the fall.

Kap-Kig-Iwan Provincial Park

Location *North of New Liskeard*

Number of trails *3*

Total distance *12km (7.2mi)*

Interesting features *Englehart River, High Falls, Horseshoe Falls, spring wildflowers, old growth eastern cedars*

Facilities/services *Parking, vault toilets*

Other *Dogs on leashes permitted*

Kap-Kig-Iwan park is a Natural Environment park. As such, it welcomes fishers, hikers, bird-watchers and canoeists. In the winter, one trail is open for cross-country skiers.

Three trails—the 4.5km (2.7mi) Cedar Trial, the 2.5km (1.5mi) Hell's Gate Trail and the 5km (3mi) Upland Circle Trail—welcome hikers interested in old growth cedars, waterfalls and bird watching.

› Getting There

Take Highway 11 north from New Liskeard to Englehart, where Highway 560 begins. Turn left (west) on Highway 560 to get to the park.

› Further Information

Kap-Kig-Iwan Provincial Park
PO Box 910, 10 E. Government Rd.
Kirkland Lake, ON P2N 3K4
☎ 705-544-2050, 705-235-1353 or 800-667-1940
www.ontarioparks.com

Killarney Provincial Park

Location *North shore of Georgian Bay, south of Sudbury*

Number of trails *4*

Total distance *109km (67.6mi)*

Interesting features *Off-white quartzite hills called the La Cloche Mountains*

Facilities/services *Parking, toilets, telephones, canoe rental, playground, fishing, swimming beaches, camping, laundry area, showers, amphitheatre, canoe launch*

Other *Dogs on leashes permitted*
Can and bottle ban in effect

Ask anybody who's been to Killarney Provincial Park and they'll tell you about clear blue lakes, white hills, pink granite ridges, cranberries and lots of sugar maples–plus pine, cedar, oak, black cherry and the occasional American beech. There's also an ecologically significant boggy area, with a hiking trail straight through it. Wolves, bears, snowshoe hares, moose, muskrats, beavers, otters and bobcats all live in the region. The 48,500ha (119,795-acre) wilderness park also provides an ideal habitat for more than 100 species of birds, including warblers, thrushes, kingfishers, terns, falcons, grey jays, chickadees, loons and sandhill cranes.

The huge, white ridges are the eroded remains of a ring of mountains called the La Cloche Mountains. Since their formation two billion years ago, four différent glaciers and 11,000 years of wind have eroded them to the ridges that appear now.

The La Cloche Mountains have always attracted visitors. Archaeological digs have established three different prehistoric periods of use by people, the first 9,000 years ago, the second 6,500 years ago and the third 1,500 years ago. The area continues to attract a diverse group of nomadic travellers, especially on the famous 100km (62mi) trail that circles the La Cloche Mountains and takes backpackers at least a week to complete. The slightly less enthusiastic hiker hasn't been left out though; the park also offers three smaller day hikes, one to Georgian Bay, one along the cranberry bog and a third along an important granite ridge.

› Getting There

Take Highway 69 south from Sudbury or north from Parry Sound to Highway 637. Turn west towards the town of Killarney. It's another 68km (42mi) to the campground.

› Further Information

Killarney Provincial Park
Killarney, ON P0M 2A0
705-287-2900 or 800-667-1940
www.ontarioparks.com

The Friends of Killarney Park
www.friendsofkillarneypark.ca

Chikanishing Trail

Level of difficulty 🚶🚶

Distance *3km (1.9mi) loop*

Approx. time *1.5hrs return*

Trailhead *From the second parking lot off the access road south of Hwy. 637, near the boat launch*

Other *Plan on taking a swim halfway through your hike*

The Chikanishing Trail, named after a creek that flows into Georgian Bay, leads up several pink bedrock outcrops and through forests in a formerly logged area. Interpretive signs point out traces of the area's forestry past, including mooring rings in the rocks where log booms were tied while waiting for tugboats to pick them up.

Cranberry Bog Trail

Level of difficulty 🚶🚶

Distance *4km (2.5mi) loop*

Approx. time *2.5hrs return*

Trailhead *Off the La Cloche Silhouette Trail or the east side of George Lake campground, just south of the La Cloche Silhouette Trail trailhead*

The trail through the cranberry bog is covered with jagged rocks in spots and crosses several wetlands, beaver ponds and beaver marshes. Leatherleaf, sundews and pitcher plants grow in the bog along with the cranberries.

Granite Ridge Trail

Level of difficulty 🚶

Distance *2km (1mi) loop*

Approx. time *1hr return*

Trailhead *South of the park office, past Hwy. 637, towards Georgian Bay*

This trail leads along the granite ridge to a great lookout towards Philip Edward Island and Georgian Bay. Several steep climbs and a rocky path will slow you down.

La Cloche Silhouette Trail

Level of difficulty 🥾🥾🥾

Distance *100km (62mi) loop*

Approx. time *7 to 10 days return*

Trailhead *The east or west side of George Lake campground*

Other *Campsites are available along the trail*

The La Cloche Silhouette Trail leads up and down the rocky granite and quartz ridges past George Lake, Threenarrows Lake, Boundary Lake, Norway Lake, Killarney Lake and a number of beaver meadows. Take a short detour to see the popular sailboat anchorage Baie Fine, or a side trail to Silver Peak, the park's highest point, at 543m (1,781ft) above sea level.

Lake Laurentian Conservation Area

Location *Central Sudbury*

Number of trails *5*

Total distance *23km (14.3mi)*

Interesting features *Ramsey Lake, Lake Laurentian, rocky plains, causeways across marshes*

Facilities/services *Parking, toilets, telephones, canoe rental, playground, ski cottage, nature chalet*

It's hard to believe that such a wonderful wilderness area would be available within the city of Sudbury. For an ideal morning, spend about four hours circling Lake Laurentian on the 12km (7.4mi) Hiking Trail and the 1km (.6mi) Lakeside Trail that loops from the Nature Chalet. You'll traverse rocky plains covered in blueberry bushes and pass through mixed forests before reaching the marshes on the south side of the lake. In this area, expect to cross at least two very wet causeways and one short bridge.

If you'd rather spend less time in the area, run along the 4km (2.5mi) Ramsey Lake Running and Biking Trail, wander along the 2km (1.2mi) Self Guided Nature Trail, or climb the 4km (2.5mi) Beaver Pond Trail.

› Getting There

Take Highway 17 West to Sudbury and exit at Lorne Street. Continue to Regent Street South (Highway 69 South) and turn right. Follow Regent Street South to Paris Street. Turn left. Follow Paris Street to Ramsey Lake Road. Turn right. Continue to South Bay Road. Turn right and continue until you get to the access road for the Nature Chalet, just before a huge hill, that leads to the Ski Cottage. Turn right onto this road.

› Further Information

Nickel District Conservation Authority
200 Brady St., 1st Floor, Tom Davies Square
Sudbury, ON P3A 5K3
☎ 705-674-5249
www.nickeldistrict.ca

Lake Superior Provincial Park

Location *Hwy. 17 between Sault Ste. Marie and Wawa*

Number of trails *11*

Total distance *128km (79.4mi)*

Interesting features *30 Aboriginal pictographs, waterfalls, floating boardwalk, a rock formation in the shape of an old woman's face, Agawa Falls, salmon spawning, Agawa Valley cliffs, Peat Mountain, Pukaskwa pits, Algoma Central Railway*

Facilities/services *Parking, toilets, telephones, playground, swimming beaches, camping, laundry area, showers, visitor centre*

Other *Dogs on leashes permitted*

In many ways, the history of Lake Superior Provincial Park, a 155,600ha (384,332-acre) region on the shores of Lake Superior, is a microcosm of Canadian history. Thanks to the volcanoes and earthquakes that moulded the Canadian Shield into towering mountains and deep canyons, and the modulating effects of four different glaciers since then, the park includes a variety of significant rock features. Two of these are Agawa Rock, which is highlighted on the Agawa Rock Pictograph trails and Agawa Mountain, which is reached via the Awausee Trail. The Awausee Trail also offers some great lookouts over the Agawa Valley and the Agawa River. Agawa Canyon is also right next to the park. Visitors who want to hike through the canyon have to take the Algoma Central Railway, which operates along the park's eastern border.

In the 18th and 19th centuries, the current day park was the site of fierce competition between the Hudson's Bay Company and the North West Company, each of which operated a fur-trading outpost in the park, one at Batchawana and the other at Agawa. The contest only ended when the two companies merged in 1821. Although the business of trapping eventually became less economically viable over the years, several people operated trap lines in the park over the next century. You can explore one such trap line by walking along the Trappers Trail, where you will have a good chance of seeing porcupines, moose and deer. Caribou and bear also live within the park's borders, as do red squirrels, martens, red foxes, Canada lynx and timber wolves. You may also spot eastern garter snakes, painted turtles, American toads and many different salamander and frog species.

Lake Superior itself played an important economic role, particularly in the late 1800s when Gargantua Harbour was the site of a significant commercial fishery. Today, hikers can view the tremendous power of the huge body of water that gives the park its name from some awe-inspiring lookouts on the Orphan Lake Trail or along the 63km (39mi) Coastal Trail that meanders along the cliff faces and bays on the north shore of Lake Superior.

Tourism was also important in the late 1800s, when wealthy patrons of the park stayed at a number of tourist lodges. Hikers should make a point of passing by the Agawa Lodge, the only remaining tourist cabin from this period, on the latest extension of the Coastal Trail between Sinclair Cove and Agawa Bay.

Logging took over as the economic force over the past century and continued to play an important role until 1989, when park authorities put an end to the practice completely. There are still several old trees in the area, however, including 80- to 100-year-old specimens along the Crescent Lake Trail.

› Getting There

Take Highway 17 north from Sault Ste. Marie or south from Wawa.

› Further Information

Lake Superior Provincial Park/ Niijkiwenhwag – Friends of Lake Superior
PO Box 267
Wawa, ON P0S 1K0
705-856-2284 or 800-667-1940
www.ontarioparks.com

Trapper's Trail

Level of difficulty 🚶

Distance *1.5km (.9mi) loop*

Approx. time *1hr return*

Trailhead *Parking lot east of Hwy. 17, 167km (103.5mi) north of Sault Ste. Marie or 58km (36mi) south of Wawa*

This trail leads through the Renner brothers' trap line, which was active until 1975. Two viewing platforms and a floating boardwalk provide a pleasant walk along the shoreline of Rustle Lake. You're likely to see beavers, otters, great blue herons and perhaps even a moose if you're lucky.

Crescent Lake Trail

Level of difficulty 🚶

Distance *2km (1mi) loop*

Approx. time *1hr return*

Trailhead *Enter from the Crescent Lake Campground, on the west side of Hwy. 17, 132km (82mi) north of Sault Ste. Marie or 93km (58mi) south of Wawa*

This trail leads through an 80- to 100-year-old birch, maple, beech and white pine forest. You'll also pass several lakes.

Pinguisibi Trail

Level of difficulty 🚶

Distance *3km (1.9mi) linear*

Approx. time *2hrs each way*

Trailhead *Access via Sand River day-use area, on the east side of Hwy. 17, 152km (94mi) north of Sault Ste. Marie or 73km (45mi) south of Wawa*

This trail leads along the shore of the Sand River to a series of waterfalls and rapids.

Agawa Rock Pictographs Trail

Level of difficulty 🚶🚶

Distance *.5km (.3mi) linear*

Approx. time *1hr each way*

Trailhead *Turn at Agawa Rock Pictograph Rd., on the west side of Hwy. 17, 82km (51mi) north of Sault Ste. Marie or 143km (89mi) south of Wawa, and continue another 2km (1.2mi) to the coast*

Climb out onto a ledge to view almost 30 Aboriginal pictographs at Agawa Rock, also known as

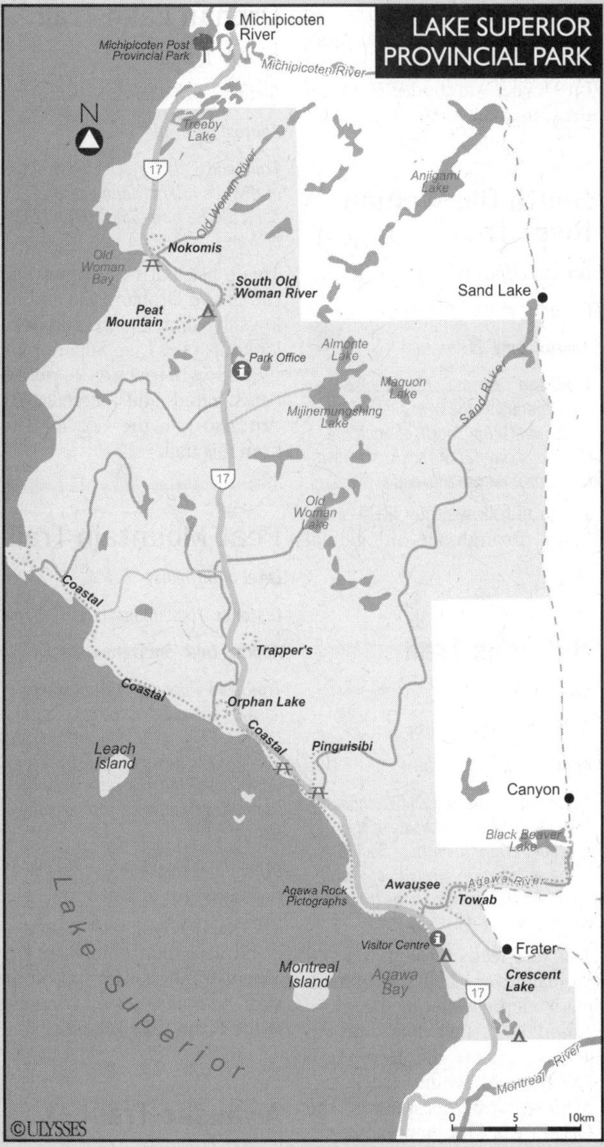
LAKE SUPERIOR
PROVINCIAL PARK
Michipicoten River
Michipicoten Post Provincial Park
Michipicoten River
Treeby Lake
17
Old Woman River
Anjigami Lake
Nokomis
Old Woman Bay
South Old Woman River
Sand Lake
Peat Mountain
Almonte Lake
Park Office
Maquon Lake
Mijinemungshing Lake
Sand River
Old Woman Lake
Coastal
Trapper's
Coastal
Orphan Lake
Coastal
Pinguisibi
Leach Island
Canyon
Black Beaver Lake
Agawa Rock Pictographs
Awausee
Agawa River
Towab
Visitor Centre
Frater
Lake Superior
Montreal Island
Agawa Bay
Crescent Lake
Montreal River
0
5
10km
©ULYSSES

the "Inscription" rock. The red ochre used to paint them probably came from a natural deposit on Devil's Warehouse Island in the Gargantua area.

South Old Woman River Trail

Level of difficulty 🚶 🚶

Distance *2.5km (1.6mi) loop*

Approx. time *2hrs return*

Trailhead *Park at Rabbit Blanket Lake Campground on the west side of Hwy. 17, 193km (120mi) north of Sault Ste. Marie or 32km (20mi) south of Wawa; trailhead is across the road*

This trail follows the Old Woman River through an old glacial spillway.

Nokomis Trail

Level of difficulty 🚶 🚶

Distance *5km (3mi) loop*

Approx. time *3hrs return*

Trailhead *Park at the Old Woman Bay Picnic Area on the west side of Hwy. 17, 200km (124mi) north of Sault Ste. Marie or 25km (16mi) south of Wawa, and cross the highway to the trailhead on the east side*

This trail leads through the Old Woman River Valley past human-made depressions in the rocks called Pukaskwa Pits, and up across a granite cliff. Here you'll see the old woman rock formation known as *Nokomis*, the Ojibwa word for grandmother.

Orphan Lake Trail

Level of difficulty 🚶 🚶

Distance *8km (5mi) loop*

Approx. time *4hrs return*

Trailhead *Parking lot on the west side of Hwy. 17, 161km (100mi) north of Sault Ste. Marie or 64km (40mi) south of Wawa*

This trail climbs to the top of a cliff above Orphan Lake and follows the shoreline to even better lookouts over Lake Superior and then down towards a pebble beach, rapids and waterfalls. You can also join the Coastal Trail from this trail.

Peat Mountain Trail

Level of difficulty 🚶 🚶 🚶

Distance *11km (6.8mi) loop*

Approx. time *5hrs return*

Trailhead *Park at Rabbit Blanket Lake Campground on the east side of Hwy. 17, 193km (119.5mi) north of Sault Ste. Marie or 32km (20mi) south of Wawa; enter the trail either from the campground entrance or from campsite no. 49*

Other *One campsite along the trail at Foam Lake*

This trail leads past a beaver pond and then climbs to Peat Mountain, the tallest spot in the park. A short side loop continues to the Foam Lake Lookout.

Awausee Trail

Level of difficulty 🚶 🚶 🚶

Distance *10km (6.2mi) loop*

Approx. time *3hrs return*

Trailhead Parking lot on the east side of Hwy. 17, 140km (87mi) north of Sault Ste. Marie or 85km (53mi) south of Wawa

This trail leads up Agawa Mountain along an old logging road and a ravine. Several lookouts along the way provide spectacular views of the Agawa River and Agawa Mountain.

Towab Trail

Level of difficulty 🚶🚶🚶

Distance *12km (7.4mi) linear*

Approx. time *16hrs each way*

Trailhead *Turn on Frater Rd., on the east side of Hwy. 17, 137km (85mi) north of Sault Ste. Marie or 88km (54mi) south of Wawa; drive 15 to 20min on a very rough road until you reach the trailhead on the north side, 4.5km (2.8mi) from the turnoff*

Other *7 campsites available on the trail*

Named after a famous Ojibwa guide, this trail leads along the Agawa River Valley to Burnt Rock Pool and Agawa Falls, climbing and descending around cliffs the entire way.

Coastal Hiking Trail

Level of difficulty 🚶🚶🚶

Distance *63km (39mi) linear*

Approx. time *7 to 14 days each way*

Trailheads *Turn at Gargantua Rd., on the west side of Hwy. 17, 173km (107mi) north of Sault Ste. Marie or 52km (32.5mi) south of Wawa, and continue another 13km (8mi) to the coast; or turn at Agawa Rock Indian Pictograph Rd., on the west side of Hwy. 17, 82km (51mi) north of Sault Ste. Marie or 143km (89mi) south of Wawa, and continue another 2km (1.2mi) to the coast*

Other *Many campsites along the trail*

The Coastal Trail leads along the shore of Lake Superior from Agawa Bay to Chalfant Cove. If you access the trail via Gargantua Road, you can either head north and hike 9km (5.6mi) to the end of the trail or head south to hike all the way to Agawa Bay. The Coastal Trail extends onto the Agawa Rock Pictographs Trail after the parking lot and then continues to the Agawa Campground.

Magpie Falls and Fort Friendship

Location *Hwy. 17, South of Wawa*

Number of trails *1*

Total distance *12km (7.4mi)*

Interesting features *Magpie High Falls, Mission Falls, Wawa Creek Falls, Dead River (Old Michipicoten River), Simmons Hill, Fort Friendship, Turcott grave, Driftwood Beach overlook*

Facilities/services *Parking, toilets and telephone at Magpie High Falls*

Other *This trail is part of the Voyageur Trail; dogs on leashes permitted*

Begin this trail at the 25m (82ft) high and 38m (125ft) wide Magpie High Falls. Cross the wooden bridge and walk along the Magpie River gorge and then up to a ridge beside the river valley. Continue through the forest to a bluff overlooking the valley gorge and then up and down hills at the base of Legarde Mountain. The Magpie River ends at a three-part waterfall known as Mission Falls. You'll see the upper falls first, as they drop 8m (25ft). Cross the road to follow a trail to the middle falls, also known as Silver Falls, which drop 5m (15ft). You'll have to bypass the trail to see the lower falls, which drop 6m (20ft) just a bit farther along the river.

To continue on the trail, turn left to follow the Michipicoten River, also known as the Dead River, to the mouth of Wawa Creek. Turn to follow Wawa Creek until it drops in another waterfall.

Continue across the bridge across Wawa Creek Falls to follow the city street to the municipal water station. There, you'll continue along a narrow gravel road that leads up a ridge. At the top of the ridge, you'll get a good view of the Dead River and the land within Michipicoten Post Provincial Park. Michipicoten Post used to house a trading post once run by the French, the North West Company and the Hudson Bay Company until it closed in 1904. Eventually, park officials hope to have hiking trails leading to and along the shore.

Follow the bluff to Mission Road, which leads to the Trans-Canada Highway. Continue along the highway to Fort Road. Turn right to reach Fort Friendship. You'll see a glass bottle chapel, historical murals and a painted water tower. Not far away is the gravesite of Bernard Al Turcott, who once owned the fort. Provincial Park officials consider this site a "safety hazard."

From there, follow Driftwood Beach Road past an abandoned water wheel to Mission Lake. Cross Mission Creek on the old beaver dam. Climb to the Driftwood Beach overlook and continue along the Lake Superior shoreline to the old gravel Bridget Lake Resources Road.

› Getting There

Take Highway 17 south of Wawa or north of Lake Superior Provincial Park to Magpie High Falls Road. Turn east to get to the falls.

› Further Information

Voyageur Trail Association
PO Box 20040, 150 Churchill Blvd.
Sault Ste. Marie, ON P6A 6W3
☎ 877-393-4003
www3.sympatico.ca/voyageur.trail

Ministry of Natural Resources
Hwy. 101, PO Box 1160
Wawa, ON P0S 1K0
☎ 705-856-2396 or 800-667-1940
www.ontarioparks.com

Mississagi Provincial Park

Location *Hwy. 639, north of Elliot Lake*

Number of trails *5*

Total distance *42km (25.2mi)*

Interesting features *Penokean Hills, Semiwite Lake and Creek*

Facilities/services *Parking, toilets, telephone, swimming beaches, camping, park store, boat launch, canoe rentals*

Other *Dogs on leashes permitted*

This 4,900ha (12,100-acre) natural reserve park through the Penokean Hills was established in 1965, a decade after the Blue Sky Mine was established by the Harvard Uranium Mine Ltd. to extract chalcopyrite, an ore containing copper. The abandoned mine site and remnants of copper drilling combine with stunning lookouts and multiple wildlife sightings for spectacular wilderness hiking. Clear water, sandy beaches everywhere and great canoeing add to the pleasure.

Most of the hiking trails stem from the park store in the campground. The park used to have six or eight defined trails but the portion of trail around the south side of Semiwite Lake and the loop beyond known as the Jimchrist Trail have been closed. The five official trails remaining offer enough beauty for a full week at the park.

› Getting There

From Highway 17 at Serpent River (between Espanola and Sault Ste. Marie), turn north on Highway 108 to get to Elliot Lake. From there, continue north on Highway 639 for about 15 minutes.

› Further Information

Mississagi Provincial Park
PO Box 37
Massey, ON P0P 1P0
☎ 705-848-2806, 705-865-2021 or 800-667-1940
www.ontarioparks.com

Flack Lake Nature Trail

Level of difficulty 🚶

Distance *.8km (.5mi) linear*

Approx. time *30 min*

This trail leads from the parking lot past an old mining camp to the boat launch on Flack Lake. Highlights include old growth trees and fossils in glacial-wave rippled sandstone.

Helenbar Lookout Trail

Level of difficulty 🚶🚶

Distance *7km (4.2mi) loop*

Approx. time *4 hrs*

This trail is the most popular one in the park, as it's the shortest link to a scenic view over Helenbar Lake.

Cobre Lake Trail

Level of difficulty 🚶🚶🚶

Distance *11km (6.6mi) loop + extension*

Approx. time *5 hrs*

The Cobre Lake trail leads around Bluesky and Tenfish lakes past remnants of the former mining and logging eras. An extension leads around Cobre Lake and to a parking lot near Highway 639.

Semiwite Creek Trail

Level of difficulty 🚶

Distance *1.2km (.7mi) loop*

Approx. time *30 min*

This short trail follows the shore of a local creek past many scenic vistas.

MacKenzie Trail

Level of difficulty 🚶🚶🚶

Distance *22km (13mi) loop*

Approx. time *24hrs*

This trail is named after Flight Lt. Hugh Mackenzie, who crashed on Helenbar Lake in 1946 and lasted for three weeks in the bush before a fishing party rescued him. Besides the crash site, it leads past an old logging camp to Upper and Lower Brush lakes and then to the top of Bear Mountain. Scenic views overlooking the provincially significant Stag Lake Peatland. Two overnight camping sites are available.

Samuel de Champlain Provincial Park

Location *On Hwy. 17, west of Mattawa*

Number of trails *3*

Total distance *12.5km (7.5mi)*

Interesting features *The Mattawa River, Campion Rapids, Paresseux Falls, Talon Chutes, potholes, glacial-era river beds, sand dunes*

Other *Pets on leashes permitted on all trails*

Facilities/Services *Parking, toilets, telephones, convenience store, laundry, maps, camping, pebble beach, canoe rentals*

The 2,550ha (6,298-acre) park along the Mattawa River protects a 600 million year-old fault and historic remnants of glaciers on the Canadian Shield. The river runs along the fault line, dividing the park between large rolling hills in the north and gentle lowlands in the south. Hikers will learn about prehistoric campgrounds, Canadian explorers, voyageur travels during the fur trade era and current canoeing on the Mattawa River, which has been designated a Canadian Heritage River. They also may see moose, bears, deer and more than 200 species of birds.

The nonprofit Canadian Ecology Centre is stationed on the site to offer nature programs to schoolchildren and meeting participants. It also rents out conference facilities and 32 log cabins.

› Getting There

To get to the park, take Highway 17 east from North Bay or west from Ottawa. The park entrance lies to the north, just west of Mattawa.

› Further Information

Samuel de Champlain Provincial Park
PO Box 147
Mattawa, ON P0H 1V0
☎ 705-744-2276 or 800-667-1940
www.ontarioparks.com

Canadian Ecology Centre
PO Box 430, 6905 Hwy. 17
Mattawa, ON P0H 1V0
☎ 705-744-7577 or 888-747-7577
www.canadianecology.ca

Wabashkiki Trail

Level of difficulty 🚶

Distance *1 km (.6mi) loop*

Approx. time *45mins return*

Trailhead *At the Bagwa Day Use area on the south side of the park, just after the main entrance*

The Wabashkiki Trail features a floating boardwalk over the marsh south of Moore Lake.

Étienne Trail

Level of difficulty 🚶 🚶

Distance *2.5 to 9km (1.5 to 5.5mi) quadruple loop*

Approx. time *From 1.25 to 5hrs return*

Trailhead *North of Moore Lake and the Babawasse Campground, off Long Lake Road*

Named after explorer Étienne Brûlé, the first European to visit the area in 1611, this trail leads to the park's most scenic views of the Mattawa River. Each loop contains a series of interpretative panels on various themes. The shortest loop is called the ecology loop and panels throughout the stand of red and white pine focus on the needs of a healthy natural ecosystem. Panels along the 5km (3mi) geology loop explains the major fault that forms the Mattawa River Valley as well as other similar features as it leads past Long and Coco lakes. The 8.5km (5mi) nature loop highlights park flora and fauna. Panels along the longest loop, known as the History Trail, describe the Aboriginals and voyageurs who explored the region.

Kag Trail

Level of difficulty 🚶 🚶

Distance *2.5 km (1.5mi) loop*

Approx. time *1.25 hrs return*

Trailhead *On the east side of the Jingwakoki Campground, just south of the Amable du Fond River*

The Kag Trail features a few steep climbs through a stand of tall red pines, past Gem Lake and the former homestead of Amable du Fond, an Aboriginal chief who once lived in the area. Interpretive panels feature Aboriginal beliefs. The word "kag" means porcupine.

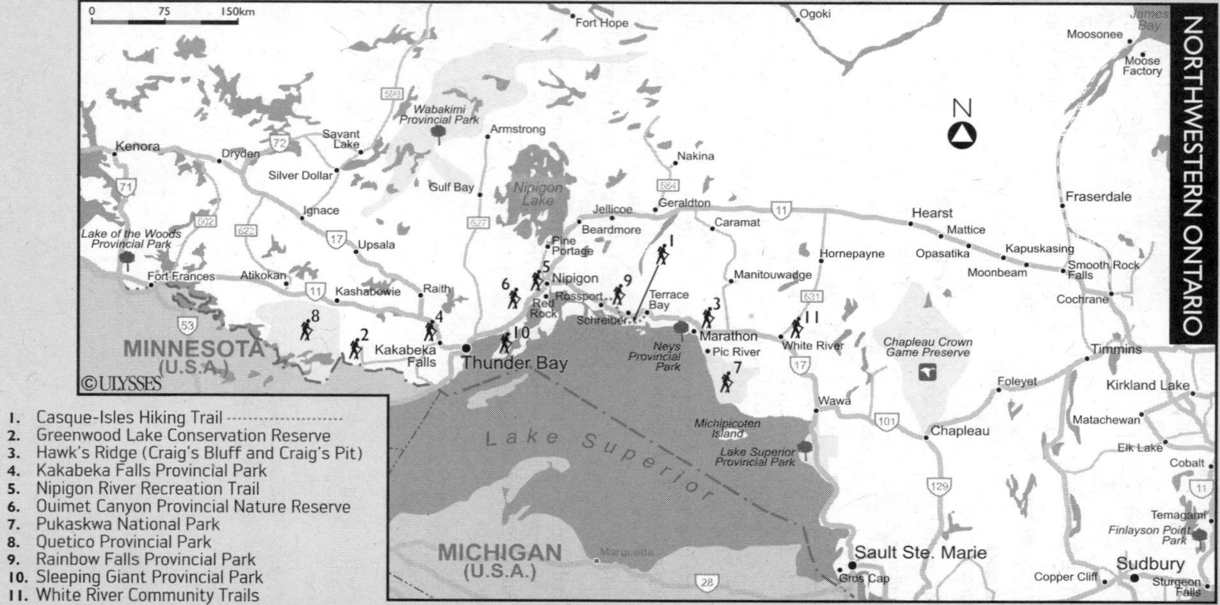
NORTHWESTERN ONTARIO
0 75 150km
N
James Bay
Moosonee
Moose Factory
Ogoki
Fort Hope
Fraserdale
Smooth Rock Falls
Cochrane
Kapuskasing
Moonbeam
Opasatika
Mattice
Hearst
Hornepayne
Manitouwadge
Caramat
Geraldton
Nakina
Jellicoe
Beardmore
Pine Portage
Nipigon
Nipigon Lake
Armstrong
Gulf Bay
Wabakimi Provincial Park
Savant Lake
Silver Dollar
Dryden
Kenora
Ignace
Upsala
Raith
Kashabowie
Atikokan
Fort Frances
Lake of the Woods Provincial Park
Kakabeka Falls
Thunder Bay
Red Rock
Rossport
Schreiber
Terrace Bay
Neys Provincial Park
Marathon
Pic River
White River
Wawa
Chapleau Crown Game Preserve
Chapleau
Foleyet
Timmins
Kirkland Lake
Matachewan
Elk Lake
Cobalt
Temagami
Finlayson Point Park
Sudbury
Sturgeon Falls
Copper Cliff
Sault Ste. Marie
Gros Cap
Michipicoten Island
Lake Superior Provincial Park
Lake Superior
Marquette
MICHIGAN (U.S.A.)
MINNESOTA (U.S.A.)
©ULYSSES
1. Casque-Isles Hiking Trail
2. Greenwood Lake Conservation Reserve
3. Hawk's Ridge (Craig's Bluff and Craig's Pit)
4. Kakabeka Falls Provincial Park
5. Nipigon River Recreation Trail
6. Ouimet Canyon Provincial Nature Reserve
7. Pukaskwa National Park
8. Quetico Provincial Park
9. Rainbow Falls Provincial Park
10. Sleeping Giant Provincial Park
11. White River Community Trails

Northwestern Ontario

Hiking has always been popular in northwestern Ontario as more than a simple form of recreation. Here, people also rely on hiking (or portaging) as an opportunity for spiritual awakening and as an essential mode of transportation that fills in when other modes disappoint.

Opportunities for spiritual awakening arise from pilgrimages to large rock formations that have inspired legends for generations. The most prominent of these varied rock formations is one that looks like Gulliver in the land of the Lilliputians at **Sleeping Giant Provincial Park** (see p. 259), near Thunder Bay. Hiking trails encircle and traverse the humongous rock formation to enable walkers to circle the giant, a feat that takes almost a week. There are also trails that enable you to climb his knees or chest in one day. The Sleeping Giant was of spiritual significance to the Ojibway, who tell stories about how the Sioux helped European miners discover the silver within its depths.

The Ojibway, the Sioux, early explorers and fur traders all travelled by canoe along Lake Superior, as well as the other lakes and rivers in this region. They created pathways along the shores and portages from one shore to another to bypass rapids, rocks, beaver dams and other inconveniences. Today, hikers follow many of the old portage routes alongside rivers, although now the purpose is no longer to avoid waterfalls or beaver dams, but to get the best view of such features that were once only natural impediments. The trails and platforms at **Rainbow Falls Provincial Park** (see p. 257), for example, provide hikers with the best possible view of a cascading river from one point and Lake Superior's shoreline from the top of a ridge at another. **Hawk's Ridge** (see p. 248) trail, in Marathon, also leads to the top of a ridge that provides both a good view of Lake Superior, and a wonderful opportunity to get close to the hawks. To relive the experiences of these early explorers, hikers can visit a rare old growth forest at the **Greenwood Lake Conservation Reserve** (see p. 246), or they can take a a two- or three-day canoeing trip with multiple portages through the scenic wilderness at **Quetico Provincial Park** (see p. 255).

Many of these scenic areas inland only became evident when the Canadian Pacific Railway began laying track across the region in the 1880s. Huge gorges of solid granite and gneiss were found. The largest of these discovered landmarks was **Ouimet Canyon** (see p. 251), a gorge 150km (93mi) wide and 100m (90ft) deep that attracts thousands of visitors a year.

Perhaps not surprisingly, such discoveries gave northwestern Ontario a horrible reputation for difficult terrain. Blasting all the rocks required to lay this part of the track demanded more money, time and labour than any other section of the line. At the peak of construction, 12,000 men and 5,000 horses lived and worked at a regional base camp in

Peninsula Harbour, now known as Marathon. The track was so difficult to lay that patches remained unfinished for years. People–including the federal soldiers sent to quash Louis Riel's Red River Rebellion–had to rely on the old portage routes. Today, hikers can follow the same route those soldiers took on the Mountain Portage Trail at **Kakabeka Falls Provincial Park** (see p. 248).

Once the rails were finished, however, they opened up possibilities for new hiking routes next to the tracks. Thankfully, views of towering cliffs and huge trestle bridges appear equally grand from outside the train as they do from inside. You'll see a couple of these views from the **Casque-Isles Hiking Trail** (see p. 244).

You'll also pass old tote roads made by lumber barons who opened up interior regions to gain access to strong stands of white and red pine. Many of today's lookouts replace those old stands, while logging roads form convenient trails to and from good views. The Coastal Trail at **Pukaskwa National Park** (see p. 253) also leads hikers along and past old logging roads to a 30m-long (100ft) suspended bridge that is 23m (75ft) above the White River for an indescribable view that everyone should see at least once. The bridge has become such a popular destination that a boat transports hikers to and from it on summer Saturdays. Current loggers have also opened up some trails for hikers. Domtar, for example, has created the **White River Community Trails** (see p. 266) on its old logging property.

Roads have come in more recently, although they still cover less than an eighth of the territory. Those that do exist run from the Trans-Canada Highway like branches from a split trunk. Driving gets quite difficult in the north because there aren't enough towns to keep drivers entertained. There are so few that even those with insignificant populations show up on the road map as comparatively giant dots. Ear Falls, for instance, has a population of only seven souls, yet on the map it appears just as large as Red Lake, a town with 4,873 inhabitants. And thank goodness it does. Drivers cheer these tiny towns' presence on the map as joyous indicators of life ahead. After an hour or two of seeing nothing but trees and giant stone ridges, a gas station or campground makes a gratifying sight. Even billboards become welcome signs of civilization, especially as the sun sets. That's when the ubiquitous yellow road signs depicting a giant moose with the words "night danger" become more and more ominous.

It's more rewarding to see moose from the trails, something you're very likely to do in this part of Ontario. There is also somewhat more "exotic" wildlife here too, such as white pelicans near Kenora and caribou near Pukaskwa. You're also very likely to see bears, wolves and other dangerous predators here, as the giant bear-proof containers placed at many campsites indicate. The north's reputation for black flies and mosquitoes seems a bit overblown, too, since insect repellent or netting is always necessary while hiking in Ontario. You may well encounter more mosquitoes in Ottawa than in Thunder Bay.

Since the roads have arrived, Ontario Hydro has created brand new paths for hikers to follow. Trail-blazing volunteers followed four Hydro poles for part of a trail, known as the **Nipigon River Recreation Trail** (see p. 250), which runs between the Red Rock and Nipigon marinas.

The Nipigon River Recreation Trail and all the other marked public trails in this region are extremely difficult to maintain. Beaver dams, fallen trees, and mini-avalanches frequently block the paths and volunteers must reblaze existing trails every spring. In some areas, hikers can expect to blaze parts of trails themselves.

The extra work is worth the effort, however. Every trail in the region highlights cliffs, outcrops, jagged terrain, lakes, rivers, waterfalls and lookouts in awe-inspiring scenery. Hiking the trails in Northern Ontario quickly becomes an obsession.

➤ Tourist Information

North of Superior Tourism
920 Tungsten St., Suite 206A*
Thunder Bay, ON P7B 5Z6
☎ 807-346-1130 or 800-265-3951
www.nosta.on.ca
www.lakesuperiorcircletour.info

Ontario's Sunset Country Travel Association
PO Box 647 W
Kenora, ON P9N 3S6
☎ 807-468-5853 or 800-665-7567
www.sunsetcountry.ca

Casque-Isles Hiking Trail

Location *Links Terrace Bay, Schreiber and Rossport*

Number of trails *1*

Total distance *52km (32mi) linear*

Approx. time *2-3 days each way*

Interesting features *Aguasabon Falls, pictographs, Rainbow Falls, lookouts over Lake Superior*

Trailheads *Terrace Bay, Worthington Bay, Schreiber, Rossport*

Markers *Blue diamond with a white hiker*

Facilities/Services *Toilets in each town, campsites*

Other *Dogs on leashes are permitted*

The Casque-Isles Trail meanders for 52km (32mi) along the northern shore of Lake Superior. Named after John Bigsby's description of the north shore of Lake Superior from Pic Island, the trail forms a significant part of the **Voyageur Trail** (see p. 70).

You'll walk through vast boreal forests, stands of birch and poplar, past sandy beaches and across barren ridges of bedrock. You'll see the remnants of glaciers, the days of logging, railway building and mining. Rare birds often show up during migration in the spring and fall. Also, look for spruce grouse, boreal chickadees and grey jays.

Mount Gwynne Lookout is the most famous of the many lookouts along the trail, both because it provides a full circular view of the area and because it contains a memorial plaque to the late founder of the trail, Thomas D. McGrath.

› Getting There

Reach the five distinct sections from a variety of access points along Highway 17, as described in each section.

› Further Information

The Terrace Bay Tourist Information Centre
PO Box 1207, 1008 Hwy. 17
Terrace Bay, ON P0T 2W0
807-825-9721 or 800-968-8616 (Ontario only)
www.terracebay.ca

Lyda Bay Section

Level of difficulty 🚶

Distance *7.6km (4.7mi) linear*

Approx. time *3.5hrs each way*

Trailheads *A side trail beginning at the parking lot on the beach at Golf Course Rd., east of the hospital in Terrace Bay; the Gorge parking lot on Aguasabon Gorge Rd., 1km (.6mi) south of Hwy. 17; Hydro Bay Rd., .5 km (.3mi) south of Hwy. 17; cross Country Ski Access Rd., near the beach, 1km (.6mi) south of Hwy. 17*

Other *3 campsites*

This popular eastern portion begins along the Aguasabon Gorge in Terrace Bay and climbs to a view along the ridge. You'll walk along raised boulder beaches and past soft sandy beaches. Expect to see lots of families, particularly on weekends. Highlights include shallow bays and the Lyda Bay lookout, a view 61m (200ft) above Lake Superior.

Death Valley Section

Level of difficulty 🚶🚶🚶

Distance *14.2km (8.8mi) linear*

Approx. time *10hrs each way*

Trailheads *Cross Country Ski Access Rd., near the beach 1km (.6mi) south of Hwy. 17; parking lot on the west side of Worthington Bay Rd., 1km (.8mi) south of Hwy. 17*

This rocky trail leads past a sandbar, a reversing tide and through an 80m-deep (263ft) gorge called "Death Valley" to Aboriginal pictographs on the west side of Worthington Bay.

Mount Gwynne Section

Level of difficulty 🚶🚶

Distance *12.2km (8mi) linear*

Approx. time *5hrs each way*

Trailheads *Parking lot on the west side of Worthington Bay Rd., 1km (.8mi) south of Hwy. 17; access trail leading west from Winnipeg St. S. in Schreiber to Fourth Lake; trail leading east from Railway St. S. to Schreiber Beach Rd. in Schreiber*

This section features many lookouts over Lake Superior, including a superb view from Gwynne Mountain.

Schreiber Channel Section

Level of difficulty 🚶🚶

Distance *14.1km (8.8mi) linear*

Approx. time *6hrs each way*

Trailheads *Access trail leading west from Winnipeg St. S. in Schreiber to Fourth Lake Access trail leading east from Railway St. S. to Schreiber Beach Rd. in Schreiber; south side of Hwy. 17 at Rainbow Falls Provincial Park access road (parking lot on north side)*

This trail begins with the rapids and cascading falls of Blind Creek and then moves along a rocky shoreline, where Lake Superior's waves often crash loudly. It then passes the foundations of an old dock at Twin Harbours, along an old tote road, and past a rock formation known as the Gunflint Formation, which contains tiny fossils dating from 1.6 to two billion years ago. You'll also see boulder beaches, giant boulders known as glacial floats, raised terrace beaches and two lookouts known as Selim and Winston that provide good views of Lake Superior near Copper and Wilson Islands.

McLeans Section

Location *West of Rossport*

Level of difficulty 🚶

Distance *12.3km (7.6mi) linear*

Approx. time *5hrs each way*

Trailheads *North side of Hwy. 17 at Rainbow Falls Provincial Park access road; Falls Trail in Rainbow Falls Provincial Park; Sox Lake Rd., 2.2km (1.4mi) north of Hwy. 17; Side Trail from Hwy. 17, 3km (1.9mi) east of A1; Wardrope Park, at junction of Hwy. 17 and East Rossport Rd.*

This trail passes glacial erratics, cobble beaches, small creeks and stands of jack pine to several different lookouts over Lake Superior.

Greenwood Lake Conservation Reserve

Location *50km south of Kashabowie*

Number of trails *5*

Total distance *20km (1.2mi)*

Interesting features *Old growth white pine, peat bogs, Greenwood Lake*

Markers *Coloured diamond with a white hiker*

Facilities/Services *None*

› Getting There

From Kashabowie, take Highway 11 west to Highway 802. Turn south and continue for 6km (3.6mi) to Burchell Road. Turn left and continue for another 25km (15mi) to Sag-Mowe Road. Turn left and travel for another 5km (3mi) to get to Sag Road. (Saganaga Lake Road). Turn right and continue for 4km to the reserve.

› Further Information

Greenwood Lake Advisory Committee

Dr. Willard Carmean, Professor Emeritus of Forestry, Lakehead University
955 Oliver Rd.
Thunder Bay, ON P7B 5E1
✆ 807-343-8110
www.borealforest.org

The 811ha (2,004-acre) forestry reserve was established in 1992 to preserve an undisturbed stand of old-growth white pine forest and several small peat bogs.

Trees in the stand are all roughly 300 years old and probably are the result of a fire in the region. Although individual specimens can grow to 450 years, many of the trees in this forest have been weakened by heart rot. Some specimens exceed 1m (3ft) in diametre and rise 40m (131ft) high. Pine warblers can be found here, even though it is at its northern edge of their range.

Orange Trail

Level of difficulty 🚶 🚶

Distance *2km (1.2mi) loop*

Approx. time *1hr*

Trailhead *Saganaga Lake Road*

The orange trail loops south of Saganaga Lake Road through an old 1991 burn. Observant visitors will notice the white pine forest regenerating.

Yellow Trail

Level of difficulty 🚶 🚶

Distance *4km (2.4mi) loop*

Approx. time *2hrs*

Trailhead *Kiosk on Saganaga Lake Road*

The Yellow Trail offers the best view through the old-growth white pine forest and includes a good lookout over a peat bog.

Blue Trail

Level of difficulty 🚶 🚶

Distance *7km (4.2mi) linear plus loop*

Approx. time *3hrs each way*

Trailhead *Kiosk on Saganaga Lake Road*

The Blue Trail begins in the old-growth white pine forest and then continues through a mixed forest. It then loops to follow the shoreline of Greenwood Lake.

West Red Trail

Level of difficulty 🚶 🚶

Distance *4km (2.4mi) linear*

Approx. time *3hrs each way*

Trailheads *Saganaga Lake Road, Blue Trail*

The West Red Trail leads through the forest to link to the Blue Trail on the shore of Greenwood Lake. Most of it lies outside of the reserve boundary.

East Red Trail

Level of difficulty 🚶 🚶

Distance *3km (1.8mi) linear*

Approx. time *2.5hrs each way*

Trailheads *Saganaga Lake Road, Blue Trail*

This trail links Saganaga Lake Road, east of the conservation entrance, with the shore of Greenwood Lake and the Blue Trail.

Hawk's Ridge (Craig's Bluff and Craig's Pit)

Location *Marathon*

Number of trails *1*

Level of difficulty *🚶 🚶*

Total distance *3km (1.9mi) linear*

Approx. time *2.5hrs each way*

Interesting features *Hawks, view of Lake Superior*

Trailhead *The end of Hemlo Drive in Marathon, in the corner of the crescent, just past house no. 127*

Facilities/Services *None*

Other *Dogs on leashes permitted*

The entrance to Hawk's Ridge Trail begins at a short stream that dries into a road of sand and continues left onto a rocky path. The most difficult portion of the trail appears at the beginning when you must use a handrail to climb onto the first rock.

The trail is easy to follow from there. The woodland path of roots and stone continues in a light ascent. Boardwalks cover muddy patches. About halfway along, a trail to Penn Lake leads northeastward.

The view of Lake Superior from the sandy basin at the top of Craig's Bluff is wonderful on a clear day, but the atmosphere is especially charged when fog rolls in, creating an immediate steam-room-like atmosphere. You can't see the hawks that live on the ledge, although they fly so close you feel the flap from their wings. Their plaintive cries will remain in your memory as a reminder of life on the edge.

The trail leads beyond the sandy basin into Craig's Pit and a scene that looks like a page from a fairy tale. The deep forest here is blanketed with wet mist from the lake, so that all the tree trunks and fallen logs are covered with a brilliant green moss and lichen.

› Further Information

Marathon Information Centre
PO Bag "TM," 4 Hemlo Dr.
Marathon, ON P0T 2E0
☎ 807-229-1340
www.marathon.ca

Kakabeka Falls Provincial Park

Location *1hr west of Thunder Bay*

Number of trails *7*

Total distance *19km (12mi)*

Interesting features *Kakabeka Falls*

Facilities/Services *Parking, toilets, telephones, visitor information centre, convenience store, playground, swimming beaches, camping, laundry area, showers*

Other *Dogs on leashes permitted*

Kakabeka Falls Provincial Park has protected one of the most beautiful waterfalls in the north since 1954. The falls are 71m (234ft) wide and drop 39m (128ft) from the Kaministiquia River into a gorge where fossils as old as 1.6 billion years have been found. Other than the nickname "Niagara of the North," these falls share some similarities with their southern cousins. Both are absolute must-sees. Both are controlled by Ontario Hydro to appear more impressive on holidays and weekends. Both have an ancient history depicted in Ojibway oral tradition. Kakabeka Falls' legend is that of Greenmantle, a 17-year-old woman who led Sioux captors to their deaths over the falls, although no one seems to know whether Greenmantle swam safely to shore or if her spirit still floats about the "thundering water." That's where the similarities end. Kakabeka Falls has a much more rustic setting than its southern version.

› Getting There

The park is located west of the town of Kakabeka Falls on Highway 17/11.

› Further Information

Park Superintendent
Kakabeka Falls Provincial Park
PO Box 252
Kakabeka Falls, ON P0T 1W0
807-475-1535, 807-473-9231 or 800-667-1940
www.ontarioparks.com

Kakabeka Falls Boardwalk

Level of difficulty

Distance *1km (.6mi) linear*

Approx. time *15min return*

Trailhead *Falls parking lot*

Other *Wheelchair accessible*

This wheelchair-accessible boardwalk provides a good view of Kakabeka Falls from lookouts on each side of the Kaministiquia River. Although it's not really a hike, the boardwalk enables you to see the falls properly from almost any angle.

Contact Trail

Level of difficulty

Distance *1km (.6mi) loop and linear extension*

Approx. time *30min return*

Trailhead *Beach parking lot*

This trail is named after the "contact," a small region where grey sedimentary rock meets pink granite bedrock. This is the best trail to take if you want to wander around a bit on exposed granite and see some tiny waterfalls.

Poplar Point (Circle Trail)

Level of difficulty

Distance *4km (2.5mi) loop*

Approx. time *2hrs return*

Trailhead *Group Campground Rd. in Whispering Hills Campground*

This trail begins on a gravel road leading from Whispering Hills Campground and then goes through a wooded forest. Chipmunks and snowshoe hares are prevalent. White-tailed deer, red foxes and black bears also live in the area. Warblers, sparrows and wrens sing throughout the summer.

Mountain Portage Trail

Level of difficulty

Distance *1.25km (.8mi) loop*

Approx. time *45min return*

Trailhead *From the picnic area beside the information centre*

Other *Wheelchair accessible*

Although now a wheelchair-accessible gravel path, this trail was once a rugged portage past the mighty Kakabeka Falls. French explorer Jacques Doyon first described the trail in 1638, although it wasn't used much by Europeans until the shorter Grand Portage Pigeon River route came under American control in the Treaty of 1783. That's when Roderick McKenzie rediscovered it. On this trail, you'll be following in the footsteps of surveyors like Simon McGillvery, David Thompson, Sir George Simpson, Sir John Richardson and Simon J. Dawson and soldiers such as Colonel Garnet Wolseley, who led 100 soldiers along here en route to Manitoba during the Riel crisis.

Little Falls Trail

Level of difficulty 🚶 🚶

Distance *3km (1.9mi) loop*

Approx. time *3hrs return*

Trailhead *Halfway along the Mountain Portage Trail*

If you want to get an idea of the kind of landscape the earlier explorers faced while they tried to get around the falls, take a detour along this path. The natural surface (read: mud) leads through a forest into the river valley and then back up again. Much of the walk is either woodland or meadow. There's a wonderful scenic lookout over the Kaministiquia River that allows you to see the changes brought on by fast-moving water. There's also a beautiful waterfall called Little Falls at the far end of the trail.

Beaver Meadows Trail

Level of difficulty 🚶 🚶

Distance *5.6km (3.5mi) linear*

Approx. time *5hrs return*

Trailhead *The group camping area or partway along the Poplar Point Trail*

This trail joins the group camping area with the Poplar Point Trail. Interesting elements include views of the Kaministiquia River from a former bank, a beaver pond and a glacial spillway.

River Terrace Loop

Level of difficulty 🚶 🚶

Distance *3.6km (2mi) loop*

Approx. time *2hrs return*

Trailhead *Partway along the Beaver Meadows Trail*

Park officials decided to add this forest loop to the Beaver Meadows Trail to provide more views of the Kaministiquia River from above. Look for examples of bur oak, which grows in this forest but is otherwise rare in the area.

Nipigon River Recreation Trail

Location *Nipigon to Red Rock Marina*

Level of difficulty 🚶 🚶

Number of trails *1*

Total distance *8.2km (5mi) linear*

Approx. time *3hrs each way*

Markers *White triangles with blue hikers*

Trailheads Nipigon Marina parking lot, Red Rock, Sawmill Point in Nipigon

Interesting features Pictographs, lookouts over Nipigon Bay

Facilities/Services None

Other Dogs on leashes permitted

The trail follows the Nipigon River's journey towards Lake Superior's Nipigon Bay. Although short, it passes through eight different landscapes: a flat marina, wetlands, open shoreline, woodlands, steep rock climbs along four poles of an Ontario Hydro line, ravines and through mature boreal forest. The trail includes three lookouts– Eagle Ridge, Nipigon Bay and Lloyd's. Lloyd's Lookout features a rest area with rest rooms and picnic tables. It is open year-round.

› Getting There

Three different access points enable hikers to get to the trail. One is located on the north side of Highway 628, just prior to the railway tracks on the way into Red Rock. The second is the Nipigon Marina parking lot. The third is at Sawmill Point in Nipigon, on a gravel road that leads from Newton Street, past the sawmill and across the railway tracks.

› Further Information

Township of Nipigon
PO Box 160, 52 Front St.
Nipigon, ON P0T 2J0
807-887-3135
www.nipigon.net

Ouimet Canyon Provincial Nature Reserve

Location North of Hwy. 17 between Nipigon and Thunder Bay

Number of trails 3

Total distance 5.5km (3.4mi)

Interesting features Ouimet Canyon

Facilities/Services Parking, toilets

Over the last billion years, wind, rain and glacial ice have hardened magma into rock and then chiselled and gouged a gorge 150km (93mi) wide and 100m (90ft) deep into the north shore of Lake Superior, near Canadian Pacific's now abandoned Ouimet Rail Station. The result is a wonder. Vertical fissures in the rock ensure that the sides of Ouimet Canyon remain vertical even as rocks drop away to the floor. Thanks to a limited amount of sunlight, lots of moss cover and cold air, arctic and subarctic plants grow on the canyon floor.

The surrounding forest is a mixed deciduous conifer forest, typical of an extensive vegetation zone north of Lake Superior. Look from the trail for snowberries, red moccasin flower orchid, blue bead lily and the calypso orchid.

› Getting There

On Highway 17, drive west from Nipigon or east from Thunder Bay. Turn north onto Ouimet Canyon Road and continue for 11km (6.8mi). The road is quite scenic; cows in pastures and rolling hills give drivers lots to look at.

Although a sign at the entrance to the parking lot says: "Attention hikers. Very steep and winding road," climb the 3km (1.9mi) road anyway. From October to May, you don't have a choice, because the access road is blocked.

› Further Information

Ouimet Canyon Provincial Park
435 James St., 221B
Thunder Bay, ON P7E 6S8
807-977-2526 or 800-667-1940
www.ontarioparks.com

Ouimet Canyon Trail

Level of difficulty 🚶

Distance *1km (.6mi) loop*

Approx. time *1hr return*

Trailhead *Second parking lot*

Other *Wheelchair accessible*

Although short, the Ouimet Canyon Trail is the only public path in this reserve. It consists of a wheelchair-accessible deck, a wheelchair-accessible gravel path leading to three lookouts, and stairs looping back. The three lookouts provide views of Ouimet Canyon, Gulch's Creek Gorge (a miniature gorge to the west of the canyon), and a rock feature known as the Indian Head.

The stone immortalizes a giant named Omett, who used to help the great spirit Nannabijou to raise mountains and create lakes. During his work, Omett accidentally killed Nannabijou's daughter Naiomi, and buried her in a shallow lake covered with stone. Feeling his daughter's spirit below him, Nannabijou used a bolt of thunder to split open the rock, exposing a giant gorge with his daughter's body at the bottom. The devastated father turned Omett the giant into stone and buried Naiomi at the bottom of the canyon, where Omett would keep watch over the grave forever.

The Marsh Trail

Level of difficulty 🚶🚶

Distance *3.5km (2.2mi) loop*

Approx. time *2hrs return*

Trailhead *First parking lot*

An on-site map shows the Marsh Trail, a trail around the edge of Gulch Lake and an unnamed lake near the parking lot at the entrance to the nature reserve. The trail is supposed to be open only for researchers, but lots of locals walk on it too.

Welburne Lake Trail

Level of difficulty 🚶🚶🚶

Distance *1km (.6mi) loop*

Approx. time *1hr return*

Trailhead *First parking lot*

This trail also appears on the on-site map and although it's not supposed to be open to the public, locals will lead you there if you ask. If you're interested in spotting some of the rare birds and subarctic plants in the area, walking this trail is a safer bet than walking along the trails that lead from the Ouimet Canyon Trail.

Pukaskwa National Park

Location *Near Pic River, south of Hwy. 17 and southeast of Marathon*

Number of trails *4*

Total distance *66.3km (41mi)*

Interesting features *Pukaskwa pits, lava rock, potholes, suspension walking bridge, views of Lake Superior, sand dunes*

Facilities/Services *Parking, toilets, telephones, visitor information centre, playground, swimming beaches, camping, showers, fishing*

Other *Dogs on leashes permitted*

Part of the mystique of Pukaskwa National Park comes from its location on the shores of Lake Superior, the largest by surface area–and possibly coldest– freshwater lake in the world. The lake's average temperature is so cold—just 4°C (39°F)—that arctic plants thrive along its coast. This unpredictable swelling sea has a reputation for storms that make its waves powerful enough to sink grand ships like the *Edmund Fitzgerald*, among many others. Even when calm, Lake Superior can be terrifying, with varied currents and swells capable of influencing coastal rivers. Pukaskwa National Park has been protecting 1,878km² (725 sq mi) of territory since 1978. The park includes 14 watersheds, five different rivers that run their full course here, from beginning to end, parts of three other rivers, more than 950 lakes and Tip Top Mountain, the fifth highest in Ontario.

An important mystery surrounds the Anishinabe people who once lived, fished, hunted and picnicked throughout the park, and the stone-lined pits they built along the shore of Lake Superior. Archaeologists still don't know what these Pukaskwa pits were used for.

Another area of mystique is the unique mix of wildlife that live within the park's boundaries, including moose, wolf, black bear and woodland caribou. In fact, in 1999 researchers completed a five-year study—The Pukaskwa Predator Prey Process Project or "P5"—to find out how these animals co-relate.

Researchers are busy solving a fourth mystery: whether prescribed burns can re-establish the white and jack pine stands once prevalent within Pukaskwa. The first experiment took place in 1998 when a 20ha (49 acre) stand of white pine near the Pukaskwa River was set alight. So far, most of the larger pines survived the fire, but whether they will continue to thrive is yet to be seen.

A wonderful backcountry trail, and three short walks enable visitors to explore some of the mysteries of Pukaskwa for themselves.

› Getting There

Drive east from Marathon or west from White River along Highway 17. Turn south on Highway 627. Drive for 15km (9mi) through the community of Heron Bay and by the Pic River First Nation and across Pic River itself. (Ignore the signs for the Pic

River historical plaque. Ontario government officials picked it up for resurfacing five years ago and they haven't yet returned it.)

› Further Information

Pukaskwa National Park
PO Box 212, Hwy. 627
Heron Bay, ON P0T 1R0
807-229-0801 x 242
www.parkscanada.gc.ca/pukaskwa

The Friends of Pukaskwa
PO Box 1840
Marathon, ON P0T 2E0
807-229-0801 x 233
www.friendsofpukaskwa.ca

Beach Trail

Level of difficulty 🚶

Distance *1.5km (.9mi) linear*

Approx. time *1hr each way*

Trailhead *Between campsites nos. 34 and 35 or between campsites nos. 53 and 54*

Walk along three different sand beaches. From the North Beach, look westward to see the Pic River Sand Dunes, Lake Superior's largest such structures on the north shore.

Southern Headland Trail

Level of difficulty 🚶🚶

Distance *2.2km (1.4mi) loop and extension*

Approx. time *1hr return*

Trailhead *Visitor centre*

The Southern Headland Trail provides the best lookouts over Lake Superior. Display panels tell how volcanoes helped shape the land into interesting features such as lava pillows and rock dikes.

Halfway Lake Trail

Level of difficulty 🚶🚶

Distance *2.6km (1.6mi) loop*

Approx. time *1.5hrs return*

Trailhead *Park Rd., opposite the campground entrance or across from Campsite no. 49*

Follow part of the path that fur trappers used to journey from Pic River to Hattie Cove on this trail, which loops the lake that marked the halfway point in the trip. Today's trail passes through many landscapes including boreal forest, grass meadows, along granite and over marsh. Look up to see scenic lookouts over steep cliffs and down to spot glacier-created potholes in some of the rocks.

Coastal Hiking Trail

Level of difficulty 🚶🚶🚶

Distance *7.6km (4.7mi) to White River Suspension Bridge (one way) or 60km (37.3mi) to Swallow River (one way)*

Approx. time *1 to 10 days return*

Trailhead *Parking lot at Hattie Cove*

The trail begins at Hattie Cove and follows the shoreline over rocks, roots and boardwalk. Large slats on the boardwalks, lots of slippery rocks, several climbs up rocky slopes, and a scarcity of hikers, combine to make this a very difficult trail. Children under 10 years of age and anyone who isn't in top shape should stick to the shorter trails.

Most visitors to Pukaskwa choose to do the White River hike, a 15km (9mi) round trip portion of the Coastal Hiking Trail that can be done in one day. Besides walking across a 30m (100ft) suspension bridge 23m (75ft) above Chigamiwinigum Falls, the trail also offers a likely possibility of seeing a bear or moose. This one-day trip has become so popular, the Friends of Pukaskwa offer boat tours to and from the suspension bridge during the summer season so that hikers would only have to walk the trail one-way.

More ambitious hikers will want to take the 8 to 10 days required to follow the entire trail, which should reopen after repairs to two bridges are completed in fall 2010. Eleven campsites along the way each offer a tent pad, bear box (for food storage), outhouse and fire pit.

Quetico Provincial Park

Location *Atikokan*

Number of trails *6*

Total distance *24km (14.4mi)*

Interesting features *French Lake, French Falls, French portage, French River, mushrooms, boreal forest, Canadian Shield, sand beaches, Steep Rock Moraine, shore fens*

Facilities/Services *Parking, toilets, telephones, visitor information centre, artists' residence, Rangers' nature centre, playground, fishing, swimming beaches, camping, laundry, showers, canoe launch, 2,200 backcountry camping sites*

Other *Dogs on leashes are permitted*

Quetico Provincial Park reserves 469,456 hectares (1,159,556sq.ft.) for canoeing, hiking and camping and is known as Ontario's best canoeing wilderness. Most visitors explore the territory via three- to five-day canoe trips, but it is also well-worth visiting the day-use area, where most of the hiking trails are located. The park will even be better for hikers once the Howard Lake and Sawmill Lake interior camping trails are renovated as planned.

The area has a prominent prehistory as a transportation hub. It served as part of the corridor between glacial lakes Agassiz and Minong for people to move northeast as the glaciers retreated. Its waters also formed part of the voyageur fur trade from Montréal. Later, settlers moving west along the Dawson Route passed through part of the wilderness in what now lies within Quetico.

Bears, wolves, moose, 122 different species of birds and other wildlife breed throughout the region. So far, 666 plant species have been found growing in the park, including jack pine and trembling aspen, and hikers will notice an unusual variety of mushrooms beside the trails.

› Getting There

Take Highway 11 48km (29mi) east from Atikokan or 152km (91mi) west from Thunder Bay to the Dawson Trail Campground entrance to Quetico Provincial Park. Turn left and continue along the park road to the Heritage and Information Pavilion parking lot to your right.

› Further Information

Quetico Provincial Park
Atikokan, ON P0T 1C0
☎ 807-597-2735, 800-667-1940 or 888-668-7275
www.ontarioparks.com

Friends of Quetico
PO Box 1959,
Atikokan, ON P0T 1C0
☎ 807-929-2571 x229
www.friendsofquetico.com

Pickerel River and Point Trails

Level of difficulty 🚶

Distance *2.4km (1.4mi) loop*

Approx. time *1hr*

Trailheads *Heritage and Information Pavillion, nature centre road*

The boardwalk section of this follows the marshy Pickerel River between the visitor centre and the day use area of the park. It is named after Sheila Hainey. A loop near the end leads farther along the river to get to Pickerel Point on the shore of French Lake. This section of the trail can get quite wet.

French Falls Trail

Level of difficulty 🚶 🚶

Distance *2.4km (8.8mi) linear*

Approx. time *1hr each way*

Trailheads *Parking lot on Hwy. 11, just east of the Dawson Trail Campgrounds entrance, French River Trail and French Portage Trail*

This trail follows the French River past the waterfalls and then links to the French River and Portage trails.

French River and Portage Trails

Level of difficulty 🚶 🚶

Distance *10.6km (6.4mi) loop*

Approx. time *5hrs return*

Trailheads *Rangers' Nature Centre, Chippewa Campground, French Lake Teaching Place or Ojibwa Campground*

The best walk for hikers in the park is a loop that links the campground road, the French Portage Trail, the Baptism Creek Trail and the French River Trail into a single walk. A short side trip can also be added to see the French Falls.

Most of the trail is relatively easy and red and yellow markers along the way are clear. The section next to Baptism Creek, however, can sometimes be extremely wet. The section next to the French River follows the former Camp 111 logging road.

Beaver Meadows and Pond Trails

Level of difficulty 🚶 🚶

Distance *2.4km (1.4mi) double loop*

Approx. time *1hr*

Trailheads *Rangers' Nature Centre, French Portage Trail*

The Beaver Pond and Beaver Meadow Trails feature forests, spruce bogs and two small ponds.

Whiskey Jack Trail

Level of difficulty 🚶

Distance *2.2km (1.3mi) loop*

Approx. time *1hr*

Trailhead *End of campground road just past the Ojibwa Campground*

This trail begins on a boardwalk and continues across rocks and through trees. Highlights include typical shield vegetation, including Labrador tea, bunchberry and tamarack. The Pines Trail begins halfway along the loop.

Pines Trail

Level of difficulty 🚶🚶

Distance *4.4km (2.6mi) linear*

Approx. time *2hrs each way*

Trailhead *Half-way along the Whiskey Jack Nature Trail*

Other *Interior campsites available with permit*

This trail begins crossing Baptism Creek and then follows the river between French and Pickerel lakes to get to a sandy beach on Pickerel Lake. Highlights are the stands of old growth red and white pine near the beach.

Part way along, you'll notice a trail leading toward the south. These are portages for canoeists to get between McKenzie, Cache, Baptism and Pickerel lakes. There are unmarked interior sites along the way.

Rainbow Falls Provincial Park

Location *Hwy. 17 between Rossport and Schreiber*

Number of trails *4*

Total distance *8.2km (5mi)*

Interesting features *Cascade waterfalls, Lake Superior Lookout, connection to the Casques-Isles Trail*

Facilities/Services *Parking, toilets, telephones, visitor information centre, convenience store, playground, swimming beaches, camping, laundry area, showers, boat launch*

Other *Dogs on leashes permitted*

Rainbow Falls is a surprise. The falls here don't begin and end all at once like those you're probably used to. Nine small waterfalls follow one after the other in a cascade of falling water. The falls look pink, as the water drops over the reddest of granites. Masses of lichen turn the same pink bedrock gray beneath your feet, as though nature knows how to present the best elements together.

Then, the cascading falls end abruptly in a local swimming hole full of rainbow trout. Known as the "deep pool," this pond is almost twice as deep–about 9m (30ft)as it is wide. A steep rocky slope and wild currents in the spring and at the beginning of summer can make swimming here treacherous.

Camping is permitted in this spot known as Rainbow Falls–Whitesand Lake location, although the park also operates another campground on the shores of Lake Superior. The other location, known as Rainbow Falls–Rossport

Campground, is 4km (2.5mi) to the west. Hikers traverse between the two along Highway 17. Entry points onto the **Casque-Isles Hiking Trail** (see p. 244) can be found about 1.5km (.9mi) east of Rossport Campground, and about 2.2km (1.4mi) north of Highway 17 along Sox Lake Road.

› Getting There

Drive 7km (4.3mi) east from Schreiber or 5km (3mi) west from Rossport along Highway 17.

› Further Information

Rainbow Falls Provincial Park
C/O Ministry of Natural Resources
PO Box 280
Terrace Bay, ON P0T 2W0
☎ 807-824-2298 or 800-667-1940
www.ontarioparks.com

Falls Boardwalk

Level of difficulty 🚶

Distance *.5km (.8mi) linear*

Approx. time *30min return*

Trailhead *Rainbow Falls parking lot*

This wooden boardwalk along the falls includes several viewing platforms to enable hikers to see all nine sections of Rainbow Falls from just about any angle. A staircase near the end of the boardwalk tends to take hikers by surprise, but builders were smart enough to paint the first and last stair with an orange line to draw attention to the sudden change in elevation.

Lake Superior Trail

Level of difficulty 🚶🚶

Distance *2.4km (1.5mi) linear*

Approx. time *2hrs return*

Trailhead *Along the road to the West Beach area between the Maintenance Rd. and West Beach*

The Lake Superior Trail is a crescent-shaped trail that leads through spruce woodlands and along a granite ridge towards several different views of Lake Superior. The trail exits at the Picnic Area Parking Lot between West Beach and the Rainbow Falls trailhead. Return the way you came, or loop back to the trailhead along the paved road.

Rainbow Falls Trail

Level of difficulty 🚶🚶🚶

Distance *2.5km (1.6mi) linear*

Approx. time *2hrs return (1.5hrs up, 30min down)*

Trailhead *Rainbow Falls boardwalk*

Get to this nature trail at the end of the falls boardwalk by crossing the bridge across the Whitesand River. The Rainbow Falls Trail begins with a climb and keeps climbing, along a wooded path covered with tree roots and rocks that like to slip away from under your feet.

Display panels along the hike indicate important rare wildflowers, such as the tiny pink twinflower that Ojibway locals use to reduce fever, single-fronded long beech fern, the oak fern with three distinct pinnate fronds, the fully-edible bunchberry, root-

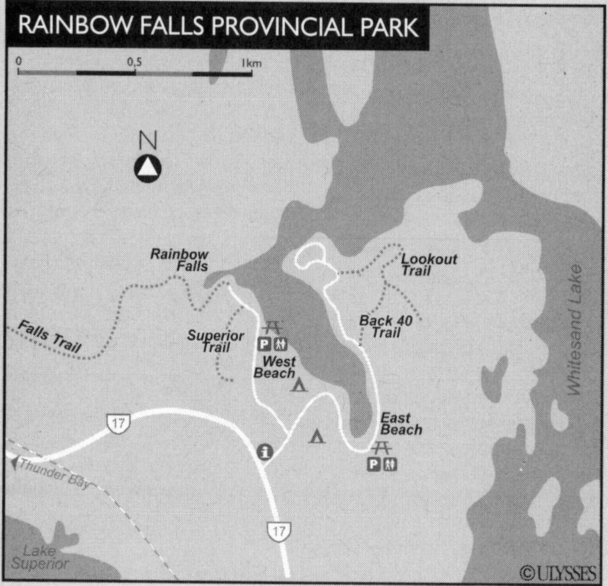

beer-flavoured sarsaparilla and the fungus/algae cooperative living system called lichens. The view at the top is wonderful.

Continue past this lookout to the Casque-Isles Trail.

The Back 40 Trail

Level of difficulty 🥾🥾🥾

Distance *2.8km (1.7mi) linear*

Approx. time *2.5hrs return*

Trailhead *Park road past the East Beach parking lot*

This very steep climb over rocky trails leads to the best lookout in the park. You'll see Whitesand Lake, Lake Superior and most of the park itself. This trail is definitely a must.

Sleeping Giant Provincial Park

Location *On the Sibley Peninsula east of Thunder Bay*

Number of trails *22*

Total distance *67km (41.5mi)*

Interesting features *The Sleeping Giant, The Sea Lion, Silver Islet Silver Mine*

Facilities/Services *Parking, toilets, telephones, visitor information centre, convenience store, swimming beaches, camping, showers, boat launch*

Other *Dogs on leashes permitted; park closed Nov, Dec and Apr*

While many have tried to explain why the peninsula across from

Thunder Bay looks like Gulliver in the land of the Lilliputians, Blackduck legend says it best. Long ago, before our time, a giant named Nanabosho led the Ojibway on to the Sibley Peninsula, a land of plenty. Soon after they arrived, Nanabosho scratched a rock and revealed silver, a metal valued highly by the Europeans. Knowing that the Europeans would destroy Sibley Peninsula to get the silver, the giant asked his friends to bury the rock and never mention the silver again. One warrior couldn't resist making himself a few weapons with the silver first, however, and that's when Nanabosho's fears began coming true. A Sioux warrior killed the vain Ojibway warrior, took possession of his silver weapons and later agreed to lead two Europeans to the source of the metal. Nanabosho saw the group as they paddled across Lake Superior to the source of the silver, became furious, and created a storm to capsize the canoe and drown the men. The Great Spirit punished the giant on the spot by turning him into stone.

Meanwhile, Silver Islet turned out to be the world's richest silver vein. Mining began on the Sibley Peninsula in the mid-1800s and ended only after the main mine shaft flooded. Logging operations followed mining until the peninsula's massive red and white pine stands were almost eliminated.

Port Arthur citizens who demanded that the pine forests be saved forced the Ontario government to create Sibley Provincial Park in 1944. The name was changed to reflect the dominant rock formation in 1998 when Sibley became Sleeping Giant.

Unfortunately, the provincial park came too late for the woodland caribou that once frequented the area. Today, you're much more likely to see white-tailed deer, porcupines, beavers, moose, red foxes, bears, martens, fishers, and perhaps timber wolves or lynx. Sleeping Giant attracts more than 190 bird species, 75 of which nest in the park. Look for solitary sandpipers, ravens, boreal chickadees, white-winged crossbills, loons, mallards, black ducks, ring-necked ducks, common goldeneyes, and common mergansers. You'll also see osprey and bald eagle nests.

› Getting There

Take Highway 17 east from Dorion or west from Thunder Bay. Turn right on Highway 587 towards the town of Pass Lake. Drive 32km (20mi) past a railway suspension bridge. The park boundary begins just after the town of Pass Lake and ends before the town of Silver Islet.

› Further Information

Superintendent
Sleeping Giant Provincial Park
Pass Lake, ON P0T 2M0
☎ 807-475-1531, 807-977-2526 or 800-667-1940
www.ontarioparks.com

The Friends of Sleeping Giant Park
Box 29031
Thunder Bay, ON P7B 6P9
www.thefriendsofsleepinggiant.ca

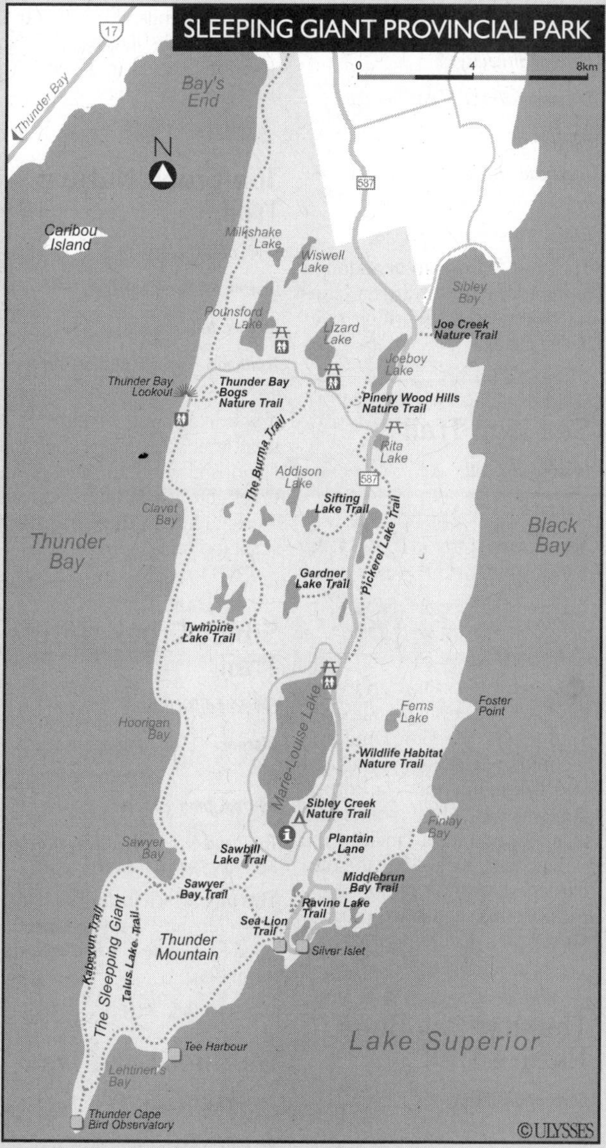
SLEEPING GIANT PROVINCIAL PARK
0
4
8km
17
Thunder Bay
Bay's End
N
Caribou Island
587
Milkshake Lake
Wiswell Lake
Sibley Bay
Pounsford Lake
Lizard Lake
Joe Creek Nature Trail
Joeboy Lake
Thunder Bay Lookout
Thunder Bay Bogs Nature Trail
Pinery Wood Hills Nature Trail
Rita Lake
The Burma Trail
Addison Lake
Sifting Lake Trail
Pickerel Lake Trail
Clavet Bay
Thunder Bay
Black Bay
Gardner Lake Trail
Twinpine Lake Trail
Ferns Lake
Foster Point
Hoorigan Bay
Marie-Louise Lake
Wildlife Habitat Nature Trail
Sibley Creek Nature Trail
Finlay Bay
Sawyer Bay
Sawbill Lake Trail
Plantain Lane
Sawyer Bay Trail
Middlebrun Bay Trail
Ravine Lake Trail
Sea Lion Trail
Silver Islet
Kabeyun Trail
The Sleeping Giant
Talus Lake Trail
Thunder Mountain
Tee Harbour
Lake Superior
Lehtinen's Bay
Thunder Cape Bird Observatory
©ULYSSES

Plantain Lane

Level of difficulty 🚶

Distance *.5 km (.3mi) semi-circle*

Approx. time *45min each way*

Trailhead *Hwy. 587, just prior to the Kabeyun South trailhead*

Other *Wheelchair accessible*

This trail follows an abandoned Silver Islet road towards a fabulous view from a bridge over Sibley Creek.

Sea Lion Trail

Level of difficulty 🚶

Distance *.5km (.3mi) linear*

Approx. time *1hr return (includes lots of time for taking in the scenery)*

Trailhead *The Kabeyun Trail, very close to the Kabeyun South trailhead off Hwy. 587*

Although quite short and easy, this hike leads from the Kabeyun Trail to the Sea Lion landform, a chunk of diabase jutting out into Lake Superior. The formation was created by molten lava that seeped into a crack in the sedimentary rock. After the lava hardened, erosion removed the rock around it to leave the sea-lion-shaped feature in place.

Thunder Bay Bogs Nature Trail

Level of difficulty 🚶

Distance *.8km (.5mi) loop*

Approx. time *30min return*

Trailhead *Kabeyun North trailhead off North Scenic Dr.*

The best things about this trail are the 18 display boards that describe glaciers in a way children can understand.

Joe Creek Nature Trail

Level of difficulty 🚶

Distance *1.6km (1mi) loop*

Approx. time *1hr return*

Trailhead *Hwy. 587, just after the park entrance*

If you like spring wildflowers or small waterfalls, this is your trail. It loops along both sides of Joe Creek through mostly woodland areas, although there are a few small footbridges over marsh.

Sibley Creek Nature Trail

Level of difficulty 🚶

Distance *1.7km (1mi) loop and extension*

Approx. time *2hrs return*

Trailhead *Hwy. 587, just prior to the Kabeyun South trailhead*

This trail, which includes a marsh, a stream and beaver dams, is good for children. You'll probably see moose.

Gardner Lake Trail

Level of difficulty 🚶

Distance *2km (1.2mi) linear*

Approx. time *1hr return*

Trailhead *Hwy. 587, just after the park entrance*

This often-wet trail follows the remains of an old logging road to Gardner Lake. Look for migrating birds, especially boreal forest warblers, since 20 species nest in the park.

Sifting Lake Trail

Level of difficulty 🚶

Distance *2km (1.2mi) linear*

Approx. time *2hrs return*

Trailhead *Hwy. 587, just after the park entrance*

This woodland trail leads to Sifting Lake, an area known to attract migrating birds, including olive-sided flycatchers and pine warblers.

Sawbill Lake Trail

Level of difficulty 🚶

Distance *2.3km (1.4mi) linear*

Approx. time *1hr each way*

Trailhead *At the south end of Marie Louise Lake Scenic Dr.*

This trail follows the remains of an old logging road to join the Marie Louise Ring Road with the Sawyer Bay Trail. If you're camping, you'll take this trail to climb the giant.

Wildlife Habitat Nature Trail

Level of difficulty 🚶

Distance *2.4km (1.5mi) loop*

Approx. time *1hr return*

Trailhead *Hwy. 587, just after the park entrance*

This trail is good for moose sightings.

Middlebrun Bay Trail

Level of difficulty 🚶

Distance *4.2km (2.6mi) linear*

Approx. time *2hrs each way*

Trailhead *Across the street from the Silver Islet Cemetery*

This trail features a fen, a non-acidic area for unusual plants. The trail also leads to a secluded beach.

Sawyer Bay Trail

Level of difficulty 🚶

Distance *6km (3.7mi) linear*

Approx. time *2.5hrs each way*

Trailhead *The end of the Sawbill Lake Trail or the Kabeyun Trail, very close to the Kabeyun South trailhead off Hwy. 587*

This trail follows an old logging road to Sawyer Bay at the base of the Sleeping Giant. Although nondescript, it's the easiest way to reach the trail that allows you to climb the giant.

Piney Wood Hills Nature Trail

Level of difficulty 🚶🚶

Distance *1.3km (.8mi) linear*

Approx. time *1.5hrs return*

Trailhead *North Scenic Drive, about 1.5km (.9mi) from Hwy. 587*

This hilly woodland trail leads to a lookout over Joeboy Lake. You have a good chance of seeing a moose here in the early morning or late evening.

Climbing the Giant via the Chest Trail from Sawyer Bay

Level of difficulty

Distance *2km (1.2mi) linear*

Elevation *250m (820ft) up the highest vertical cliffs in Ontario*

Approx. time *2hrs each way*

Trailhead *At the end of the Sawyer Bay Trail*

This steep climb up the chest of the giant leads to Nanabosho Lookout. The view here is of the park and Sawyer Bay, although on a clear day you can glimpse the eastern shore of Thunder Bay to your left and Black Bay to the right.

Pickerel Lake Trail

Level of difficulty

Distance *10km (6.2mi) linear*

Approx. time *4hrs each way*

Trailhead *Hwy. 587, just after the park entrance*

This trail was designed for cross-country skiers, but it leads to some of the park's largest white pines.

Ravine Lake Trail

Level of difficulty

Distance *1.5km (.9 mi) loop*

Approx. time *3hrs return*

Trailhead *Kabeyun South trailhead*

Two different lookouts, a view of Ravine Lake and a shaded cedar grove make this steady climb and sharp descent worth the effort.

The Burma Trail

Level of difficulty

Distance *11.4km (7mi) linear*

Approx. time *6hrs each way*

Trailhead *Near the end of Louise Lake Scenic Dr.*

Birdwatchers will love the variety of species along this trail, which leads along rocky ledges, to lakes, and through stands of mature red and white pine.

Kabeyun Trail

Level of difficulty to *very difficult between the giant's feet and Lehtinen's Bay*

Distance *40km (25mi) linear around the coast, 9.2km (5.7mi) to the Chimney Trail*

Approx. time *1 to 5 days each way*

Trailhead *Kabeyun South trailhead off Hwy. 587 or the Kabeyun North trailhead, off North Scenic Dr.*

The Kabeyun Trail, which leads from the Silver Islet Cemetery near the Sea Lion all the way around the coast, around the Sleeping Giant, to the Thunder Bay lookout, is the park's most popular trail to climb the giant. Although there are 11 campsites along its route, you can also do portions of this trail to limit your trek to less than one day. The most popular stretch is, of course, the 9.2km (5.7mi) stretch from the south trailhead near Silver Islet to the Chimney Trail.

Climbing the Giant's Knees via the Chimney Trail

Level of difficulty 🚶🚶🚶

Distance 1km (.6mi) linear

Elevation 250m (820ft) up the highest vertical cliffs in Ontario

Approx. time 1hr each way

Trailhead Kabeyun Trail, 8km (5mi) from the Kabeyun South trailhead off Hwy. 587

This is by far the best way to climb the giant. A large crevice in the rock (the "chimney") leads over a talus slope of boulders, through and onto the giant's knees. As you come out of the chimney on the east side of the knees, you'll see Lehtinen's Harbour, Tee Harbour, Silver Islet and the rest of the peninsula. The island out in Lake Superior is Isle Royale, a U.S. national park. Take the short trail to the west side of the knees to view Thunder Bay (both the body of water and the city), Pie Island and Mount McKay. Pay attention for signs of both beavers and porcupines, both of which live here year-round.

Twinpine Lake Trail

Level of difficulty 🚶🚶🚶

Distance 4.7km (7.6mi) linear

Approx. time 3hrs each way

Trailhead Either the Kabeyun Trail about 8km (5mi) from the Kabeyun North trailhead off North Scenic Dr. or the Burma Trail about 2.6km (1.6mi) from the Louise Lake Scenic Dr. trailhead

This very wet trail connects the Kabeyun Trail and the Burma Trail. You'll pass a very large double lake, where white-tailed deer are known to feed.

Talus Lake Trail

Level of difficulty 🚶🚶🚶

Distance 5km (3mi) linear

Approx. time 3hrs each way

Trailhead Either the Kabeyun Trail about 7.5km (4.7mi) from the Kabeyun South trailhead or the Sawyer Sawbill Lake Trail about 5.8km (3.6mi) from the Louise Lake Scenic Dr. trailhead

This trail leads along cliffs and through meadows between the Sleeping Giant and Talus Mountain. Highlights include three lakes, talus slopes, and a waterfall.

Climbing the Giant's Knees via the New Top of the Giant Trail

Level of difficulty 🚶🚶

Distance 3km (1.9mi) linear

Approx. time 2hrs each way

Trailhead At the end of the Talus Trail

Volunteers spent a summer building the stairs along this twisting vertical climb to the top of the giant. Their efforts give visitors a very pleasant alternative to the rapelling climb of the original Chimney. Once you get to the top of the giant, it's another 2km across to the spectacular views of the harbour on the west.

White River Community Trails

Location *White River*

Number of trails *4*

Total distance *20km (12.4mi)*

Interesting features *Beavers, wolves, porcupines, rabbits, blue herons, relative seclusion*

Facilities/Services *None*

Cross-country skiers maintain these trails on crown land, but locals frequently mountain bike and hike on them during the summer. You'll see lots of wildlife, very few (if any) people and interesting vegetation. In exchange, you must be willing to blaze your own trail in spots and accept the occasional rickety footbridge.

To get to three of the four trails, you'll cross a 30m (100ft) beaver dam with no rails and a lot of loose branches.

› Getting There

Drive east of the information centre on Highway 17 in White River to Highway 631. Drive north for 2km (1.2mi) towards Hornepayne. The parking area and sign is on your right.

› Further Information

The Corporation of the Township of White River
PO Box 307, 102 Durham St.
White River, ON P0M 3G
☎ 807-822-2450

Timberwolf Trail

Level of difficulty 🚶🚶

Distance *10km (6.2mi) loop*

Approx. time *4hrs return*

Trailhead *Hwy. 631*

This very long loop leads up and down a boreal forest ridge where wolves are known to live. It's also a very popular trail for mountain bikers.

Jackrabbit Trail

Level of difficulty 🚶🚶🚶

Distance *4km (2.5mi) loop*

Approx. time *2hrs return*

Trailhead *Hwy. 631*

This trail is the main trail crossing the beaver dam and circling an unnamed lake. You'll see lots of boreal chickadees and gray jays. Look for bunchberry, yellow clintonia and large-leaved aster in the boggy lowlands.

Beaver Trail

Level of difficulty 🚶🚶🚶

Distance *2km (1.2mi) linear*

Approx. time *1hr each way*

Trailhead *Partway along the Jackrabbit and Whiskey Jack trails*

This very wet trail joins the Jackrabbit and Whiskey Jack trails to form a very short loop closest to the unnamed beaver lake. You'll see lots of beaver dams and beaver meadows and most likely some beavers as well.

Whisky Jack Trail

Level of difficulty

Distance *4km (2.5mi) linear*

Approx. time *2hrs return*

Trailhead *Halfway along and near the end of the Jackrabbit Trail*

This trail joins two portions of the Jackrabbit Trail to form a shorter loop and avoid a bridge crossing.

Appendix

Index

Bold numbers refer to maps.

A

B

C

D

E

F

G

H

I

J

K

L

M

N

O

P

Q

R

S

T

U

V

W

Order at www.ulyssesguides.com

Shipping is free if you use the following promotion code: **GDEHI**
(limit of one promotion code per customer)

Ulysses guides are also available in all quality bookstores.

ULYSSES TRAVEL GUIDES

Montréal
$24.95 CAD
$22.95 USD

Ontario
$32.95 CAD
$28.95 USD

Québec City
$24.95 CAD
$24.95 USD

The Traveller's Journal
$12.95 CAD
$12.95 USD

ULYSSES GREEN ESCAPES

Cross-Country Skiing and Snowshoeing in Ontario
$24.95 CAD
$22.95 USD

Hiking in Québec
$24.95 CAD
$19.95 USD

ULYSSES GREEN ESCAPES

National Parks in Gaspésie and Bas-Saint-Laurent
$19.95 CAD
$21.95 USD

Ontario's Bike Paths and Rail Trails
$22.95 CAD
$17.95 USD

FABULOUS GUIDES

Fabulous Canada
$29.95 CAD
$29.95 USD

Fabulous Montréal
$29.95 CAD
$27.95 USD

Fabulous Québec
$29.95 CAD
$22.95 USD

Fabulous Western Canada
$29.95 CAD
$32.95 USD

Fabulous Québec City
$24.95 CAD
$24.95 USD

ULYSSES PHRASEBOOKS

Canadian French for Better Travel
$9.95 CAD
$6.95 USD

French for Better Travel
$9.95 CAD
$6.95 USD

Italian for Better Travel
$9.95 CAD
$7.95 USD

Spanish for Better Travel in Latin America
$9.95 CAD
$7.95 USD

Universal Communicator
$9.95 CAD
$11.95 USD

ULYSSES FOR KIDS

My Vacation Journal
$14.95 CAD
$16.95 USD

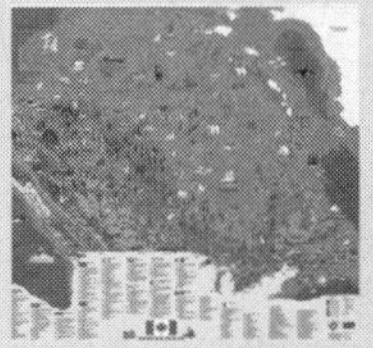

Illustrated Canada Map for Kids
$22.95 CAD
$24.95 USD

ULYSSES ONE-OF-A-KIND-TITLES

Delights of Old Montréal - Arts, History, Design, Gastronomy
$19.95 CAD
$19.95 USD

Montréal in Mi
$12.95 CAD
$13.95 USD

otes

Notes

Notes

Table of Distances (km)

Example: The distance between Montréal and Toronto is 547km.

	Chicago (Il.)	Hamilton	Kingston	Kitchener / Waterloo	London	Montréal (Qué.)	New York (N.Y.)	Niagara Falls	Ottawa	Sault Ste. Marie	Sudbury	Toronto	Thunder Bay
Hamilton	788												
Kingston	1100	338											
Kitchener / Waterloo	767	69	369										
London	661	140	451	110									
Montréal (Qué.)	1383	621	299	650	738								
New York (N.Y.)	1294	765	583	838	911	618							
Niagara Falls	896	77	408	156	227	689	690						
Ottawa	1242	480	203	511	600	202	719	544					
Sault Ste. Marie	780	748	894	777	699	1003	1498	814	806				
Sudbury	1079	460	609	490	572	700	1212	529	508	302			
Toronto	855	75	263	123	198	547	829	144	410	696	411		
Thunder Bay	1058	1469	1623	1496	1414	1638	2212	1534	1516	723	1019	1421	
Windsor / Detroit (Mi.)	460	318	626	306	191	912	1018	413	773	584	751	386	1310

Hiking Trails

See the colour map on the back cover.

Southern Ontario

1. Avon Trail
2. Backus Heritage Conservation Area
3. Bruce Peninsula National Park
4. Elgin Trail
5. Fanshawe Conservation Area
6. Gordon Glaves Memorial Pathway, Brantford
7. Long Point World Biosphere Reserve
8. Luther Marsh Wildlife Management Area
9. Lynn Valley Trail
10. Maitland Trail
11. McKeough Conservation Area and Floodway
12. Pinery Provincial Park
13. Point Pelee National Park
14. Rondeau Provincial Park
15. Thames Valley Trail

Greater Toronto and the Niagara Peninsula

1. Albion Hills Conservation Area
2. Ball's Falls Conservation Area
3. Cootes Paradise, Royal Botanical Gardens
4. Crawford Lake Conservation Area and Iroquoian Village
5. Darlington Provincial Park
6. Dufferin Islands, Niagara Falls
7. Dundas Valley and Tiffany Falls Conservation Areas
8. Durham Regional Forest
9. Ganaraska Forest
10. Glen Haffy Conservation Area
11. Humber Valley Trail
12. McLaughlin Bay Wildlife Reserve and Second Marsh Wildlife Area
13. Mountsberg Conservation Area
14. Niagara Glen
15. Niagara River Recreation Trail
16. Rouge Trail
17. St. Catharines Trail System
18. Seaton Hiking Trail

Central Ontario

1. Algonquin Provincial Park
2. Arrowhead Provincial Park
3. Awenda Provincial Park
4. Ferris Provincial Park
5. Georgian Bay Islands National Park
6. Georgian Trail
7. Haliburton Forest and Wild Life Reserve Ltd.
8. Lake Simcoe Trail
9. Mono Cliffs Provincial Park
10. Nokiidaa Trail along the Holland River
11. Old Nipissing Colonization Road
12. Petroglyphs Provincial Park
13. Seguin Trail
14. Springwater Provincial Park
15. Warsaw Caves Conservation Area
16. Wye Marsh Wildlife Centre

Eastern Ontario

1. Bon Echo Provincial Park
2. Charleston Lake Provincial Park
3. Foley Mountain Conservation Area
4. Frontenac Provincial Park
5. Gould Lake Conservation Area
6. Hell Holes Nature Trails, Caves & Ravines
7. Lemoine Point Conservation Area
8. Mac Johnson Wildlife Area
9. Morris Island Conservation Area
10. Murphys Point Provincial Park
11. Ottawa Greenbelt Trails
12. Perth Wildlife Reserve
13. Rideau Trail
14. Sandbanks Provincial Park
15. Shabomeka Legpower Pathfinders
16. Sheffield Conservation Area
17. Silent Lake Provincial Park
18. Voyageur Provincial Park

Northeastern Ontario

1. Chutes Provincial Park
2. Cup and Saucer Trail
3. Elliot Lake Hiking Trails
4. Halfway Lake Provincial Park
5. Hiawatha Highlands Conservation Area
6. Kap-Kig-Iwan Provincial Park
7. Killarney Provincial Park
8. Lake Laurentian Conservation Area
9. Lake Superior Provincial Park
10. Magpie Falls and Fort Friendship
11. Mississagi Provincial Park
12. Samuel de Champlain Provincial Park

Northwestern Ontario

1. Casque-Isles Hiking Trail
2. Greenwood Lake Conservation Reserve
3. Hawk's Ridge (Craig's Bluff and Craig's Pit)
4. Kakabeka Falls Provincial Park
5. Nipigon River Recreation Trail
6. Ouimet Canyon Provincial Nature Reserve
7. Pukaskwa National Park
8. Quetico Provincial Park
9. Rainbow Falls Provincial Park
10. Sleeping Giant Provincial Park
11. White River Community Trails